Average Married Dad's Guide to Health, Wealth, and a Sexy Marriage

FOR 30- TO 40-SOMETHINGS

Alex Peck

Published by Good Life Vision, LLC
GoodLifeVisionLLC@gmail.com

AverageMarriedDad.com

Average Married Dad's Guide to Health, Wealth and a Sexy Marriage/Alex Peck. —1st ed.
ISBN 978-0615999593

Contents

PART 2: MARRIAGE

PART 3: FINANCIAL MATTERS

PART 4: PARENTING

PART 5: PUTTING IT ALL TOGETHER

To Holly, who helped get this crazy thing off the ground.

Disclaimer

I'm not a doctor, psychologist, nutritionist, pharmacist, personal trainer, financial planner, marriage counselor, politician, journalist, or any certified or trained expert in these matters. I do not dispense medical or counseling advice, nor do I recommend your use of any technique contained herein as a form of treatment for physical, emotional, or medical problems without the advice of a physician or other professional. What I am is a professional engineer with a thirst for knowledge in these areas, and have devoted the last 10-plus years of my life to incorporating the various strategies of this subject matter into my own life. I have read hundreds of books and studies on the topics within the book and have boiled it down here. I have spent well over a thousand hours participating in various learning environments devoted to the individual parts and pieces presented here. I have no agenda to push except to further educate the masses of men who have no clue how to improve their situations as people, fathers or husbands, and to help them improve their life and financial situation.

In no way is this book intended to replace expert advice or instructions from your medical practitioners, nutritionist, counselors, financial planners, or other trained or licensed providers. If information in this book educates you on potential issues that need to be evaluated further, please seek the appropriate input from those trained in that field, and continue to educate yourself.

My intent is to offer information of a general nature to help you in your quest for physical, financial, emotional, spiritual, and relationship wellbeing. Viewpoints may be contrary to popular beliefs and are not necessarily based on laboratory research or scientific evidence. To the extent possible, scientific research and anecdotal evidence are provided to support the claims in this book, but like many things, opinions may vary. Should readers elect to employ suggestions contained within this book, they should hold this author harmless for negative outcomes or results. If in doubt about employing any methods contained within, please consult with a professional.

Preface

I stumbled upon my own self-improvement journey that led to writing this book entirely by accident. During a time in my marriage and life when I was trying to figure out why everything wasn't as good I had hoped it would be, I discovered a whole new world that was out there: a loosely organized group of (mostly) men who discussed men's issues on life, love, and relationships that ran contrary to common perceptions. This led to a complete reworking of my own perceptions of women, interpersonal relationships, health, and parenting. I fell down the rabbit hole, spending hundreds of hours reading books, websites, forums, and blogs and became a blogger in my own right, chronicling my own experiences of navigating the complex and fast-paced life of a suburban father of two. During my interactions, both with real life people and those internet friends I've made, it has become apparent that the vast majority of men are completely unaware of the way of seeing things that, while unproven, fly in the face of conventional wisdom but make intuitive sense at the core. As a result of this finding, a seed was planted and I began a journey that resulted in a Whole Life improvement.

The journey begins with a shift in how men see the world. The traditional rules of our generation result in lackluster marriages, overconsumption of both food and "things" intended to fill some internal hole in our lives, and chronic under-saving. The trickle-down effect is that many are just a fraction of the man, husband, and parent they could become. The messages contained herein are not unique, and if you had the time, you could change your way of thinking without reading this book by doing your own research and critical thinking. I am attempting to bring all these ideas into a Whole Life approach so that married men can improve themselves and subsequently their family life. Using my own experiences and interpretations of the resources available, I am repackaging them up here to hit all the core areas necessary to be a better man, better husband, and better father. Perhaps you simply haven't run across the resources that are available (books, websites, forums, blogs). Perhaps you don't have the time, or desire, to devote to sitting in front of a computer and sifting through the thousands of pages continuously growing content on these subjects. For me, stumbling upon the ideas presented here, along with reflection and discussion with friends, iFriends and my wife, was a game changer.

I feel it is absolutely necessary to continue to try and spread the messages contained in this book for two reasons. First, I think we men are at a critical sociological stage and education is necessary so that our generation, and the one we are helping to raise, can cultivate the masculine values and behaviors that are getting figuratively beat out of us by feminist doctrines and laws. Second, at the time of this writing, actual published book resources on some of these concepts are few and far between, and if published in book form, tend to focus on one topic instead of how they are interrelated. For example, books that focus on mental health or dietary guidelines don't integrate the impact these subjects have on marriage or parenting. Books that focus on marital sex or parenting topics don't get into details on how to achieve the healthy mental and physical wellbeing for a full healthy life. Add into the mix that our country's current state of financial savings is very poor and for my generation (those in their 30's and 40's), the possibility of Social Security providing tangible benefits when we retire is a crapshoot at this time. I'm attempting to mix the cocktail together in a detailed matter that hits the key salient points of being a healthy, complete father and husband; a Whole Life approach to being a happy and fulfilled family man; and the foundation to have a strong financial platform to build your family and life. While not a religious man myself, I believe those who follow their Godly beliefs will also benefit greatly from this message. You may need to make certain minor modifications to my messages to adhere to your religious beliefs, but it shouldn't diminish from the value or message I'm trying to impart to you.

The research I conducted while writing this book opened my eyes in so many ways and took me in directions that I didn't expect. This book attempts to give you knowledge of the situation we as men and husbands are up against, to provide the key concepts and very specific tools necessary to start you on your journey, and to directly improve you and your family life. At the end of the day, I'm just an Average Married Dad finding my way through this world. This book is written to benefit the man I was five, ten, fifteen years ago; while at the same time to serve as a reminder to myself on how to live each day today. As may be expected with my vocation, I'm not always an eloquent writer with great prose and you may find I don't always follow strict adherence to the *Chicago Manual of Style*. My writing is often clumsy and clunky, but what I lack in vocabulary, good grammar, complete and coherent thoughts, and literary creativity, I hope to make up for in content.

Think of this book as a brief introduction to these topics, one that maybe opens your eyes to the possibilities. You can take me at my word (which is pretty good), follow the instructions, and you will likely make some huge improvements in your life. Or you can be skeptical (not a bad choice either), do your own research and test your hypothesis on your own life. Either way, I think you'll likely come to the same conclusions I did: the world is much different than we're led to believe and by knowing the rules it is possible to get pretty far along in your life. Think for yourself. Don't believe anyone. Remove yourself from the herd of sheeple. Find out what works for you. That is my message here.

Foreword

It's Father's Day, as I write this, the day we set aside to pay our respects to our sires for their invaluable support and guidance. For far too many people this day is empty, their fathers estranged or missing from our lives. In the context of the Sexual Revolution's chaotic dance with divorce, for millions Father's Day is empty and hollow, the disappointment and regret mocked by this holiday. Dads are important, and no one knows this better, perhaps, than those who have grown up without the influence of one.

But fatherhood, like marriage, has changed since the Sexual Revolution. Where once fathers would impart to their sons the vital information necessary for them to start their own adult lives, now even where there are fathers – dedicated, loving, passionate fathers – there is a gap in this communication which has crippled us. A sense of confusion and caution pervades fatherhood these days, and in the wake of their own (sometimes disastrous) relationships, few of our fathers feel confident in passing along their wisdom to their sons. The much-maligned Patriarchy is shattered. So for many of us, finding and marrying a wife (and then staying married), building a family and keeping a household are exercises in which we are making it up as we go along. We navigate between what we think we're supposed to do and what actually works without the benefit of paternal advice and guidance . . . and we tend to screw up a lot.

But as the shards of the Patriarchy strive to knit themselves back together into something workable, the internet comes to the rescue. Brave men who aren't afraid to share their valuable wisdom and paternal knowledge are coming forward. This book is the result of one brave man who decided to stop worrying about what other people thought and ran his life – and his marriage and family – the way he needed to.

For those unfamiliar with the Red Pill, it's simply an outcome-based, pragmatic approach to living with an emphasis on personal responsibility. But it demands we be accountable to ourselves, and hold our mates accountable as well. It accepts the gender differences we've inherited and acknowledges that men and women do things differently. That is not politically correct. It advocates firm male leadership in the household. It does not place a high value on equality, instead striving for marital equilibrium. It does not encourage our daughters to aspire to be corporate CEOs, and does not condemn our sons to a spineless existence of self-loathing and fear. It embraces the traditional elements of masculinity and femininity without being bound by them.

That's a controversial topic, and under the auspices of the gender war it's one that even reasonable people can get upset about. But Alex, the Average Married Dad (AMD), attacks the subject honestly, humbly, and with a great deal of thought. Building on the growing body of work concerning the practical side of fatherhood, husbandry, and masculinity, AMD takes a thoroughly Red Pill approach to married life in the 21st century – as it is, not according to a lofty ideal. The "lofty ideal" here is making stuff work, and while some of the ideas and techniques described might not be novel to you, together they weave a tapestry of well-reasoned and tested methods of a most practical nature. This is the stuff your father would have told you, had he known it and known how to articulate it.

Not everything in this book will work for your personal situation. Everyone's relationship is different. But there are enough true gems of insight and guidance that you will not complete this book without having gained some profound understand of how your own relationship and family life works – or doesn't. AMD's life isn't perfect, but he's not striving for perfection. He's striving for a workable solution, no more, no less, to the practical problems of married life and fatherhood in our troubled age. While the inability to produce magical results might make him less likely to make Oprah's book club, this book wasn't designed for that. It was designed for you, the man or woman searching desperately for the whispers of paternal advice that you missed . . . or you weren't paying attention to. That makes this book more valuable than gold, to those who need it.

AMD doesn't claim any special credentials beyond being an average married dad who is determined to do right by his family, his wife, and himself, and is willing to share the benefit of his experience. That, in and of itself, makes this an important book. On this day in which we pay respect to our hallowed fathers, or regret their lack, here is the authentic voice of Patriarchy 2.0 helping to guide us and our sons into the dangerous gloom of family life, and out the other side to the real Happily Ever After we are all seeking.

Pay attention. Don't make him stop this car.

Ian Ironwood

June, 2014

Introduction

I am an average married dad. I am 38 years old, have been married 12 years to my wife Holly, have a daughter (for privacy reasons we'll call her Birdsnest; 8 years old) and a son (we'll call him LoudBoy; age 6). We live in that middle area of the country over which you fly between New York and L.A. called "the Midwest." Maybe you've heard of it, or driven through it on the great American vacation. Both my wife and I work full time at professional jobs where we commute about 25 minutes each way for work. Our kids go to public schools. I enjoy football during the weekends, drinking beer, swearing, and carrying on just like most men. I'm probably a lot like you.

I'm going to be honest here and say it's not going to be all touchy-feely. My blog, www.AverageMarriedDad.com, is a place for me to dump my thoughts on life in semi-coherent - sometimes poignant - ways. It is often PG-13, but also R-rated some days, as I discuss sex, marriage, kids, money, diet, fitness, and whatever other random topic comes into my head. And I cuss sometimes, so be warned, this book isn't all puppy dogs and rainbows in the vocabulary and subject matter department. While one of my big points is improving your life and marriage, many of my writings run against the grain of traditional "be nice, be yourself and people will like you; your wife will like you" thinking. Because of that I've been called sexist, misogynist, an idiot, a pig, and many other insults from people who disagree with my thoughts. Before you get too far into this, I simply wanted to let you know what you are in for. I can be incredibly dry, detailed and boring. I like to think that I can also be witty, funny or thought provoking. I'm all over the board, but I think many of us are like that.

There are a million books on any subject you can possibly think of, but when I look at issues that I think are the foundation of happiness for the average married dad, they aren't usually integrated with each other, and most don't provide specific or detailed tools to use. Nor are these books written for the audience of their peers. Most speak from the pulpit down to the masses, making them hard to relate to. While I've pondered on these topics extensively, I am one of the masses for whom I'm writing for - the 30- to 40-something parents of kids still at home, with strong family values who are just sort of floating through life.

Let's get something straight – life in our situation is hard. If you want to be happy, it does take hard work. But the payoff is totally worth it.

Unlike most authors who site all sort of prestigious awards, PhD's and call themselves "experts" in whatever subject they are waxing poetic on, I'm not going to do that. The only two licenses I have are my engineer's license and my driver's license. I consider myself a very well read amateur who has, through trial and error in my own experiences, found some valuable knowledge in a lot of areas that can benefit many men (and women). However, according to the definition that Tim Ferriss describes in *The 4-Hour Workweek*, I guess I *do* qualify as an expert. I've read a shit-ton of books. My blog has over 400,000 page views (as of summer 2014), and I've guest-blogged on sites receiving more than 600,000 unique visitors and 2 million page views a month. I have been invited to appear on Huffington Post podcasts and national radio shows like Steve Harvey. I have been interviewed by, and mentioned in an article within, *Men's Fitness* magazine. I have a mix of women and men on my site, some Paleo (diet), some Christian, some exhibitionists, but most just regular people and all of them trying to be the best they can in today's crazy world. While I like to believe my message is appropriate for those ages 20 to 70, my primary demographic is the 24 million married men aged 30-50 who really want a better life and a happier marriage.

In my profession, I'm more of a generalist than a specialist, but like Liam Neeson in the movie *Taken*, I have a "very particular set of skills." Skills that make me a unique and valued employee despite the fact I don't dig really deep in any one area. I need to know a lot of technical and detailed information in a lot of areas and manage people who are specialists. For the topics I'm presenting in this book, it's similar. I may not be able to get into the detailed scientific formulas, sociological theories, or economic algorithms like the experts. Instead, I possess a thorough understanding of the key concepts in these matters. And for the purpose of self-improvement and life improvement, that is what matters for the common man.

The three pillars that support a happy life in our situation are health, a happy marriage, and financial security. While your work life is also a large part of this life satisfaction equation, I had to cut this book off somewhere. So work is beyond my scope here, though you should expect to see some ancillary benefits at work from self-improvement in other areas. You may not have given it much thought, but all of these pillars (health, marriage and finances) are interrelated. If you have two out of the three, you're likely unbalanced like a two-legged stool. Having health and a happy marriage, but without financial security will lead to stress and cause issues throughout your life. Having a happy marriage and financial security may be good for a while, but being unhealthy, fat, and weak will catch up to you and may rock your financial security if you end up diseased or on prescriptions due to poor life choices. Having great health and financial security doesn't matter either if your marriage sucks, since it that also takes a huge toll on your mental health as well on your financial picture - especially if you get divorced. And all three pillars lead to being a great parent, thus giving your kids an advantage in succeeding in life through learned lessons, having basic needs met, and having an example of how marriage should be.

Let me paint a picture of my typical day and see if this sounds familiar.

I wake up at 5:30 a.m. to give a quick kiss to my wife Holly as she heads out the door to the gym and then directly to her job. This will be the last time I see her until the evening. In preparation for school, I make the kids' lunches and see what I can throw together for my own lunch. Around this time, my kids Birdsnest and LoudBoy are waking up, and if not, I have to rouse their groggy and grumpy bodies up and start making breakfast. After breakfast we all get dressed, and if it's a good day they have brushed teeth, matching socks and combed hair before we scramble out to the school bus. I then commute into work about half an hour away. At lunch, I may try to sneak in a workout of some sort. If not, I'll simply eat lunch at my desk to make sure I've maximized my productivity and complete my various work projects. Throughout the day, Holly and I are communicating like air traffic controllers about various schedule items and household needs.

Upon leaving work, I may need to stop and get groceries or other items; otherwise, I simply head home to start dinner while Holly picks up the kids. Depending on the day, I may get to lift weights or exercise in the afternoon after work if I didn't in the morning or lunch. If not, the late afternoon/evening is spent getting Birdsnest and LoudBoy fed and shuttled to their various activities. After coming home, they have a quick snack before bed, get into pajamas, read a book, and brush their teeth before falling asleep (hopefully without a hassle). At this stage of the day, Holly and I are again communicating about the next day, cleaning up what we can to keep the household disaster to a minimum, and maybe decompressing a little before finally heading to bed to start it all over again the next day.

Whew! I got tired just writing that. Kids are a game changer to marriage, and you don't really realize this until you're right in the middle of the action. Is it any wonder that, with so much other "stuff" for which we're responsible for, that we lose touch with our partners, harbor hidden resentment, or see each other more as roommates than as spouses? Our once beloved spouses tend to get lumped into the landscape of this day-to-day jungle. With so much going on, it's easy to let yourself go, too: to put on some pounds, and generally stop focusing on yourself for the so-called betterment of the children. With or without kids, it's likely that the animal attraction that was present when you first started dating your wife has melted away a long time ago, perhaps replaced with a general feeling of comfort or contentment. The excitement that once made you break into that abandoned apartment building so you could have sex is now replaced by some resentment, and she's always making excuses why she's *not* in the mood to have sex. Feelings of inadequacy can build, and as a man who *needs* sex, how you view yourself is diminished to some degree. This can then manifest itself into depression, with grumpiness towards your wife or children, further undermining what you're trying to achieve (a happy marriage, happy kids) and keeping the vicious circle spinning, perhaps even ending in divorce.

As Warren Farrell describes the plight of the married man in his book *The Myth of Male Power*:

> He kept to himself his hurt that his wife seemed more interested in the children, in shopping, and in herself than in him. That he felt criticized for working late rather than appreciated for working late. To him, his wife seemed to define communication as her expressing her negative feelings but not him expressing his. She seemed to avoid sex more than enjoy it. He felt hurt that soon after marriage his wife paid less attention to keeping weight off and started dressing sloppily unless she was meeting other people.

It doesn't have to be like that. Your changes aren't guaranteed to change other people, but likely will. Making these changes requires a lot of evaluation and introspection, breaking free from societal and historical norms or expectations, and possibly physical changes, too. The key points in this book present a new way to see the world and a process through which you can start making improvements. Be forewarned though, this new world view is going to be a little bitter, but you need to have this education so you can know the biological and evolutional rules we are up against and therefore know how to deal with them. Though I call myself average, I strive to be excellent. If you are reading this book, you don't want to settle for being average either.

The impacts of failing at any one of these activities reverberate not only throughout your life, but the lives of your kids and your spouse – or if things go badly – ex-spouse. The bibliography at the end of this book and the Recommended Reading tab on my website will provide some excellent additional resources for those looking to expand their knowledge in any particular area. Cited sources and studies are noted here where appropriate, as well as anecdotal evidence and internet sources that are available.

If you were so inclined, you can score your life happiness on some sort of chart, like I created below. Think of happiness as being the total area of the middle segment – the larger the middle area, the happier you are. Really, life boils down to maximizing happiness and minimizing the shit that sucks and drains that happiness from us. If you really have your stuff together, your happiness area in the chart below is going to be large. If you have categories that need improvement your area may be much lower. Also, these areas are not independent of each other. If you have poor health, your sex life will suffer. Maybe you have doctor bills that hurt your finances or you can't be a good parent and your marriage suffers. Likewise, if you have a crappy sex life, maybe your marriage begins to suffer, or you have anxiety and depression issues that carry over into how you behave with your children. Success in one area begets success in others, just like failure begets failure.

Life Happiness Ratings

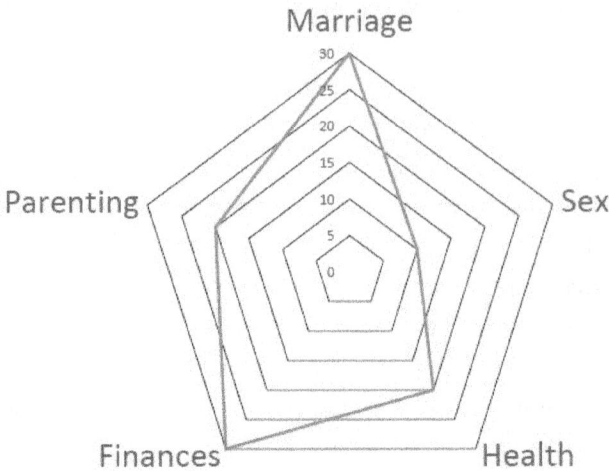

This book is broken down into four main parts: health, marriage, financial matters, and parenting.

Part 1: Health

Part 1 will focus on improving your health, body and mind.

Shoring up your weak areas or completely overhauling major flaws in yourself is often the first step before you can improve in other areas of your life. This portion of self-improvement will focus on both the physical body and mental aspects, and I'm guessing unless you are a contrarian thinker, will fly in the face of conventional wisdom and even governmental recommendations. We'll turn the USDA recommended diet on its head well as the typical thinking of "fat is bad, low-fat is good." I'll also focus in this section on finding and developing an exercise plan, as well as getting your mental and emotional house into a state where you are calm, strong and confident.

Part 2: Marriage

Obviously, married fathers coming into this book without any of this knowledge of the inter-gender Game will gain the most, and unmarried, childless younger readers that have already read most of the books, websites, and blogs on the subject matter will gain less. However, regardless of whether you're a newbie or an expert in these matters, I hope you learn something and pass along some of the knowledge you've gained to other men who haven't yet unplugged from conventional wisdom.

The first step of my own marital improvement journey, and yours here, is bringing you up to speed on the men's movement and reality of inter-gender relationships. This initial foray into the abyss can be bitter as it flies in the face of conventional wisdom and societal norms that we've been fed our whole lives, but is necessary to see the world for what it is. These concepts lay the foundation for understanding why women behave the way they do and subsequently, how a man can modify his behavior to get the response he desires. Think of this section as The Ghost of Marriage Past.

Next will be The Ghost of Marriage Future, where I extrapolate on what could happen if you continue to make the same mistakes over and over again. Marriage future could be great, very average, or, as many people can attest, end in divorce. While my goal here is very much pro-marriage and making it work, like Charles Dickens' *A Christmas Carol*, sometimes you need to see the flip side to appreciate and improve on the situation you are currently in. You will learn more about divorce, not just as an abstract concept, but the ways in which it can be especially devastating to the father and adversely impact the children. I hope that by seeing divorce in concrete form it provides you with the necessary motivation to do whatever you can to improve your marriage.

Finally, I'll explore how these key concepts apply to marriage and sex in what could be described as The Ghost of Marriage Present. Understand that you can only change yourself, but you will learn about how your behavior is likely impacting the woman you are with and her interactions with you. You'll learn about the potential major pitfalls hormonal birth control and other drugs can have on a woman's libido as well as why your wife may not enjoy sex until after you're in the act.

Part 3: Financial Matters

Personal finance is as important to a happy life and security as anything else. Without a plan, direction or basic knowledge of what to do, it's easy to be intimidated and do nothing. Then one day you wake up, you're fifty and have that "Oh Shit!" moment where you realize retirement isn't just a concept but a tangible thing staring you in the face and you have nothing saved. My wife and I have made our share of poor financial decisions but have been saving since we had any tangible income to speak of, and are starting to see a decent positive net worth prior to turning 40. I'll provide some basic strategies for getting out of debt, as well as basic saving strategies. Then I will outline key tools and concepts to save for retirement and kids' college in a straightforward way. This will provide some guidance on how to meet your financial goals in a simple way so that you, the average guy with no particular skills, can get started. If you are already well versed in this section, it should be a good reminder to keep the pedal to the metal and to be the tortoise, not the hare.

Part 4: Parenting

Last, but not least, I'll get into how parenting has changed today, how to be a better father and what this newly acquired knowledge means in raising children. Being a father doesn't come with an instruction manual and most of the knowledge gained is from the school of hard knocks. If we can improve as fathers and impart some of the wisdom and the thinking presented to our sons and daughters, the next generation will be improved; they will understand the rules of the game regarding the opposite sex, money and healthy living.

Takeaway

If you take only one thing out of this book, it's this: you can only control yourself, your thoughts, your actions and reactions, and your overall happiness and wellbeing. You can't change anyone else. Your changes may result in improved behavior and responses in others, but as they say, you can lead a horse to water but you can't make them waltz...or something like that. You need to let go of the fact you can't control other's happiness and instead focus on your own. That is the core of this book. As you'll find though, as you take control of your own life and put things in order, you set the tone and example for your family to follow. The new structure you provide for yourself will result in a cumulative impact to those in your direct circle of influence. It's pretty powerful to know that you can start the snowball rolling on life improvement for other people. What are you waiting for? Let's get this party started!

Part 1: Health and Wellness

CHAPTER 1

Diet

Most of us are aren't stupid, we're just weak willed in some regard. But we've also been fed a whole smorgasbord of lies by our government and doctors that drastically reduce our ability to get healthy. In general though, we know that we should be eating better, drinking fewer distilled spirits and soda, and many of us are carrying around at least a few extra pounds. Obesity has become an epidemic in America and throughout the world, and it's impacting not just adults but kids too. A 2013 American Heart Association fact sheet noted that 33% of boys ages 2-19 and 30% of girls that age are overweight or obese. Among adults, between 65-69% of men and women are overweight depending on what source you use. Basically, you are in the top third of the country health-wise if you simply aren't overweight or obese and how we behave towards health and diet is the example we're setting the next generation as a society. We should do our best on an individual level to promote good practices so that our and our family's health and thoughts on diet improves.

Besides looking like a fat pile of poo (I don't mean to fat shame, but that is what's ingrained in our lizard brain in terms of what is attractive, or rather what is not attractive), being overweight or obese is very unhealthy. You increase your risk for gallstones, Type 2 diabetes, high blood pressure, high cholesterol, coronary artery disease, stroke and sleep apnea. As you'll see in the upcoming section, being attractive to your spouse is a critical component to marital dynamics and happiness. So then, how hot is it when you have to be hooked up to a continuous positive airway pressure (CPAP) machine every night? Lots of hot sex right? "Let me just take my oxygen mask off and turn off the machine that keeps me alive at night before I make sweet, sweet love to you babe!" are words that aren't often spoken.

The Body Mass Index (BMI) isn't perfect, but is at least a guideline to use when assessing your weight. At 5'7" and 165 pounds (2014), I am technically in the "Overweight" category myself. However, I lift weights 3-5 days a week and gained nearly 30 pounds of mostly muscle over the last couple years compared to my lean underweight endurance days. While I may not have a six-pack, I still fit into the same waist size as I did in high school. When people who haven't seen me in a few years note I've gotten "huge," it's not because of my gut. For those participating in high-intensity sports that value large muscles and power such as sprinting, football, weightlifting or hockey the BMI chart may not accurately depict if you are at an unhealthy weight. However, for those not participating in much of anything (except life), the BMI chart carries a lot more value in your assessment. Look at the BMI chart to see where you fall, and look at recent pictures of yourself. Be honest – brutally honest – with yourself and see if there is room for improvement...there likely is.

Besides the cost that society bears in supporting overweight and obese people, individual costs are high as well. According to a 2010 study by George Washington University School of Public Health and Health Services, the annual individual cost of being overweight is $524 for women and $432 for men. For obese individuals, the annual costs jump to $4,879 and $2,646 for women and men respectively. The cost drivers are primarily direct medical costs incurred by the individual, though things like lost wages from absenteeism and short-term disability also contribute. Besides other factors such as premature mortality, being overweight or obese may increase your insurance costs for both health and life insurance.

For those of you who are parents, being able to watch our kids grow up, get married and have kids of their own is obviously a priority. While most may not have to worry too much about living to see grandkids, what about keeping up with your kids running around at the park, playing football or pond hockey or tag, or just being a good example for your kids? I see fat kids at our kids' sporting events all of the time, and most of the time they go hand in hand with fat parents. While I was never a fat kid, being one must not be fun and I'm guessing they probably have a harder time in life and in building self-esteem versus a "normal" weight kid.

Finally, besides the health benefits of feeling good, saving money, and keeping up with our kids, we really just want to look good for vanity reasons. We want to look better than our peers, we want to stand out at the community pool or at the beach on vacation, and we want to look good for our spouses. Basically, looking good naked is a very simple goal that most of us are trying to achieve. Not necessarily benching two-times our bodyweight, but looking better than most of the regular guys. If it results in being noticed by other women (especially in front of your wife), it may have the unintended impact of creating jealousy or tension within your own wife, which may not be a bad thing.

Diet

Looking good and losing weight is dictated primarily by diet. There's a saying in the bro-gym community: "abs are made in the kitchen." The word diet automatically insinuates a lot of negative reaction in people. They diet in short term fits and spurts to try and fit into that dress that will turn heads at their 20 year reunion. They diet to look good at the beach in the summer. They diet to not embarrass themselves on vacation. Often, as soon as a person has returned from this event, his or her motivation disappears and he or she goes back to their old eating habits, subsequently packing back on that 20 pounds or more. In the context of this book, diet is something entirely different. A diet isn't something you do (it's not a verb), but rather a noun to describing the way you intake nutrition. Diet should not be something we do for a temporary period of time to lose weight, it should be our standard way of eating that is healthy and balanced in perpetuity.

The thing about nutritional science and diet is that it's not black and white. You could get 10 scientists in the room familiar with low-carb, high-carb, low-fat, high-fat, paleo, primal, fruit, vegan, pescatarian, vegetarian or raw meat diet and they probably couldn't agree on whether the sky is blue. We average people don't have the time or expertise to read technical scientific papers on the latest studies conducted that say meat is good, or that eggs are bad, or that soy is sent from Jesus to save our arteries, or that soy is the devil and will make men all have boobs. Instead, we're left in the weeds, reading articles in magazines, listening to Doctor Oz or our own doctor, or perhaps venturing off into the internet to try and find answers. It is all very confusing, and for every "expert" opinion, you'll find another refuting it, often with both sides raising good points. Additionally, with the anonymity of the internet, you never know if any special interest groups are behind these so-called experts, or if these experts are taking their positions with some ulterior motive such as selling you something.

So who are you to believe? First, I think you need to take a look at the government recommendations and see if those nutritional recommendations hold water. Second, if you acknowledge that perhaps the United States Department of Agriculture (USDA) doesn't have the best scientific support for their recommendations, and society today has gotten much unhealthier as a result of following their recommendations, then you need to research alternatives that may improve your health. Having done that research, you'll really only know if it works by testing it out on yourself and seeing if your health is better or worse after incorporating those changes, making further modifications as necessary. It doesn't really need to be that complicated. In general though, a good diet does require self-education and critical thinking, and will take a disciplined effort to implement. It's about time you stopped being a sheeple and following the unhealthy herd.

My opinion on diet has changed a great deal over the years, and I believe we've finally found a sustainable and healthy diet that works very well for us. This is supported by our own anecdotal evidence, cause and effect adverse relationships with certain food, and by basic blood work conducted as part of regular physical exams. The diet we follow flies completely in the face of our own government's USDA recommendations, but is strongly supported by actual scientific, as well as tons of anecdotal evidence, of its whole life benefits. It behooves you to at least read this section and consider giving it a shot to see if you benefit as well. Again, finding full consensus on any diet recommendation will be impossible, so it is up to you to separate the wheat from the chafe (probably a poor analogy given my lack of love for wheat, as you'll see). It is up to you to determine if the dietary changes result in positive life changes or negative, and will be supported by your own experience, health and blood work.

Just to warn you, this diet section does get sort of science-y at times, but I'm really only giving you the very tip of the iceberg from the resources I've read (and recommend you read as well) such as Denise Minger, Robb Wolf, and William Davis. If you take this section at face value, you'll have the building blocks to succeed, provided that you commit to making some potentially large diet changes. Alternatively, if you don't think a broad, whole life diet change will be of much benefit, I strongly encourage you to reevaluate your health and see if there are things you'd like to address. It is up to you to learn about nutrition's impact on health on your own and decide if a change is necessary or not. Perhaps your current diet is working for you. Perhaps your research will push you to a plant-based diet. It's your life, so educate yourself for your own health and the health of your family and children. Whatever you decide, have good reasons for following that plan; hopefully it's not just because "the government told me to eat this way."

While I'm more of fan of clinical scientific studies, let's be honest in stating that trying to get any large control group to consistently eat exactly what the scientists want over a period of years is impossible. All of our lives have inherent environmental variables that research can't control, so while we can find likely correlation effects of various items to adverse health impacts, it is much more difficult to prove causation. With that said, anecdotal evidence should at least be considered when finding out if a particular way of eating may work. These anecdotal writings may also indicate how strict you may really need to be before you feel the health impacts. Many of the so-called "Paleo" authors and bloggers post success stories on their sites, perhaps the longest running is a page on www.marksdailyapple.com. Like anything else, take this somewhat with a grain of salt. Many of these authors and bloggers have products they are selling. I have personally found great value in these resources and they are well worth reading in my opinion. With that said, I believe everyone would be better off eating as I will outline versus eating the conventional USDA diet. For our family this diet has been an easily maintainable approach to health and wellness, one that we've been following for years.

Before we start, let's look at nutrition at the most basic level. Nearly any food can be broken down into three macronutrient categories: carbohydrate, protein and fat.

Carbohydrate - (or "carb" for short) provides 4.2 calories per gram and consists of simple sources such as sugar or honey, or complex sources such as grains, beans, peas or potatoes. So called "simple carbs" are simple chemical structure made of one or two sugars - monosaccharides and disaccharides. Monosaccharides include fructose, galactose and glucose. Disaccharides include two linked monosaccharides and include lactose, maltose and sucrose. These latter types of carbs include table sugar, white flour, honey, milk, fruits and soda.

"Complex carbs" are of a more complex chemical structure containing three or more sugars, but break down to simple carbs in the digestive process and provide immediate energy (they spike insulin). Complex carbs are found in vegetables, whole grains, milk and legumes. Carbs fuel certain brain functions that are dependent on glucose, a simple form of sugar. However, unbeknownst to most, carbs as a food source aren't necessary in our diet, since our body can break down proteins and fats into simple carbs, even from our own muscles, and can replenish muscle glycogen from conversion of other macronutrients, albeit at a slower rate. Glycogen is a sugar that is made and stored in the cells of the liver and other muscles. For humans, it serves as an immediate energy storage tank so that when we bike or run, we have an immediate fuel source for outrunning the saber tooth tiger, or staying ahead of Jan Ullrich up L'Alpe d'Huez. Once depleted though, you are dependent on digested glucose or fat as a fuel source.

The other thing to consider about carbs is their glycemic index (GI), or how quickly blood sugars rise after eating certain foods. Lower GI foods take longer to raise blood sugar take more time to digest, such as beans, seeds, and vegetables including sweet potatoes. Medium GI foods are those that elevate your blood sugar in the middle, like potato, prunes, enriched wheat and bananas. High GI foods get into your blood stream the fastest and spike blood sugar quickly and include white bread, corn flakes, breakfast cereals and most of the crap we eat that is high-carb combined with low-fat, like pretzels. Low GI foods release glucose slowly and steadily while high GI foods are like rocket fuel.

Adding fat and protein to any carb source will lower the GI rate since fats and protein take longer to digest. So a potato with full fat sour cream, cheese and bacon will have a lower GI than just a plan one. Lower GI diets have been shown to reduce type 2 diabetes, heart disease and other adverse health impacts. Getting further into quantifying the impacts of GI on food is called "glycemic load," where it takes the quantity of a particular food (the number of carbs it contains) as well as the quality (GI level) to determine its overall ability to raise blood glucose and insulin levels. Hence, a bagel has a higher glycemic load than a serving of the higher GI corn flakes despite the fact that the corn flakes have a higher GI score (but smaller serving size).

Protein – Protein is basically an organic compound that has one or more chains of amino acids that support the structure, function, repair and regulation of the body's organs and tissues. There are 20 different types of amino acids that make up a "complete protein" and are found in most meats and eggs. Many plant foods contain incomplete amino acid profiles and, need to be combined with others to provide the full profile needed for full amino acid distribution. This is often a problem that vegans or vegetarians encounter and requires basic understanding of food combinations. Proteins are an essential human nutrient and provide 4.1 calories per gram, very similar to carbohydrates (in fact both are generally considered 4 calories per gram).

In the absence of carbs, your body can still convert protein to glucose by a process called gluconeogeneses (GNG). It takes place in the liver and is associated with ketosis, which I'll talk about later. The conversion of protein to glucose doesn't happen just from food sources, but can also happen with your muscles in the case of starvation, fasting, or intense exercise. Have you ever done a three hour hike or bike ride where you haven't eaten enough and smelled like ammonia afterwards? You just experienced gluconeogenesis.

Fat – Fats are esters of glycerol and one, two or three fatty acids; occurring widely in organic tissue of animals as well as seeds, nuts, vegetables and some fruits. Nearly all foods contain fats, and it's not something to avoid. In fact, fats are vital to our diet. Fats move fat soluble vitamins, stores energy, are essential for our growth and development, help maintain skin and cells, and regulate many of our body's processes. There are two different types of fat based on the different carbon/hydrogen ratio: saturated (each carbon atom in the fatty acid chain is "saturated" with hydrogen) and unsaturated, with the latter broken down further to monounsaturated and polyunsaturated.

Unsaturated fats can be converted to behave like saturated fats (and in some instances to become saturated) by artificial hydrogenation or partial hydrogenation, which is how trans fats are created. Many types of foods have fats with both types (saturated and unsaturated), and even trace amounts of trans fats can naturally occur in meat and dairy products though it is unclear if these naturally occurring versions have similar adverse health impacts compared to artificial sources (and it is difficult to evaluate since consumption of artificial sources of trans are orders of magnitude higher than the naturally occurring trace amounts in certain meats).

Saturated fats are typically solid at room temperature and naturally found in animal products like meat, milk and eggs as well as plant products such as coconut oil. Margarine is also a type of saturated fat due to the artificial hydrogenation process.

Monounsaturated fats are typically liquid at room temperature and are found in olive oil, avocados and rapeseed oil (aka canola oil).

Polyunsaturated fats are found in foods like fish, nuts, seeds and vegetable oils. Polyunsaturated fatty acids are usually broken down into two main types: Omega-3 and Omega-6. These are very important to bodily function, and must be made up entirely from food sources since our bodies are not able to synthesize it. Oily fish like salmon produce a lot of Omega-3 fatty acids which have many health benefits. Significantly higher ratios of Omega-6 fatty acids are found more in vegetable and seed oils like canola, corn, sunflower, peanut or soy.

The ratio of Omega 3s to 6s is also important. Studies conducted on polyunsaturated fatty acids (or PUFA) show statistical importance of this ratio on brain function, cholesterol, Alzheimer's disease, seizures, quality sleep, cortisol (stress), cancers, and cardiovascular diseases. Basically: the higher the ratio of Omega-3s the better, and the higher the percent of Omega-6s the worse. Historically, our ancestors' ratio of Omega-3s to 6s was nearly 1 to 1; currently in today's society, estimates range from 1:10 to 1:15. One estimate indicates "the diet by the typical American tends to contain 14 to 25 times more Omega-6 fatty acids than Omega-3 fatty acids." This is not a good thing and is a contributor to many of our western society health woes as Omega-6 is related to inflammation and inflammatory diseases. These diseases include type 2 diabetes, irritable bowel syndrome, rheumatoid arthritis, asthma, cancer and autoimmune diseases to name a few.

Animals that are raised on farms (processed chicken, beef and salmon for example) have a much higher Omega-6 content versus wild or organic animals fed grasses or natural diets. You can supplement with fish oils (Omega-3s) to increase this ratio – though the studies demonstrate mixed results of the effectiveness of this approach. The easier way to adjust the ratio though is to reduce the Omega-6 number by stop eating processed crap. A study published in the May 2006 Journal of American College of Cardiology showed that replacing high Omega-6 polyunsaturated corn oil with monounsaturated olive and canola oils, thereby decreasing the Omega 3:6 ratio, led to a 70% decrease in total mortality compared to the control group in the study timeframe.

While trans fats are chemically unsaturated, they behave so differently than unsaturated fats that they cannot be labeled as such. Trans fats are primarily artificial, and are found primarily in fried, fast foods and commercial shit-products like cookies, donuts and chips. Trans fats are made by adding hydrogen to liquid oil, which turns it solid like margarine or Crisco©. This processing makes the fat easy to handle, extends the shelf life, and is inexpensive. Any time you read "hydrogenated oil" or "partially hydrogenated oil" that is a trans fat. Doctors from the Mayo clinic to your local practitioner, consider trans fat "bad" as they raise your LDL (considered the "bad" cholesterol) and lowers your good HDL cholesterol (but it's not so black and white as you'll see). Trans fats are also very high in Omega-6's, further contributing to the issues noted above.

The USDA Food Guidance is a Crock of Shit

Here's a short snapshot of the USDA and their role in this mess. The United States Department of Agriculture has had a long and sordid history in terms of the scope of their original responsibilities and the role they currently perform. Originally established in 1862 by Abraham Lincoln to aid in agricultural development and assist in the distribution of new plants and seeds, it expanded its role with federal funding to teach agriculture, home economics and similar topics to the public throughout the U.S. The USDA assisted in the Great Depression with loans and other programs that helped assist small farmers with food production and distribution. Today, the USDA still assists farmers and food producers with the sale of crops domestically and worldwide.

That is only part of their responsibility, which has also morphed into the agency providing nutritional guidance to Americans. Prior to 1977, the Department of Health, Education and Welfare (HEW) and the USDA were both involved with health and diet education and diet-disease research. But a 1977 farm bill pushed the research responsibilities primarily to the USDA due to the perception that HEW was not doing much to advance disease prevention research. This put USDA in the position of both needing to appease agricultural interests (their primary "official" responsibility up to that point) while at the same time guiding the principles related to United States human health and diet – which as you will see has significant conflicts of interest.

In the late 1970's Luise Light was hired as the head of the USDA's nutritional team to revamp the old "basic four" food guidance (originally established to deal with preventing malnutrition) into the "food pyramid" most of us are familiar with; this pyramid was only recently replaced with the USDA "My Plate" program we see today. Light and her researchers analyzed scientific literature on the links between disease and diet, reviewed dietary standards from the National Academy of Sciences, and worked with a variety of scientific experts to develop what was believed to the be the best dietary guidance to prevent chronic diseases from nutritional sources. What she came up with and presented in the late 1980's was recommendations that we consume:

- five to seven ounces daily of protein foods like meat, eggs, beans and nuts
- five to nine servings of fruits and veggies
- two to three servings of dairy

She also recommended eating natural fats and four tablespoons of "good" fats like olive oil, as well as limiting both processed junk foods and refined carbs – like white flour products – that she considered in the same category as the junk food (those at the pointy end of the pyramid, which we were supposed to eat only in moderation). Cereal grains were still present, but were limited to three to four servings per day. Read that part again: based on the expert they hired, and years of research, they recommended a diet that primarily consisted of protein, fruits and veggies, with minimal amounts of dairy and cereal grain. After review by higher-ranking (but with less scientific knowledge) officials in the USDA, the resultant recommendations weren't even close to her original recommendation.

It was as if Light's pyramid got flipped upside down. Instead of 3-4 servings of grains closer to the top of the pyramid, it was changed to 6-11 servings and served as the base of the pyramid. Protein sources were cut in half and kept near the top of the pyramid with the unchanged dairy servings. Fruit and veggies were right near the top too at 2-3 daily servings, but were later changed to 5-9 servings due to pressure from cancer prevention organizations. This Frankenstein's monster of a pyramid was released in 1992, was taught in schools, and became the dietary guidelines most Americans took as law.

According to their website, the current 2014 USDA propaganda, err...recommendations, on grains are as follows:

- "Most adult men and women should have 5-8 ounce equivalents of grains, at least half being whole grains." What the hell is an "ounce equivalent" you ask? Why that's one slice of bread, one cup of cereal, or a half cup of cooked pasta. So a man my age should be eating 7 slices of bread, 7 cups of whole grained cereal like Cheerios, or three and a half cups of pasta. Per Day! Does that even pass the sniff test? Do you think eating a third of a loaf of bread a day makes sense for your health? Because that is what the USDA is selling you.

- The health benefits of whole grains: *may* reduce risk of heart disease, *may* reduce constipation, *may* help with weight management, and fortified whole grains help prevent neural tube defects during fetal development. [Italics my emphasis, conclusions are taken directly from USDA].

- Nutrients include: fiber, several B vitamins and minerals. Fiber, fiber, fiber. This is the drum they beat for good bowel function, the reduction of blood cholesterol, and to help make you feel full. You'll see that the fiber story isn't so black and white. Even if you determine that fiber is critical for your health, vegetables, and to a lesser degree fruits, can provide all the fiber and nutrients you need, and in the correct amounts, for proper health.

These three recommendations constitute the cornerstone of the USDA's guidance on why we should eat a lot of wheat product, or at least what they are presenting to the public. Because of this big push for breads, cereals and pastas (remember the previous food pyramid had this category at the base, with 6-11 servings recommended, so I guess that's an improvement since the MyPlate program has it down to 5-8 servings a day), we are bombarded from grade school to adulthood with the message that this is the correct way to eat. We, and our kids, are literally brainwashed with this idea as being infallible. If this is the healthiest diet, then why were these changes made against the advice of the team hired to make these decisions in the first place (Light's team)? As in most things, you can follow the money to get your answer.

As mentioned earlier, the USDA has a large conflict of interest in promoting health versus serving its real master of agricultural industry. Firms like

Monsanto, Kellogg's, ContiGroup and Cargill carry a lot of political power and subsequently can and do put a lot of pressure on USDA. With $15 billion in farm subsidies at stake, the Big Ag group has a lot of interest in making sure they get as much of this share as possible for the crops they grow. So their lobbyists and politicians-in-hand pressure the USDA to pass bills and push subsidies to a large share of their interests at the expense of more healthy options. These crop subsidies help pay farmers to produce large quantities of corn, soy and wheat, instead of other crops like fruits and vegetables that tend to be less stable and a have a more limited shelf life without freezing or other processing. In other words, crops like fruits and vegetables are more expensive and more of these products are thrown away, or don't even make it to market, versus the more stable corn, soy and wheat. According to a study from Yale University, four crops (corn, soy, wheat and rice) receive 60% of subsidy payments. Of these subsidy payments, 54% are now going to "large," presumably corporate, farms, consolidating and shoving out what were once small family farmers. The bottom line is that USDA is controlled by companies that have a vested interest in having you eat the way they want you to eat so their profits are maximized – namely eating lots of corn, soy and wheat products.

You can begin to see at least the tip of the iceberg in who is influencing policy, and receiving the benefits of said policy. You might be saying "Who cares? The USDA is looking out for my best interests and these are healthy foods right?" Whole grain has to be healthy, because they say it is? First off, how can you trust a group who has such a vested interest in selling something from which they benefit financially? And second, so much research to the contrary exists, which I will touch on momentarily. I'm not a food scientist and have eaten many different diets, including moderate-to-low fat, vegetarian, high-carb, low-fat, high cardio programs. Today, diet following Paleo principles has left me and my family feeling healthier than we ever have felt.

According to Michael Pollan's book *In Defense of Food*, the average adult in the U.S. consumes approximately 67% of their calories from corn, soy and wheat (and their derivatives). Studies on our ancestors showed they ate about 80,000 different species of plants, animals and fungi and that approximately 3,000 (3.7%) of those are foods widely seen in our current human diet. Based on those studies, Pollan estimate that over tens of thousands of years of eating this type of diet (which varies based on climate and geography) derived only 1% to 5% *maximum* of total calories from corn, soy and wheat.

Whole books have been written on the fallacy that wheat is good for us: *Wheat Belly* by cardiologist Dr. William Davis may be the most well-known. I had the opportunity to see Dr. Davis speak on this subject in 2014 and while it's an uphill battle, more and more people are seeing that wheat is a direct contributor to poor health conditions.

Wheat: A Food Demon

Consider the other dietary information the opening band for the main event. Really, if there is one thing I'd urge you realize about your diet it's that whole grains and wheat-based products are likely one of, if not THE KEY detractors to losing weight, why you sleep poorly, and factors into inflammation and adverse autoimmune response. The website WholeHealthSource.blogspot.com has a nice introduction on grains quoted below. Remember that modern man has been around for about 200,000 years, so even your longest consuming ancestors have only been eating wheat for a small fraction of their existence. You can find something similar from any number of books from Cordain to Wolf.

> "Although wheat had its origin 11,500 years ago, it didn't become widespread in Western Europe for another 4,500 years. So if you're of European descent, your ancestors have been eating grains for roughly 7,000 years. Corn was domesticated 9,000 years ago, but according to the carbon ratios of human teeth, it didn't become a major source of calories until about 1,200 years ago! Many American groups did not adopt a grain-based diet until 100-300 years ago, and in a few cases they still have not. If you are of African descent, your ancestors have been eating grains for 9,000 to 0 years, depending on your heritage. The change to grains was accompanied by a marked decrease in dental health that shows up clearly in the archaeological record."

One of the books that has helped to support vegetarian and vegan diets is *The China Study* by T. Colin Campbell. The book includes a lot of interesting discussion on diets around the world, promotes a plant-based diet, and tries to make meat to be the boogeyman. It is forthcoming and outright in its belief that a vegetarian and no-dairy diet is ideal for preventing western diseases and leads to better health. It correlates the hypothesis that all meat is bad, often supporting this conclusion with data showing a single protein type in milk (casein), that seems to correlate with increased health risk (because obviously, eating casein - a cow milk protein - is the same as eating that same cow for beef). Anyway, some of the data in the book is really interesting in support of why wheat is bad. Consider the following data from the 1989 China Study II questionnaire (credit to Denise Minger for breaking this down and doing the heavy lifting of crunching data from the Clinical Trial Service Unit and Epidemiological Studies Unit of the UK):

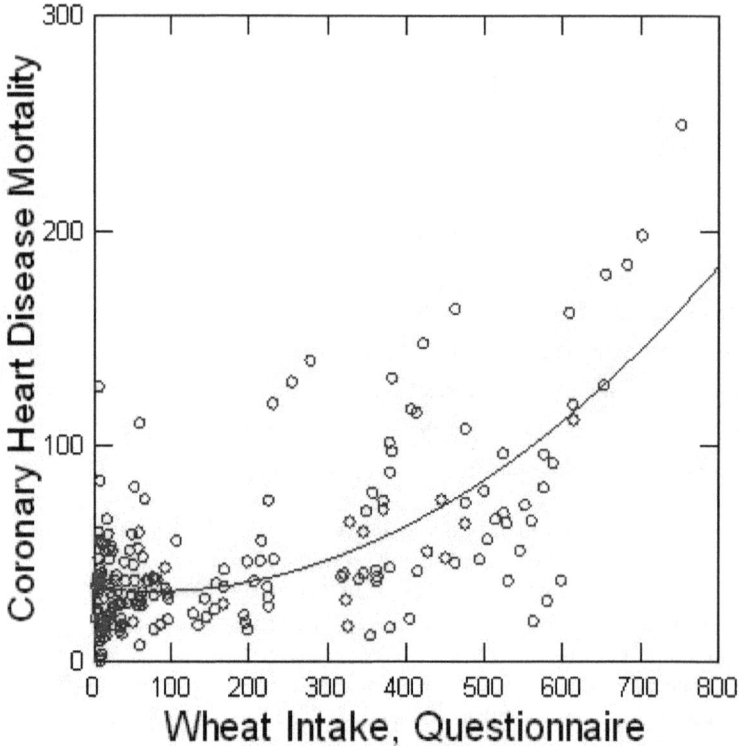

This chart basically shows that as self-reported wheat product intake increases, death from heart disease goes up. That is pretty compelling data, especially when considering that, like heart disease, stroke and hypertensive heart disease are also strongly correlated with consumption of wheat flour. What's also interesting is that higher body weight and higher BMI have been correlated strongly with higher wheat intake, but not higher calories. Meaning that despite eating the same or fewer calories as other types of diet with less wheat, the wheat-eaters tended to be heavier.

Dr. Davis, author of *Wheat Belly* ("Lose the Wheat, Lose the Weight" as the jacket says) claims that wheat is a highly toxic genetic abomination. Current strains of wheat are bred to be more resistant to pests and for increased ability to withstand powerful herbicides, and are all around very different than historical strains, even which, as you may recall, our ancestors ate in very small amounts. Wheat causes varying degrees of inflammation in virtually every person who consumes it. Despite what wheat defenders are starting to put out to the public about lack of a "smoking gun" in people without Celiac disease, wheat does have adverse impacts for most people. It can cause problems with immune, endocrine, nervous, and digestive systems, though certain people are more susceptible than others. Just because you don't have full-blown celiac disease doesn't mean your digestive system won't appreciate you cutting it out. Dr. Davis has discussed situations where people have had varying nasty autoimmune diseases and have been tested for celiac multiple times with negative results. After cutting out all wheat products (white flour, processed foods, everything that has wheat – even as a minor ingredient such as canned soups) these disorders "magically" disappeared without requiring expensive and unnecessary medication or surgical intervention. Wheat is also very high on the GI index, spiking blood sugar higher than even table sugar. Spiking blood sugar leads to crashing blood sugar later.

Just why wheat is toxic to us needs to be broken down further here. Unlike some foods, like berries, that establish a symbiotic relationship with predators (they are allowed to be eaten so the seeds can be spread and fertilized by the animal moving and pooping), grains are designed to prevent predation. A basic grain is a domesticated grass that we can process and subsequently eat, and includes such staples such as wheat, rye, barley, oats and rice. All grains have three main anatomical parts: Bran is the outer covering of the whole grain and contains proteins and anti-nutrients designed to prevent a predator from eating the grain; Endosperm makes up 83% of the grain kernel and is primarily a starch with a small amount of protein; Germ is the reproductive part of the grain and makes up only 3% of the kernel.

Grains have a variety of proteins called lectins, one of the nastier ones is called wheat germ agglutinin (WGA), and is well studied. Gluten is a cousin of lectin and just one of these nasty proteins found in wheat, rye and barley, and unless you just awoke Rip Van Winkle style, you've heard at least of gluten. Like gluten, lectins are problematic in that they don't break down in the gut. Subsequently, the large, intact proteins attach to receptors and are transported through the intestinal lining. Basically, these proteins trick our intestinal lining and allow passage through the intestinal walls into our bodies, and once through, our bodies see them as similar to viruses or parasites and attack them. Both gluten and WGA increase intestinal permeability and damage gut lining, causing it to become more porous and contributing to leaky gut syndrome. Our immune system then initiates an immune response by creating antibodies to fight these passed-through proteins. Unfortunately, these proteins appear very similar to proteins in our own body, and the antibodies made to fight the WGA will also attach to proteins in our pancreas. When this happens, pancreas starts to become damaged and a whole host of health issues can follow.

Gluten or WGA may not knock you out of the water, but it may still impact you. Celiac is an autoimmune disease caused by gluten. People who suffer from celiac have severe digestive issues such as bloating, stomach pains, diarrhea, weight loss, constipation, fatigue, and irritability. In children, celiac disease may result in growth problems, trouble maintaining or putting on weight to the point that they show signs of malnourishment. This disease prevents the body from absorbing essential nutrients and in adults, if left untreated, can result in iron deficiency, arthritis, depression and even erratic menstrual periods. Because they actively and adversely impact the body's ability to absorb nutrients, these proteins are often referred to as anti-nutrients. Now don't think that just because you don't have celiac you are home free. Gluten, WGA and other lectins can significantly impact enzymes that can subsequently modify every protein in our body. The autoimmune response and passage of these proteins through our gut lining can result in the development of allergies to foods that are normally benign due to the increased porosity of the intestines. If you are especially sensitive, even small amounts of gluten or WGA (found in many foods) can adversely impact your gut lining, and those who have a reaction effectively have to remove 100 percent of it from their diets. As Robb Wolf states in *The Paleo Solution*:

> "You only need to be exposed to things like gluten once very ten to fifteen days to keep the gut damaged. This can bedevil people as they 'cut back on gluten' but do not notice an improvement in their overall health. You need to be 100 percent compliant for thirty days, then see how you do with reintroduction."

If you are a sufferer of one of the more than 100 autoimmune diseases, you understand how inflammation is part of your everyday life, and for the worse.

Dr. Davis states the following on his blog: "For every person... who is diagnosed with celiac disease, there are nine more that don't know they have it but suffer with various misdiagnoses, suffer silently, or end up with non-celiac form of the disease, such as cerebellar ataxia, peripheral neuropathy, type 1 diabetes or gastrointestinal cancer in some form."

Based on these symptoms, doctors are likely to prescribe drugs or put you on some therapeutic remedies, but most sufferers have no clue about how diet may be contributing to their plight. I'm not saying diet can solve everything, but until you try eliminating highly inflammatory items such as wheat from your diet, you will not know what impact it may have. Most people don't want to do this though since they get used to baking, to eating three square meals, and three snacks a day – most of them including quick and easy wheat or flour products. Then there's the matter of the sugar rush (and it is a real rush – the grains contain molecules that fit into the opiate receptors in your brain) of wheat or flour in their diet. This rush is also addicting and unknowingly creating millions of food zombies.

My wife and I have explained how diet can have adverse impacts – immune disease, obesity, and other health issue – with several of our own family members. And while they respect our diet beliefs, they unfortunately won't pull the trigger themselves. It isn't easy to make the change, but if your health is impacted, I sincerely believe many people would see very strong positive correlation with better health with complete elimination of wheat or wheat byproducts (including regular flour) from their diet.

You may be thinking then "How will I get my fiber if I take out wheat? That's what is so healthy about whole grains in the first place!" Author of *Your Personal Paleo Code* Chris Kresser sites many examples of the overstatement of the nutritional benefits of fiber, and even paints them as a detriment to health. Research showing the benefits of dietary fiber concludes that the link between eating fruits and vegetables (which have natural fiber) lower obesity, heart disease and colon cancer. Despite what the USDA says though, controlled trials that add fiber supplements to otherwise nutrient dense diets did not show these similar protective impacts. Fiber is not digestible, and insoluble fiber in larger quantities can actually bind to important minerals like zinc, iron, magnesium, and calcium, preventing their absorption in our bodies. Fiber does have benefits of maintaining good gut bacteria, but many vegetables provide both soluble and insoluble fiber in the quantities necessary for healthy digestion. Eating fibrous whole plant foods (yams, sweet potatoes, carrots, leafy green vegetables, apples, and berries) is a much better way to get your fiber, without the need to supplement, compared to relying on wheat or other cereal grains that are high in anti-nutrients.

Besides wheat, other common foods that sometimes wreak havoc on peoples' bodies include soy, dairy, and nuts. Food allergies are more and more common, and just because you haven't been diagnosed with one, doesn't mean you don't have sensitivity to common foods that are in so many things. Take a look at the ingredient label for anything processed, like that artisan loaf of bread or that cake from Costco, you'll be surprised how many contain soy or nut products. Many people are able to tolerate and enjoy dairy, but your body may still be better off without it. Some people find there is some inflammatory response from unfermented dairy products and when they eliminate them from their diet, they see an immediate result in feeling better, better stools, and even leaning out. Others are able to tolerate fermented dairy like Greek yogurt or sour cream, which add some physical properties to cooking that are beneficial from a texture or flavor standpoint. Even nightshades like potatoes, tomatoes, peppers, and eggplants can cause some people problems. So don't lock yourself into any hard and fast rule on diet. I'm a fan of going to very "clean" eating for 30 to 60 days – that is, no dairy, no wheat or gluten, no soy, no legumes. Just eggs, high quality meat and fish, vegetables, fruits, bone broth, and healthy cooking fats like coconut oil. If you see improvements eating strictly clean, maybe add foods back in one type at a time to see if you are able to tolerate them or see if they have any impact on your health. That's the only way to see what we actually have sensitivity to and what we're better off eliminating from our diet permanently.

Many Paleo authors echo these same recommendations of removing wheat (and other possible common food items that cause issues) from your diet for 30 days to see if you feel better. Better yet, remove all processed foods, flour (breads and pastas included), and soda and see if it doesn't start a new way of eating that makes you feel better. Healthy skepticism is OK. In fact it's good in many ways. You are a one person experiment, and if you want to drop pounds and feel better about yourself, I strongly believe eating a whole food, nutrient dense diet is the way to go. And eliminating wheat and all-purpose flour is the easiest way to start and see significant improvements. It is tricky to find food alternatives to sandwiches and pizza and bread, since they are so prevalent in every type of traditional diet (that is making us fat and unhealthy), but we've adjusted and so can you. See more about "What to Eat" in that section below.

But I Thought Saturated Fat Causes Heart Disease (or otherwise titled: Fat is a Four-Lettered Word)

Another thing USDA has strived to reduce is one of the key aspects of a healthy diet: fat, and especially saturated fat. Fat has been demonized and "low-fat" is put up on a pedestal as something for which we should strive. Our family followed this type of eating for years. Low-fat skim milk, lots of pasta and breads, lean cuts of meat... and ended up in a binge and purge cycle where we would eat super "healthy", but then break down and eat sweets and pizza and junk. We were constantly unfulfilled, had intense hunger after the initial burning of food fuel was completed, and were in the "eat, crash, eat" cycle that is so common in this type of diet. Though we felt somewhat ashamed every time we fell off the low-fat, healthy grain wagon for junk food, in reality, it really wasn't our fault, nor is it yours. While we exercised a lot, we always were carrying around a few (sometimes more than a few) extra pounds usually around our collective waists. Sleep at night wasn't great and we would wake up starving. Holly was convinced she was an undiagnosed hypoglycemic (low blood sugar) condition, where she felt as though she would faint if she didn't eat at regular intervals. Like many other adverse effects of the low-fat way of eating, most of the symptoms went away completely once we changed our diet to include more fat and lower amounts of refined carbs.

While the USDA now has strong recommendations to reduce trans fats like partially hydrogenated oils, which is a good thing, saturated fats from eggs and meats are still ostracized. Here's what the USDA has to say about saturated fats (from the 2010 USDA dietary guidelines publication):

> "A strong body of evidence indicates that higher intake of most dietary saturated fatty acids is associated with higher levels of blood total cholesterol and low-density lipoprotein (LDL) cholesterol. Higher total and LDL cholesterol levels are risk factors for cardiovascular disease.
>
> ...

> To reduce the intake of saturated fatty acids, many Americans should limit their consumption of the major sources that are high in saturated fatty acids and replace them with foods that are rich in monounsaturated and polyunsaturated fatty acids. For example, when preparing foods at home, solid fats (e.g., butter and lard) can be replaced with vegetable oils that are rich in monounsaturated and polyunsaturated fatty acids."

So based on these recommendations, you should not fry your food in saturated fat-laden, coconut oil (stable at high cooking temperature) and instead use canola or soybean oil or shortening. You will see this is bad advice.

"But the doctors say saturated fat is bad!" you say. Let me fill you in on something about doctors and nutrition: most don't know much about it. Over 70 percent of medical schools in the nation, including Harvard, have no requirement for nutrition-oriented classes to get a medical degree. As such, they may understand the biological aspects of bodies and diseases but may not even realize how nutrition plays a role in that, so instead they follow the group-think of health recommendations from organizations like the USDA. Add to that the fact that physicians (94% or more) have regular contact and relationships with "Big Pharma" pharmaceutical representatives. It is more likely physicians get biased nutritional and medical advice from them versus from actually reading nutritional journals. I don't plan to digress too much into this incestuous relationship, where there is no incentive for the doctor to treat the cause, only the symptom (often for their and their clinic's profit) but it bears mention here.

Fat and saturated fat didn't become demonized without reason; in fact, it has been well studied. Two key hypotheses were developed to explain the cause of heart disease. **The Lipid Hypothesis** states that high cholesterol in the blood causes heart disease. **The Diet-Heart Hypothesis** states that high saturated fat intake *causes* high cholesterol in the blood, which causes heart disease. It may seem like a minute difference, but the difference is very important. Mainstream media gets the Lipid Hypothesis, which has some pretty good scientific support, confused with the Diet-Heart Hypothesis, which is grounded in very flimsy data. So it's widely and mistakenly, believed then that saturated fat hikes up blood cholesterol. This isn't the case, and we should be sure to distinguish between the two theories. Even in the absence of saturated fat, cholesterol and other lipids can cause heart disease. To restate this again in another way: high cholesterol of the wrong type has been shown to be a key cause of heart disease; but despite the propaganda of the USDA, saturated fat hasn't been shown to definitively contribute to blood cholesterol increase of the type that results in heart disease.

Let's talk about cholesterol for a moment. Cholesterol is a vital part of the body's chemistry and is critical for life. It is used to produce steroid hormones for normal development and functioning, including the sex hormones estrogen and progesterone in women and testosterone for men. Other hormones produced from cholesterol includes cortisol which assists in regulating blood-sugar levels and defends the body against infection. I'll talk about the bad part of excess cortisol later, but on its own, cortisol is a necessary hormone for bodily function. Cholesterol is also important in synthesizing vitamin D, a vitamin in which many people are deficient, especially in winter. Vitamin D impacts mental health, immunity, bone and muscles, and helps with disease prevention such as diabetes, cancer and heart disease. Cholesterol is also used to make bile, an important substance used to digest foods.

As you're likely aware, two types of cholesterol are present in our bodies, with the "bad" kind (low-density lipoprotein, or LDL) has been shown to be a legitimate contributor to heart disease. Heart disease is also known as cardiovascular disease, and includes the condition atherosclerosis where the arteries are hardened, thereby contributing to heart attacks and remedies such as bypasses. High-density lipoprotein (HDL) is the "good" type. It cruises the bloodstream and removes the larger "bad" LDL type, from where it doesn't belong. It has been concluded through multiple studies that elevated LDL is a contributor to heart disease. In times past, they didn't have the capabilities of distinguishing HDL from LDL and so all cholesterol was lumped together, hence the start of "high cholesterol is bad" doctrine that carried over from an earlier time. With modern medical techniques, doctors can now distinguish between HDL and LDL, resulting in treatment of patients that have elevated LDL levels and not condemn someone with higher levels of HDL to a life of drugs like statins.

Most parties general agree on this point. But did you know there is more than one type of LDL? In fact, some LDLs are relatively safe and some are dangerous. It is easier to describe them as good and bad than to break them down further and confuse the masses. Since you are more than average, you should know that LDL cholesterol shouldn't all be treated the same. When you go to the clinic for a blood draw to check your cholesterol, and get a cut and dry three-part lipid panel (HDL, LDL and triglycerides), it classifies all LDL as the same and subsequently, your doctor may want to put you on statins or some other drug. These treat the symptoms, not the problem. But LDL comes in primarily two different forms: the big, fluffy particles (largely benign), and the small, dense versions that are the devil about which to be concerned. A 1988 study published in the *Journal of American Medicine* showed that the small, dense LDL particles are three times more likely to cause heart disease than normal puffy LDL.

The typical lipid panel doesn't differentiate between LDL types, so you may incorrectly be put on medications when you don't need them. What's even more interesting is that studies have shown that while saturated fats make your overall LDL levels rise, they only increase the larger LDL particles (LDL Pattern A, sometimes known as LDL-R subclass pattern A) and not the smaller devil LDL particles (LDL Pattern B, or LDL-R subclass pattern B). This indicates that saturated fats by themselves are neutral (or better) in your cholesterol as they aren't increasing the quantity of the LDL-B particles. Like most things, this theory is by no means 100% agreed upon within the scientific community, but seems to be generally accepted by many in the nutritional sciences and is supported by research.

There are several special blood tests that identify between pattern A and pattern B. Some of these tests are proprietary, such as the Vertical Auto Profile (VAP) cholesterol test. Another is called polyacrylamide gradient gel electrophoresis. Costs may range from $100 to several hundred dollars. If you think you've been eating pretty well (i.e. few, if any grains, little or no trans fats, few or no fried foods, more saturated fats, a more traditional "paleo" type diet), then this type of test may potentially pay off significantly in short order if it allows you to avoid taking drugs and incurring their associated costs. The research I could find indicated that misdiagnosis based on lumping all LDL together is fairly common, and issues could often be addressed beyond the standard approach by tailoring treatments specific to individual factors. However, there are still a lot of other factors potentially at work here impacting LDL levels including poor thyroid function, infections, leaky gut (which could be caused by wheat intake), and genetics. Follow the advice of your doctor in these matters.

Blood cholesterol is certainly a key contributing factor to heart disease, and things like stress, poor diet, smoking, physical inactivity, obesity and genetics play a great part in the blood cholesterol levels and types. Diet is a key factor in this, but not in the way the USDA or conventional wisdom presents it; in fact it's nearly the exact opposite.

The USDA and, by extension, conventional wisdom paint the saturated fats from red meats, eggs, and other fatty meats as the culprit for high cholesterol. This is taking the Lipid Hypothesis (elevated cholesterol is correlated with and a contributing factor to heart disease – an agreed upon truth), ramming saturated fats as the *cause* of the elevated blood cholesterol based on flimsy research and then selling it to the public as being chiseled into the diet 10-Commandments tablet from God himself. The USDA that guides U.S. dietary guidelines states saturated fats are the primary contributor of higher amounts of LDL (regardless of if the LDL is "neutral" or "bad") in many people. They subsequently connect the dots and say then that saturated fat is a leading cause of heart disease and heart attacks. So what does conventional wisdom tell you when you have high cholesterol? Give up meats and eggs, and then go on a statin drug like Lipitor or Zocor which helps to clean out those nasty LDLs. The winner in this scenario and choice of diet (treat the symptom, not the cause) is the drug industry. *Forbes Magazine* stated statins earn drug companies $26 billion in annual sales. If the sheeple are kept in the dark about how diet impacts their cholesterol, they'll continue staying "ill" and feeding the corporate drug companies, who subsequently lobby the government and your doctor (hot drug reps anyone?) to keep the gravy train rolling in any number of ways.

The USDA hangs their hat on the "saturated fat is bad" approach on 12 scientific studies. Author and researcher Denise Minger breaks down all 12 of these studies on her website rawfoodsos.com (in a post titled: "The New USDA Dietary Guidelines: Total Hogwash and Here's Why"). Discussing these 12 studies is beyond the scope of what I'm trying to accomplish here, but suffice to say every one of those studies has flawed assumptions, data or conclusions, and in some cases the USDA conclusions were way off base. For example, one study that replaced the percentage of saturated fat with high GI carbs was associated with a 33 percent *greater* risk for heart attack. This meant that if you ate fewer eggs and more white bread you would be 33% more likely to have a heart attack. Despite the results of this study, no carb trends were discussed nor were carb or flour-based dietary items discouraged by USDA. Instead the "whole grain equals healthy" trend continued. One of the 12 studies even stated:

"In conclusion, our meta-analysis showed that there is insufficient evidence from prospective epidemiologic studies to conclude that dietary saturated fat is associated with an increased risk of CHD [coronary heart disease], stroke, or CVD [cardiovascular disease]."

As Minger points out, it is very difficult to unravel saturated fats from all the other ingredients that make people unhealthy. The second-largest contributor of saturated fat intake (besides direct sources such as meats or eggs), is "grain-based desserts" such as cookies, pies, cakes and strudels, which, in addition to whole food saturated fat such as eggs, use fats such as shortening, margarine and of course have tons of flour and sugar. Coming in at number three on the saturated fat list is pizza; number four is cheese, then processed meats and french fries. Nearly half (45%) of our saturated fat comes from starch-based meals like pies, cakes, and pizza, versus only about a third from solo items like butter, whole milk, eggs and meat. Without strict controls, coconut oil and animal products get lumped with things like Pizza Hut ® and donuts on the saturated fat spectrum.

The bottom line is don't believe what they say about animal based saturated fats. Be much more wary of partially hydrogenated oils, which are bad for you, and wheat or all-purpose flour's role in our dilemma, as discussed earlier. Monounsaturated fats such as olive oil and some polyunsaturated fats can be good, though many studies on even those fats are inconclusive. A good rule of thumb is that if you know what the oil came from you're probably ok putting it on or in your food. So fish oil is good, olive oil probably good, coconut oil is good, canola oil is...well what the heck is a canola? It's rapeseed oil (apparently the manufacturers of this product didn't think rapeseed was a good brand identity so rebranded it as canola), and isn't good for you. Likewise, vegetable oil is a pretty generic term. Can you tell me what vegetable it comes from? No? You're not alone. Most of the time it's from seed and nuts. I would avoid if I were you. The only cooking oils in our kitchen are coconut oil, olive oil, real butter, and bacon grease.

What to Eat

So I've talked briefly about what not to eat, but haven't talked about what *to* eat. Simple: nutrient-dense, whole foods. Think: things you could still find in nature, or at a minimum, live on the outside aisles of the grocery store.

Vegetables, fruits, meats (grass fed is ideal), eggs (buy locally raised from free ranged chicken if possible), and some fermented dairy if it works for you. Bone broth and organ meat is wonderfully healthy for us. You can pick veggies and fruits, hunt animals for meat, harvest eggs, and milk cows. This is what our ancestors ate (maybe without the domesticated cows for milk), including seeds and nuts, and this dietary approach has unchanged for thousands of years. Though don't assume that this diet will be 100% right for you, and don't be afraid to make tweaks. Maybe at the end of the day you'll find a careful plant-based diet is what works best from you, but many find keeping animal proteins from meat, fish and eggs allow you to feel your best. Another diet to consider if you are reluctant to eat much (or any) red meat is pescatarian, or basically plant-based diet with seafood, as many have had great health success on this approach.

Meat provides a complete protein source, and if wild game or organically or grass fed, has a decent ratio of Omega-3's to omega-6's compared to the store bought the stuff. Even if it isn't pasture raised, meat provides very good proportion of nutrition to cost and if you keep processed foods out your Omega 3 to 6 ratio will still be pretty good. A lot of high-quality macro nutrients (protein/fats) come from meat depending on the cut, which can range from below 50/50 (protein to fat) to over 90/10.

Whole foods like vegetables and fruits provide many micronutrients important for health. Eating mostly greens and veggies would address many of the nutrient deficiencies seen in people today. Nutrient deficiency is on the rise due to the replacement of nutrient dense foods (meats, veggies) with flour, grains, fruits and processed junk. While I don't put a lot of credence in the Food and Drug Administration's (FDA) Recommended Daily Allowance (RDA), some conclusions can still be drawn showing we aren't eating well enough. For example, most people are 40-100% deficient in folic acid, a nutrient that can cause a loss of appetite, headaches, weakness, apathy, anemia and insomnia. Leafy greens and beans are a great source to fight this deficiency. People are often magnesium and iron deficient, too often by 50% or so. Iron deficiency leads to anemia, increases heart disease, cancer, osteoporosis, depression and digestive problems. Magnesium is key to maintaining a healthy nervous system and deficiency can increase potential to heart attacks, type 2 diabetes, colon cancer and asthma. Foods like nuts, seeds, beef, dark turkey, and leafy greens (spinach,

Swiss chard) can provide these. Those are just a few example of how diet impacts health.

What this means for your daily meals is up to you, as you may really have to change how you do things, but it doesn't have to be hard. If you have a favorite burger joint (with real ground beef), simply order it without a bun. If you like spaghetti or pasta, simply make your standard meat pasta sauce and substitute sliced, zucchini fried in coconut oil instead of noodles. Fish, quality poultry, eggs, meat, and vegetables leave you extensive meal choices – from stir-fry, to steak and sweet potatoes, to stews. Many websites and books have good Paleo recipes for comfort foods. For a pancake recipe you may substitute flour for things like bananas and nut butter (and it tastes really good; this is one we use sometimes). You can often substitute almond flour or coconut flour in baking or in pizza crust, but when you see the prices of some of those alternatives, you'll likely cut down on traditional baking altogether.

The hard part is starting. The mental hurdle of throwing out all your processed foods and saying no to the bagels and donuts and treats at work is difficult, but can be done. If you get through a few weeks of eating "clean" without this processed stuff, you'll start to feel better and you'll find continuing on this path is easier. Then, you'll fall off the wagon and have a donut or pizza at work, and you'll then see first-hand how bad that food makes you feel, reinforcing the fact that you were on the right track. They say that habits take 60 days to fully integrate into your life, so by day 30 you'll see that you probably feel better, and by day 60 eating this way will be second nature.

What Not to Eat

While this may be redundant if you've been paying attention and connecting the dots as we went along, I'll wrap this up by beating you over the head with this information. If you follow the guidelines on what to eat such as getting most calories from "real" meats (not just muscle meat, but organ meats and bone broth, which has a lot of documented health benefits as well), leafy greens, vegetables, and fish, you'll be doing pretty well. But most people believe either the fallacies fed by the USDA – of what and what not to eat. As I mentioned earlier, the war against eggs, beef and saturated fats has been waged for years and is based on untruths. In 1950, obesity and diabetes were not the public health atrocity that they currently are. In the mid-part of the 20th century, proteins and fats dominated the dinner table – meat (including organ meat), fish, eggs, whole milk, and cheese – were staples. Vegetables, from broccoli to potatoes, were a part of most meals. Whole foods. Foods with proteins and fats that left you satiated. What was missing from the diet of yesteryear were trans fats, high fructose corn syrup, Franken-chicken and high quantities of grains.

The USDA has a really interesting publication called the *Agriculture Fact Book*. Chapter 2 of the book breaks down food choices over the years. If you look at why we're fat today, it's because we essentially have a caloric surplus. Per capita, we eat more meat today than in the 1950s, primarily from a huge increase in chicken (over 300% more in 2000 than in 1950s). Chickens that are commercially raised to fatten up quickly can't even stand, and are fed corn and soy enriched with antibiotics. I would highly recommend reducing or eliminating the amount of chicken sourced from large producers from your diet. We Americans also eat one-third fewer eggs now, and four times as much cheese. We also eat more fruits and vegetables now, with most of the increase from non-citrus fruits and other fresh vegetables like corn. Grain products are consumed at a 30% higher rate, and use of corn sweeteners like high fructose corn syrup (HFCS), which was basically non-existent in the 1950's, increased by nearly 800% by 2000. Finally, let's not forget about fats. We eat 67% more fat in 2000 than we did in the 1950's. This increase is made up almost entirely by salad and cooking oils and shortening (hydrogenated or partially hydrogenated oils), while the saturated fats such as lard, beef tallow and butter have actually decreased. Way to go USDA: your demonization of saturated fats appears to be working and we're so much healthier now!

So what conclusions can we make comparing our diet from the 1950's and our diet today? Basically we eat more (duh!), but more importantly, it is what we are eating *more* of that counts. We eat more grains, more corn sweeteners (especially HFCS), and have replaced saturated fats with fats that are chemically processed and/or modified in most cases. As a result our western society is fatter, more disease ridden, and unhealthier. Wouldn't it stand to reason then, that if we eliminated processed foods, grains, and processed fats in our diet, we would start to be healthier and have the stronger and leaner bodies most people had 60 years ago?

One final micro-topic on diet before we move on; what not to eat if you are interested in losing fat. Up to this point, I haven't discussed carbohydrates, as people tend to get hung up on what it means in the context of a healthy diet. People have had success eating a broad range of proteins, fats, and carbohydrate ratios so it's more important to focus on getting a broad range of foods that provide macros (fats, proteins) and micronutrients (vegetables, fruits) and let the carb side of things fall where they may by eating tubers (sweet potatoes) and other fruits and veggies. With that said, if you are interested in dropping fat in a more rapid manner, going lower carb may be right for you.

Controlling Carbohydrates and Impact on Weight

Before I discuss the concept of using diet to lose weight, I want you to realize that focusing on losing weight or losing fat as the end goal usually doesn't work. Sure it can be a motivating factor, but if that is the only reason you eat the way you do, it likely won't last long term. You need first to internalize that you are eating for long-term health, and in doing so, you will likely naturally lose excess weight.

Using diet to control or reduce weight doesn't have to be complicated, especially if you've already eliminated processed foods and the carb-straviganza that is the standard American diet. Simply cut down on the higher carb vegetables and minimize fruit. Primal entrepreneur Mark Sisson recommends 0 to 50 grams of carbs a day to induce ketosis and accelerate fat burning. Ketosis is a state of switching from dietary carb to fat for energy. The liver converts fat into fatty acids and ketone bodies that replace glucose as an energy source. You may very well go through what is commonly referred to as "low carb flu" as your body gets used to using fats as fuel instead of primarily carbohydrates. Experiencing headaches, nausea, brain fog, and fatigue are not uncommon. It may last for several days to several weeks. Just stick with it if this is your goal.

While we've used this approach in the past in our house to some success, I don't believe this is a good long-term practice. Cutting out higher carb foods like fruits or some vegetables result in reduction in many micronutrients present in these foods. Having adequate protein is also important to spare muscle mass from being used as an energy source while at the same time increasing fat content (fat is a large percent of calories in this diet). When trying to switch to this sort of fat-utilized diet, even consuming a few too many carbs or protein can kick you out of it, so if you want to employ this for a while, you need to be committed and consistent over a period of weeks; maybe even months. If employing this approach, using a Keto Calculator website (such as http://keto-calculator.ankerl.com/), my macros would be fewer than 25 grams of carbs, 140 grams protein (for an active lifestyle), and 170 grams of fat which would leave me slightly calorically deficient given my activity level. When I've incorporated a low-carb approach, I didn't read Atkin's diet book or really think too hard about it; I just simply tracked my carbohydrates and kept them low. You may smell like ammonia and your breath may stink, so be aware that this is a normal part of the process. Many, many people have had success with this very low carb approach in making quick work of dropping weight, but as I mentioned, I haven't found this to be sustainable. After the first wave of weight loss, you're likely better off adding a few carbs back into your diet and taking the slow-and-steady approach.

For those looking for a slow, easy way to instigate fat loss using a high nutrient density whole food diet I think you'll naturally gravitate to between 50-100 grams per day. This approach minimizes insulin production while at the same time maximizes, to a large degree, fat metabolism. With this approach, you can likely lose one to two pounds per week without too much trouble. Neither of these lower carb diets are recommended if high intensity exercise (like Insanity or CrossFit) are on your plate, so back off on these types of workouts. Longer, slower, steady state cardio such workouts – such as biking – are more suitable when following a ketogenic diet, provided you keep intensity appropriately low to promote fat burning instead of glycogen burning. You may still hit weightlifting workouts with limited impact. If you want to gain muscle, many find the need to add back in carbs to provide enough energy for fueling the body and leaving adequate protein untouched for muscle rebuilding.

Finally, the "maintenance zone" in keeping a steady bodyweight will likely be around 100-150 grams per day of carbs. When combined with lifting heavy weights, moderate amounts of cardio exercise, and lower intensity activities such as walking or simply moving, this approach is highly sustainable and is typically where my wife and I are at on any given day. As you start to increase carbs above 150 grams/day, (for reference, the USDA ChooseMyPlate website recommends for a 2,000 calorie diet macros that contains average daily carb intake of 275 grams. Ouch.), you'll start to see higher insulin response, lower fat burning ability and most likely, long term weight gain. In some instances, higher carbohydrate (from good sources such as fruits or tubers like sweet potatoes) may be necessary if you are say, one who needs fast replenishment of glycogen following intense, frequent workouts (like CrossFit or other HIIT). For most of us though, keeping in the maintenance zone of 100-150 grams of carbs per day is the key for feeling satiated and happy and is easy to maintain.

One macro diet consideration is how much protein you should be consuming if you are exercising or lifting weights regularly. Whether your goal is fat loss or putting on muscle, a good starting point is 1 gram of protein per pound of bodyweight. This level will keep you satiated, while at the same time being anabolic enough to contribute to muscle gain as well as preventing muscle loss under calorie restriction while lifting weights. Some may find they need to bump this up, but protein not used for muscle building will turn back to energy in the form of fat or potentially inhibit ketosis if you are going low-carb. Don't be afraid to supplement with protein powder post-workouts or as a meal replacement to make sure you are getting enough, especially if you follow a strength training protocol. Most agree, however, that whole-food sources are still preferable for protein intake.

Cortisol

I've referenced cortisol several times up to this point but haven't gotten into what it is and what it means in our life. Cortisol is a hormone produced by the adrenal glands in response to stressful situations, and subsequently increases blood sugar, suppresses the immune system and decreases metabolism. Basically, our bodies utilize the cortisol response (otherwise known as the "fight or flight" response) for a quick burst of energy, heightened brain function and lower sensitivity to pain. This response allows our bodies the ability to survive in the short term. These are all good things in acute situations.

For our modern life though, stress seems to be constant and persistent given the daily commute, work, kids, having only small amounts of time which to relax, and the onus of balancing family finances. The constant cortisol release brought on by these daily stresses requires other bodily functions to shut down or decrease. Things like digestion, immunity response, and endocrine function are all impacted. The conversion of protein to glucose by gluconeogenesis triggers the breakdown of muscle mass. Cortisol's constant release also leads to weight gain and the inability to lose fat. Furthermore, cortisol and testosterone compete for the same resources, so if cortisol goes up, testosterone comes down. For men, low testosterone impacts ability to maintain or grow lean muscle, libido, energy, red cell production, emotions and quality sleep. For women, this can also impact lean body mass, libido, produce PMS, and contribute to polycystic ovary syndrome (PCOS), fibroids, and infertility.

How do we address this cortisol issue, then, in our busy lives? First, do your best to get a handle on your stress. Getting your marriage and sex life in order, making progress on your financial house, exercising, and having kids who are growing up to be good people have a huge ability to reduce stress. A good pet helps too as cortisol response decreases when petting your animal. The best any of us can do is to try to limit most of our worries to work issues and minor life/family things that come up. That should be your goal. I've included some mental health ideas to calm your mind and try and keep the stress wolves at bay in Chapter 3.

Other ways we can reduce cortisol release is through our environment. Eliminating grains and other foods that may be problematic – such as legumes and diary – will reduce cortisol as well. Consuming these foods actually results in stress on your body and the corresponding reaction is a release of cortisol. Sleeping in a dark room for eight to nine hours a night will contribute to improving adrenal functions and reducing the release of cortisol. Studies have also shown that active video and light sources before bed (phones, tablets, television) impact the ability to get quality sleep by suppressing the secretion of melatonin thereby disturbing your natural circadian rhythm. Instead, switch to books or quiet activities to unwind before bed. We've also found that melatonin supplements have helped both the kids and adults in our house get to sleep more easily (1 mg for the kids, on occasion, and 3 mg for the adults).

Ironically though, one symptom of chronically elevated cortisol is insomnia and the inability to get quality sleep, so it can be a vicious cycle if you are dealing with similar issues. You are stressed so cortisol is chronically dumped in your system, therefore you have poor sleep, which means your human growth hormone (HGH), which gets released at night, isn't as high. When that happens, you don't recover from that workout as easily, and you wake up tired and stressed. Repeat ad nauseam. Getting out of this cycle can be tricky. First, despite being counterintuitive, cut out your high intensity exercise such as CrossFit, and chronic cardio such as frequent running or biking. These are both large cortisol contributors. Some specialized heart rate monitors and phone apps can provide some sort of indication the level of stress your body is under and if you should even be exercising at all. Too much of a good thing (working out) can even cause adrenal fatigue, which may take some time to dig out from. The saying is that "if you find yourself in a hole, stop digging." Work toward using some of the strategies for stress reduction and sound sleep such as a dark room, meditation or relaxation exercises, trying to leave work at the office, and eating well so that your body can recover and you aren't introducing more stress from foods like wheat. Eventually you should be able to recover and reintroduce your exercise regimen.

CHAPTER 2

Exercise and Fitness

Secondary to eating whole, nutrient dense foods and cutting out wheat, flour and all the processed crap, is exercise. Eating will take your body to a great place, lean out, and look good naked. But it won't give you muscles or give you the cardiovascular benefits that the right fitness routine can provide. Fitness can be as a divisive topic as any. Let me first say that if you have some fitness activity that you like to participate in, you're able to stay healthy and happy doing so, then by all means keep doing what you're doing. My intention here is to provide some basic framework for a fitness or exercise program if you don't really know what you're doing, as well as to dispense some more up to date knowledge on the potential adverse impacts following the conventional wisdom on a fitness program that has you doing a lot of cardio for much of the year.

My Background

I'm not some Johnny-come-lately to the fitness side of things. Most of my life has been a pursuit of various exercise or fitness related competitions and making my own body capable of doing both regular and amazing things. As a man of relatively small physical stature (I'm only 5 feet, 7 inches tall – 1.7 meters) I was drawn to pursuits such as running and wrestling in my youth. It became apparent that I was pretty uncoordinated during youth team sports like flag football and soccer. This fact, as well as being small for my age, led me to running 5k events in grade school and then cross country in junior high. I also added in wrestling at that time, which I continued through high school and actually did fairly well at on the state level. Wrestling introduced me to weight training and I did some basic movements from High School through College. During college I played various intramural and club sports from soccer (indoor and outdoor) to volleyball to Judo.

After college I was a slug before catching the triathlon bug. At that point, and for about five years thereafter, I dedicated myself to long-distance running, biking, and triathlon events, which culminated in high level placement in two Ironman Triathlons, which consisted of a 2.4 mile swim, 112 mile bike, and 26.2 mile run. My times qualified me for the age-group World Championships in Hawaii (an event many triathletes chase their entire "career") but I chose not to go, as I had a newborn at the time and was very burnt out training and pursuing these goals. I had been training with professionals in the sport, had taught myself key aspects of kinesiology for long distance endurance athletes and was considering going into coaching. I was, at the time, super-fit and very, very skinny with not much meat on my bones, which ironically was not attractive to my wife Holly as she liked me with more mass. Eventually the long 10-20 hours of training per week got to be too much and I felt like I was spinning my wheels going nowhere fast.

For several years after completion of these events, I stayed in shape without any real goals, always capable of being able to drop into a 50 or 100 mile bike ride with friends, or sign up for a half-marathon (13.1 mile run) on a whim. This "chronic cardio" still took a fair amount of my time, from 5-10 hours of training a week, and despite this caloric expenditure, I became what is commonly referred to as "skinny-fat." This term is typical of those who do a lot of cardio, have limited muscle mass and carry extra weight around their mid-section. Millions of people have fallen into the conventional wisdom that cardio plus a low fat diet will yield results of being "not fat." While this may work for those vigilant in counting calories and being blessed with good metabolism, for the vast majority of us this doesn't work. The chronic cardio eats muscle for fuel and you end up with limited muscle mass and usually an emaciated look. Even worse than that, with often higher levels of cortisol being released it usually results in storage of fat on the midsection or butt.

I was searching for something that would catch my passion again. Enjoying Mixed Martial Arts (MMA) on television, and already having spent about 7 years of my life doing grappling (wrestling mostly, but some Judo), I signed up for

Brazilian Jiu Jitsu (BJJ) with a club in my area. Competing again on a regular basis was something that really fired me up again as was learning a martial arts that had practical application as self-defense in the real world. Around this time Holly jumped into some Judo classes on her own at another gym, and we had some interesting living room grappling sessions from time to time. Due to change in employment that made it next to impossible to maintain classes and home life, I had to discontinue BJJ after less than two years, but led to the next fitness chapter.

During and after the Judo sessions my wife was taking, she was also doing a regular group class at a local fitness center that focused on body weight movements like pushups, pull-ups, running, kettlebells, and rope climbs that were centered on shorter, high-intensity sessions. She made some great fitness, strength, and body composition improvements and really liked the group environment. I dropped in for a few classes, which I really enjoyed, and saw the benefits of changing the routine. Upon researching high-intensity training a little more, I decided to jump in and completed the Beach Body series *Insanity*. If you aren't familiar with this program, it is a high-intensity, body-weight DVD program that cycles between a number of different workouts over 60 days. I got stronger, in much better shape, and it continued to spark my motivation, including competing in a very challenging half-marathon trail run with a lot of elevation gain. In my opinion, unless you have very high level of mental fortitude, staying motivated with a DVD program is very difficult past the first cycle. However, I recently ran into a former colleague of mine, we got to talking about weight lifting and fitness, and he said that he had made it a point to complete 365 straight days of *P90X*, another of Beach Body's DVD programs. So it is possible to sustain something like this for much longer if that is your sole motivation.

After *Insanity*, I had gotten rid of much of my skinny-fatness, and had some muscle definition. At this point I then started weightlifting again; something I hadn't done with any vigor since my high school and college years 10+ years earlier. Unlike my teenage and college years where I followed typical bro-workouts (bench, bicep curls, pec-deck) I actually learned what to do to get stronger and bigger. Under a linear-progression program, which I'll describe later in this chapter, and focused eating, I was able to put on about 30 pounds of mostly muscle (compared to my Ironman weight) over the next 6 months, much to Holly's delight. Since this time, I've maintained this weight, leaned out a little more and gotten stronger using a heavy weightlifting slanted strength and conditioning program. For a while I had a CrossFit membership, and competed at several CrossFit competitions, but I found the strength component the best part about that program. In addition, I have a number of issues with some of the CrossFit training practices. In general though, CrossFit does a lot of things right and is a program some may consider instead of what I present here. I am still trying to gain strength and keep lean muscle mass, but I'm really happy with where I'm at and have accomplished my baseline goals set a couple of years prior.

My intention here isn't to back-door brag about my accomplishments, but to show you that I've followed many fitness- and exercise-centric paths nearly continuously since 1988, and have seen firsthand where the various paths can lead. Very simply, I think you'll generally be healthy and happy if you can do the following:

- **Passion** - Find a sport or activity that inspires you to show up and improve
- **Play** – Your chosen sport or fitness activity should be fun. If not what's the point? Seeing the changes you can make in your body through hard work can be fun in its own right, as is having the ability and fitness to participate in fun activities or races on a whim while on vacation or with friends. My wife often needs more of a group activity for it to be fun, while for me, really putting myself through the gauntlet either alone or with others is my version of fun. The occasional bike ride or trail run with friends is fun. Playing tag with the kids is fun.
- **Goals** – if you don't have specific goals you are going to flounder and eventually give up. "Getting stronger" isn't a goal, it's a wish. Tangible, attainable and time-sensitive goals are needed to motivate.
- **Avoid Chronic Cardio** – Don't follow conventional wisdom if possible that running every day or performing other cardio activities frequently is good for you. If you enjoy running or biking as a hobby or sport, please continue, especially if you perform these activities outside. If you think running on a treadmill or biking inside is fun, you should probably have your head examined. On the other hand, if you want to get into shape, and have something that

still carries over to the occasional 5k run your time is better spent doing other things. In most cases, chronic cardio causes more harm than good, at least compared to other alternatives.

- **Lift heavy weights** –frequently enough as heavy weights promote increased testosterone, better body composition, and a tough guy mentality that sets you apart from the 5k wimp at your office. Plus, chicks (like your wife, whether she admits it or not) dig muscles.
- **Walk** – walking is easy, sustainable and you can add things like a weighted vest if you want to make it a little more interesting. Our ancestors mostly walked, occasionally sprinted and sometimes lifted our hauled things, but mostly walked. It has a foundational role and isn't utilized enough in today's society.

That's it. You'll likely stick with an activity that is sustainable and fun for *you*, and not an activity or sport that I say is the best for you. With that said, I highly recommend involving weight lifting movements in some fashion into the routine and I'll explain why. Most of us like the pump and fulfillment of lifting, and the changes it makes to our bodies.

Below I've provided a Basic and Advanced sections to start you on your way if you need a workout program that fit into your busy lives. You can continue with the Basic program lifelong if you'd like and be perfectly fine. Advanced is for those that want to challenge themselves and be that dad at the local pool that everyone says behind your back "he must work out!"

If you've been living a sedentary lifestyle, put on a lot of weight over the years and generally are starting from ground zero, you should be starting in the first category and work your way up to the second. This means crawling before you walk and walking (literally) before you run. If you're like many men and are semi-weekend warrior types, you may likely be able to jump right into the higher movements with just a little bit of time.

While it's certainly not necessary, I do encourage competition to get the juices flowing a little, and you learn a lot about yourself in competition. When I ran cross country in Junior High I sucked. I mean I really sucked. Like last place in every race sucked. It wasn't for lack of trying, I simply wasn't very good, but I didn't get discouraged and came back each time fighting harder than ever. There's no miraculous ending here, where I came on to win the final meet of the season or anything. The lesson that can be gained here is that unless you put yourself out there, learn to deal with winning or losing in competition, you can't really know how you'll react. Competition, regardless of the outcome, results in higher testosterone levels, with the winner usually seeing a larger improvement. It colors life a little differently when you've been choked out grappling, or attempted a 230 pound bench press that nearly crushed you (thank God for spotters) or placed in the top half of WHATEVER competition versus continuing to stand on the sideline and spectating. Trust me here, even if you are risk averse and never competed in anything in your life, you'll come out feeling more like a man after conquering your competition fears. There's nothing in the world, besides maybe public speaking in front of a large audience, that compares to standing at the starting line of a race or staring that opponent down before the start of a competition, be it a person or a target or a barbell.

Whether you compete or not, there are a number of key things you can do to set yourself up for success. These things will essentially create mental rewards that recognize your accomplishments frequently, which creates a positive feedback loop and will therefore make it more likely that you'll stick with it. These include:

- **Make exercise a ritual** – do it at a set point on certain days. Make it a habit and commit to a 60 day window to make it stick (again, studies have shown 60 days is the time it takes to make a habit seem second nature and therefore require less willpower to continue)
- **Set mini goals** – as basic as a goal to increase bench press by five pounds by the end of the month, or trying to walk a certain amount of miles in a week. Keep mini goals simple and basic, but something to motivate you to crank out that last set and to work hard
- **Track progress** – you need to keep track of each workout so that you can see the progress you make. Maybe you're an Excel geek and wants to graph your lifts, or maybe you want a basic software app like *Beyond the Whiteboard* or some free app that does the work for you. Even if you're like me and still use the old school spiral notebook, just write down your workouts, how you're feeling and so forth. It can help guide you as you get further into the process and you can see where maybe you can tweak things to reach new goals

- **Accentuate the positive** – if you miss a workout or aren't feeling it some days, don't sweat it. I like to imagine that I'm one of the small percent that is making an effort to stay on top of health and to look good and say things to myself like "Look at Me! I just deadlifted 300 pounds!" Do whatever you need to do to give yourself an "Attaboy" when things are going well, or even if they aren't. You are at least grinding out progress while others aren't.

- **Keep it entertaining** – listen to music, find a workout partner, mix up your short cardio workouts. Don't always do the same thing as that just gets boring. Don't' be afraid to mix things up once in a while, even if it goes against the designed program. I always do a "Twelve Days of Christmas" workout with 12 different exercises around Christmas and look forward to that every year. Have fun with this.

- **Set macro goals** – have big, large goals that you have to work and stretch to achieve. Maybe it has to do with weight loss, maybe a number on a barbell, maybe it's to compete. The mini goals should lead to these big goals, but shoot for something to keep that carrot out in front of you to chase.

One thing to remember, before starting any exercise program, please check with your doctor or have a basic physical exam to make sure you don't have any major issues that could be exacerbated if starting a program. Additionally, clogged arteries, heart disease, and diabetes is so prevalent so don't take it for granted that you are ready to jump right in and start an exercise program. I've known several men who recently had close calls (heart attacks) doing relatively light to moderate activities such as golf. I've known skinny-fat marathoners -and my supposedly healthy as a horse father-in-law - end up with multiple bypass surgeries. The most common symptoms of a heart attack are chest pain, chest discomfort and chest pressure. If you feel these symptoms, don't wait – call your doctor or 911 immediately.

Playing

Before I get into discussing the serious topic of fitness and exercise, let's say a few words about play. Sports as children are all about play, and at some point we lose this lightheartedness and make them way too serious. I think it's important to be fit enough to be able to play on a whim, be that biking down to the park, running with the dog, or playing tag with the kids. Our children and the neighborhood kids are at the stage where tag and outside games like Ghost in the Graveyard are all they want to do after school. It's always a huge hit when one of the parents joins the play and is the Ghost. Being able to run around the house and not be winded so the play can continue is the type of thing I take for granted but you may not. Play is fun, whether you have kids or not. Pickup softball or basketball games or Frisbee at lunch; running, jumping, PLAYING should be done more by all of us grown-ups. A healthy lifestyle should not end at trying to be the best tennis player in your neighborhood, but should be the first step in a lighter, more enjoyable adulthood. We're all under tremendous pressure to be responsible, hard working adults. Work often sucks the lifeblood out of us, as does regular household and child-rearing responsibilities. By remembering to play, we reduce stress and if it's an outside, physical play, it can count as exercise – two birds with one stone!

Walking – so easy a caveman could do it

Slow steady locomotion (AKA walking) has been part of our ancestral life, and should be a regular part of ours no matter if we're a desk jockey or stay-at-home dad. Walking will always be part of my routine in some fashion. I walk our dogs, go on walks with the kids all the time, and enjoy hiking in parks and trails in our area. It's low-impact and everyone can do it. If you're just starting out and are in a bad place physically, and overweight, walking is the ideal starting point along with a clean food and low-carbohydrate diet. Benefits of walking include strengthening that muscle we call the heart, reduction of LDL cholesterol while increasing HDL levels, burning some calories (150 calories per hour), boosting vitamin D levels if walking outside during the day, and like most exercising, releasing endorphins in our blood and making us feel happier. Be warned though, for the time invested, walking is not a great calorie burner and doesn't provide that much benefit in the way of higher intensity cardiovascular endurance. Walking is certainly a good lunch time activity and getting out into sunshine while not having to find a shower can be a year round healthy activity. Most would do perfectly well simply weight lifting, walking and doing some short sprinting efforts from time to time.

A good pair of comfortable shoes are what you need. If you want to increase the pace, and actually get a sweat going, by all means do that, but you may want to reconsider the cotton socks that are typically part of men's athletic shoe wardrobe. You can find synthetic socks that wick moisture at any department store for pretty cheap, and this will help prevent blisters and make your feet happier.

Basic Bodyweight Strength Protocol

This is where things start to get fun. Say you just started moving again after a long length of time being sedentary. You and your friend or wife started up tennis, since you both enjoy it and you played when you were younger. Great start! Now it's time to add in a little resistance training. You don't have to pay any sort of membership fee as long as you have a floor, a wall, a chair and a pull-up bar. You can find pull-up bars to go in your doorway for under $30 at most sporting goods stores or if you're handy you could probably make one yourself with some steel plumbing pipe and fittings, but that's for you to engineer.

Keep playing tennis or softball or walking at lunch, and of course eating right. If you're just starting, a twice a week body-weight exercise program will be plenty. This will begin to make you some muscles while at the same time, giving you options for a short-intense workout, again killing two birds with one stone. If you advance further or want to throw in an extra workout, by all means do so. I've included some of my favorite bodyweight workouts below, feel free to mix and match, but be sure to hit legs twice per week minimum. These movements will focus on primarily the large muscle groups and compound motions. We're not doing calf raises or forearm curls. Instead, we'll focus on the legs (squats), chest, back, arm and shoulders (pushups, pull-ups, chin-ups and handstand pushup progression) and core (plank, toes to bar, knees to elbows, ab wheel if you've got one). That's it. You should be able to knock out a full bodyweight routine in under 20 minutes, and if done right you're going to be breathing hard and sucking wind.

The key movements, for body weight or weight training stay the same. A push, a pull, a squat and an overhead press works your chest, back, legs and shoulders and in general strengthen your whole body equally. I've linked YouTube videos on my website at AverageMarriedDad.com, "Exercise Examples" tab at the top.

Squats

Start standing up, arms at your side. Your feet should be approximately shoulder width apart, with toes pointing out at a 30 to 45 degree angle (think 1' to 2' O'clock for your right foot and 11' to 10' O'clock for your left). Bend at the hip, keep your weight on your heels and bring your butt back, bending at the knees. Try and get your butt as low as possible, and the crease in your hip at the bottom should be below the top of your knee. Your back angle should be fairly vertical. It is important to do these correct now, since you'll want to develop good habits as you progress to weights. As you bend down, you'll likely find that bringing your hands forward and ending up parallel to the ground provide a nice counter-balance to this movement. To come back up, simply reverse that movement.

The squat progression is A) leaning back against the wall, lower yourself down into the squatting position to legs at parallel and raise yourself back up B) using a pole or pillar or chair to hold on to with your hand, lower yourself down in the squat and use your hand/arm as assistance to rise back up C) regular "air" squat. Most will be able to air squat right away.

Push-ups

There are many variations of the push-up, but we'll focus on the most basic one. If you advance, you can add plyo-pushups (high speed push-up where you clap or touch your chest at the top), diamond pushups (narrow hands, with index fingers and thumbs together to make a diamond) or wide width pushups. For the basic version, hands are shoulder width apart, fingers pointing forward. Body and core should be tight, hands directly below your shoulders. As you lower yourself, bring elbows back towards your butt and not to the side as this will engage the triceps more. You may have to play with bringing them straight back parallel to your spine, or if you want them more at an angle, away from your body. Simply touch your chest and push back up locking elbows at the top.

The pushup progression is A) Leaning against a wall at an angle pushing off B) on your knees but keeping the core from knees to shoulders tight with no hip bend or butt in the air C) a regular pushup with your hands on an inclined surface like chairs or a bench D) Knee pushup, and finally E) a regular pushup on the ground. In all cases, keep core tight, butt down. If you can't do a good pushup without your butt down, bump up to an earlier progression.

Pull-ups/Chin-ups

Again, there are many variations of the pull-up, including changing of hand width, chest to the bar (instead of just the chin over the bar) and weighted pull-ups. The basic pull-up is palms facing out, hands shoulder width apart, simply pull up to chin over the bar. CrossFit, uses a kipping movement. This allows for you to get some English with your body, basically changing horizontal momentum to vertical momentum. For beginners, I don't recommend this as it puts a lot of stress on your shoulder girdle. It's better to strengthen that shoulder girdle with traditional strict pull-up before whipping out the higher skill movements that have a higher risk of injury. Chin-ups are the same general movement but with palms facing in towards you. Note that palms in results in more bicep recruitment and essentially can replace bicep curls.

The pull-up progression is A) chair beneath the pull-up bar, using your legs as little as possible to provide some upward lift to complete the pull-up motion. Slowly lower yourself back down B) Reverse pull-up/chin-up – jump up or use your legs to lift you over the bar, and without your legs, slowly lower yourself back down C) use of a band – basically a large rubber band mounted with one end on the pull-up bar and the other wrapping your leg or feet to give you a little help. They have different strength bands and can find them at sporting goods stores or online D) regular pull-up or chin-up.

Shoulder press

If you don't have dumbbells, you can use a chair. With your feet on the chair, place your hands on the ground and pike at the hips, inverting yourself like a jackknife. At that stage you can lower your head to the ground and press back up. Preferably though, you have a barbell or dumbbells to do shoulder press with. A dumbbell or barbell press are both pretty straightforward, take from resting on shoulders press overhead. In the barbell version, as the bar passes your forehead your head pushes through the window created. I don't particularly think the piked press, or especially handstand pushups, are safe since your upper vertebrae of your neck is not designed to support your body weight, which eventually happens if you rest your weight on your head. This is one of criticisms of CrossFit and what I told *Men's Fitness* in my interview with them.

The standard progression for shoulder press is A) pike press B) handstand pushup (which I don't recommend). Instead I'd prefer you work the pike press, getting progressively steeper, and then work to dumbbell (or other odd object) or barbell press. Resting your object in front of your shoulders and pressing vertically. Use old milk jugs filled with water or whatever you can get your hands on if you don't have anything. Play-it-Again Sports (or other used sporting goods stores), garage sales and Craigslist all have weights and dumbbells at reduced prices. Unless you are really budget-tight, I encourage some weights for shoulder work instead of trying to make bodyweight stuff work.

Plank

If you aren't lifting heavy weights yet with such exercises as squat or deadlift, doing some core work is a good idea. Front plank is like a pushup position with a rigid body (like a plank of wood) and side plank is one arm down, body rigid, feet together, facing the wall. For now I'll focus on the front plank.

The standard plank progression is A) knee pushup position, arms extended B) knee pushup position, forearms on the ground C) arms extended, feet on floor, like rigid regular pushup position D) forearms on ground, feet on floor, rigid and straight bodyline.

Basic Bodyweight Workout

Before getting into the actual Basic bodyweight workout protocol, I wanted to note a few things. First, this workout is something that is designed to be sustainable over the long term and fit into a busy lifestyle. Second, I'll show you some modifications to add challenges and further fitness as you progress. Third, get it out of your mind that you need to spend 30-60 minutes in the gym to get a fitness or strength benefit. In many ways, doing a hard, bodyweight workout twice a week can be more beneficial than grinding out miles on the treadmill for an hour a day 6 days a week. My high-intensity cardio workouts are nearly all 5-15 minutes in total work duration (not counting rest intervals). Remember, weight loss (or gain) is made in the kitchen, muscles are made in the gym. The protocol will add muscles, and you will be sore, but there is only so far it can take you. For many, that toned, lean rock-climber type look with real-world strength this protocol provides is perfectly fine. If you want bigger muscles, and really want to take the next step in physique, Advanced is where to go from here.

The protocol itself is pretty simple to start. It is a basic circuit:

- One minute of as many repetitions of that exercise as you can do and 30 seconds of rest before starting the next exercise.
- Exercise order should be: pushups, pull-ups, squats, shoulder press or variation (jack-knifes/pikes) and plank
- After you get through the first round of all five exercises take enough time to fully recover and catch your breath to give it your all before the next cycle
- Start with the highest level on the progression you can, and modify through the minute to try and keep moving. For example: you start with pushups, and can knock out 10 before you fatigue where you can't do them anymore, then you move to knee pushups where you knockout another 15 before fatiguing then finish the minute with leaning wall pushes.
- Complete two rounds of this

Pretty simple. You'll need a watch, stopwatch, phone app or a $5 kitchen timer that keeps a running minute and second's digital clock. This is 10 total working minutes of time, and if you keep your rest interval between rounds 6 minutes or less, you'll be done with the whole thing in 20 minutes or less.

When you can complete a full minute doing mostly the highest level of the movement, or feel you are limited more by your muscles than by your cardio, I would start to drop your rest between each exercise. The goal would be to take the rest down to zero and go from one exercise to the next without rest. If you feel like you are still strength limited, keep the rest before that particular exercise to give you the best opportunity to use the harder movement throughout. Getting to a minute on plank may come the quickest, so feel free to hold plank as long as you can (up to 3 minutes) after you get to one minute hold.

If you progress to the point of knocking out mostly the highest level bodyweight movements for two full rounds, without rest, I would add another half (30 seconds of work interval per exercise) to full round. No need to go beyond that. You can add clapping pushups, chest-to-bar pull-ups, or wear a weighted vest to the exercises to add challenge. Really though, you're better off making the jump to Advanced weight training at that point.

This protocol in Basic is an abbreviated version of what *Insanity* is. Basically short, high intensity bursts of large-moving muscles using bodyweight. The difference is, *Insanity* has you moving six days a week, fewer rest intervals and much longer workouts. This beginner workout is designed to promote sarcoplasmic hypertrophy, that is, focusing more on increasing the size of the muscle and less on increasing strength. Basically, designed to make you look better, with some strength increase. It also increases fitness with the higher intensity cardio component. A basic bodyweight strength and fitness regimen doesn't have to be complicated people. KISS: Keep it simple stupid! And yes, 10-20 minutes of work is enough to make a difference, and unlike something like *Insanity*, allow ample time for recovery with minimal bad things happening from doing too much (excessive cortisol excretion, poor sleep, eating a lot to recover).

The Advanced protocol mixes both sarcoplasmic (muscle size increased more than muscle strength) and myofibril (more strength increase and less increase in size) hypertrophy. Sarcoplasmic hypertrophy is what bodybuilders are going after (bigger muscles with a larger cross-section, with less emphasis on strength – 8-12 rep scheme at the heaviest weight you can hit), and myofibril hypertrophy is what power lifters are going after (very strong, dense muscles – lower reps in the neighborhood of 1-6 achieves this goal).

Advanced Strength Protocol

If you want to get strong, fight aging, keep lean muscle mass as you get older, and keep or increase testosterone production (good for men and women, as both lose testosterone as they age which is not a good thing), you have to move weight. Period. This requires some type of home gym, or going to a gym. It doesn't require anything fancy, but you will need a squat rack and weights. If you are trying to build a home gym, stick with Olympic-style bars and plates (7 feet long and approximate 2 inch inner diameter of plates) and ignore the "standard" style (shorter bars, 1 inch inner diameter) as they aren't nearly as good unless that's all you can get for your budget. I have the Olympic-style bars and bumpers at home, but keep a cheap weight bench and a couple hundred pounds of Standard-style in our mud room at work and probably use that once a week at lunch, so Standard-style still is useful if that's all you have.

Four of the exercises in the Basic strength protocol, along with deadlift, make up the program. We're not doing the bodybuilding bro-lifting of five different exercises for biceps, four for triceps, three for forearms, six for chest, and so on since as family men, we don't have the time for that. The focus is on making maximum strength (and size) gains for the most minimal amount of time. Squats, bench press, shoulder press, pull-ups (or bent over row) and deadlift is all we're doing. Going beyond the Advanced protocol is beyond the scope of this book, but for those that are interested, there's many other strength cycles, training programs, and lifts that will further fill out your physique or increase your strength, whatever your goals are. This is really Advanced only in the sense that it is advanced beyond bodyweight training, and will result in someone who has never followed a "real" program getting strong. If you are already strong, you probably know enough to be dangerous. Though the point of the program can still be applied in several month cycles even if you are on a different strength program. I think most people don't milk out this linear progression enough, and this approach should be the foundation of strength before moving on to other programs.

If you are just starting out on the strength protocol, I can't recommend Mark Rippetoe's *Starting Strength (3rd edition)* book enough. While a book can't replace a competent coach, I'd say it's a good substitute on implementing proper form along with videotaping your lifts and watching them back. It is likely that you'll learn better form from his book than from a personal trainer who is there to sell his services and may have never learned a proper deadlift himself. *Starting Strength* breaks down these key lifts in excruciating detail and can really advance a novice lifter's ability to get set up properly and to use good form.

Rippetoe is a powerlifter and thus, my only criticism of the book is in regard to squatting. His goal is to make lifters squat as much as possible (three days a week), and he trains what is called the "low bar back squat" with the bar resting lower on your back. I think for most people, competing in powerlifting is likely not a goal so should not be using the low bar back squat. Instead, a high bar back squat where the bar is higher on the traps translates better to a larger amount of life and sports movements, and should be used exclusively unless you have dreams of powerlifting or putting up a huge one rep max for the squat.

It is beyond the scope of the book to get into form of the lifts as whole books have been written (as mentioned, Rippetoe's is one of the best on this in my opinion) on the intricacy of these few lifts. However, you can find a fair amount of information on the internet (as mentioned, some YouTube videos are linked to my website), and honestly, it's not rocket science. Put weight on the bar, move the bar. A word of caution though: using proper squat and deadlift form are important, as using poor form those can really mess up your back. Keep core tight, back rigid, don't round your back and you'll generally be ok. If in doubt, and form starts to fall apart, drop the weight or stop the set. Also, use a spotter, especially on bench press, and learn how to dump the barbell properly when squatting.

The approach I recommend for all those who haven't lifted before is called linear progression and is a very simple concept. You start at a fairly light weight, you do some lifts at that weight. Next time, you add a little more weight than last time and do some more lifts. Essentially, you challenge your muscles, break them down, recover, and add more weight. Repeat cycle. Eventually, you will get to the point where you can't complete the lifts at that incremental weight increase. At that point you drop the weight approximately 10% and start again. I recommend a minor change in protocol on the first, and subsequent resets.

The protocol I recommend is flexible depending on your time to commit to getting stronger, recognizing everyone is in a different position to devote time to this endeavor. At a minimum, you'll need two days a week for heavy lifting. Three days will require a better diet and more attention to recovery (sleep), but will allow you to progress faster.

For strength training (1-6 reps per set) use approximately three minutes (and up to five) of rest between every set. The reason is that strength training uses your body's full adenosine triphosphate (ATP – a biochemical way to store and use energy) reserves to achieve maximum power in that rep interval at heavy weights. They need this long to replenish and you aren't maximizing your ability to move heavy weights if you rest shorter than this. For hypertrophy training (6-12 reps per set), you should be shooting for 60 to 90 seconds per reset between sets. You aren't relying just on the ATP mechanism for energy, you tap into mechanisms for endurance training and therefore don't need as much rest. In using these rest intervals so, your body produces more growth hormones and you will experience a more rapid growth in muscle size or strength.

I will present a few different options for Advanced Programming, so depending on your time available and your goals, you should be able to find something that works for you. You will see programming for:

- Linear Progression (twice per week)
- Linear Progression (three days per week)
- Advanced Heavy Lift Lifestyle (a low time commitment approach to maintaining or increasing strength and size for a regular guy)
- Advanced Cardio (for those that want a fat burning boost beyond just walking, and who may not have other sport hobbies where they get higher intensity, brief cardio sessions naturally)

Despite what program you decide to do, I recommend reading through the first Linear Progression protocol as it has nuggets of rationale and thoughts on why it is laid out that way that apply to the other programs as well.

Advanced Linear Progression Twice-a-Week Protocol

Workout #1 (of 2):

- **High Bar Back Squat 4 sets of 5 repetitions (reps):** For all exercises: warm up with lighter weights, up to maybe 10 reps starting out, progressively adding weight (and lowering reps) until you are ready to start your "work set." I like to warm up to a single rep of a weight 10 or 20 pounds lighter than my work set for most exercises. The work set will be four sets at the same weight.

  Next session of the same squat type, add 5 pounds. Starting work set weight should feel pretty light and that you aren't really doing much. That's good. As you keep adding weight over time in the linear progression protocol, you'll be surprised at how hard it gets. It's slowly stretching the rubber band, instead of starting out too high and having to reset early. Think about it, if you are adding 5 pounds a week, that's 50 pounds after the first two and a half months, and 100 pounds after five. Don't be in a hurry to stall out and reset. Slow and steady wins the race. If you have a rough feel for your 1 rep max, starting out a 60 to 65 percent of that weight for your initial work set is conservative but will start to establish good muscle movement patterns and will allow you to grow into your routine and body. Too many people start out too heavy and are resetting after just a month or two of the program. Take your time and you'll likely establish better form. The weights aren't going anywhere but you might if you get frustrated at lack of progress.

- **Bench Press 4 sets of 5 reps**. Add 2.5 pounds (two 1.25 pound plates – sometimes called fractionals. You may need to purchase a pair of these and take them to and from the gym with you) next session. Bench and shoulder presses are much slower to increase strength and fractional weights help a lot.

- **Pull-ups 4 sets of maximum reps** (or 4 sets of 5 reps of bent over barbell row – alternate between pull-ups and barbell rows week-to-week). Use pull-up progression from Basic protocol if you can't do at least five pull-ups.

So Workout #1 (of 2) of the week has a squat, a push and a pull (full body workout). Note that I recommend 4 sets of 5 reps for the two day-a-week protocol and 3 sets of 5 reps if you decide to lift three days a week (below). Some linear progression recommends 3 sets of 5 and others 5x5. I recommend those set/rep schemes for recovery since as a lifter past 35 recovery is paramount, and those are is easier to recover from compared to a 5 set, 5 rep scheme. Another issue with 5x5 is that it's hard to maintain good form at heavier weights across that set and rep scheme. Since I am a slightly older lifter, injury prevention is a key consideration in my workouts. I think you are getting nearly the impact with four or three sets as you are from five and still allows good form throughout the set/rep scheme while allowing ample recovery between sessions.

Workout #2 (of 2):

- **Front Squat 4 sets of 5 reps.** Note: alternating back and front squats provide better leg balance. Back squats place more of a load on the posterior chain of glutes and hamstrings while front squats place more emphasis on quads. Additionally, the low bar back squat has much more hamstring involvement than the high bar, and the high bar's more vertical back angle does tend to share more in common with the front squat, but is not identical. Do both. Hell, try all three types of squats (low bar, high bar, and front). At a minimum I recommend incorporating front squatting, and use the same protocol as the back squat – start with a conservative weight, add 5 pounds next week.

- **Strict Overhead Barbell Shoulder Press 4 sets of 5 reps.** Add 2.5 pounds next session.
- **Deadlift 1 set of 5 reps at your working weight.** Warm up like you would the other exercises, but only complete one set at your working weight. Deadlifts stress your central nervous system (CNS) very highly. I personally often replace deadlifts with the faster and lighter pulls from the ground that cleans provide, but deadlifts themselves are a man maker. Some may find that a once-a-week frequency to be too stressful with inadequate recovery when the weights start to get heavy. If that is you, then push these out to once every 10 days instead of once every 7.

So Workout #2 (of 2 for the week) of the week has a squat, a push and a pull (deadlift pulling from the floor – a full body workout). Notice a pattern here?

Advanced Linear Progression Three Days-a-Week Protocol

Workout #1 (of 3):

- **High Bar Back Squat 3 sets of 5 reps:** Next back squat session add 5 pounds.
- ***Bench Press 3 sets of 5 reps**. Add 2.5 pounds next session.
- **Pull-ups 3 sets of maximum reps**. Use pull-up progression from Basic protocol if you can't do at least five pull-ups.

So Workout #1 (of 3) of the week has a squat, a push and a pull, another full body workout. I switch to 3x5 for this protocol since you now have more volume and recovery is still where your muscles are made. You have more wiggle room on sleep, nutrition and general recovery with three instead of four or five sets while still making good progress.

Workout #2 (of 3):

- **Front Squat 3 sets of 5 reps.** This is 5 pounds heavier than last week.

- ***Strict Overhead Shoulder Press 3 sets of 5 reps**. Add 2.5 pounds next session.
- **Deadlift 1 sets of 5 reps at your working weight**. See note on deadlifts in the twice a week protocol if you skipped that.

Workout #3 (of 3):

- **High Bar Back Squat 3 sets of 5 reps**: Yes, we are squatting three days a week. You may still be stressed from deadlift previously so you may play a little bit with what days you rest. For example, you may do Workout #1 on Monday, #2 on Wednesday and wait until Saturday to do Workout #3 to give you an extra rest day from deadlifts. Your call. Also, if you are struggling to add 10 pounds per week, simply repeat the weight from Workout #1 once in a while.
- ***Bench Press 3 sets of 5 reps**. Add 2.5 pounds next session.
- **Bent over barbell row 3 sets of 5 reps**. Add 5 pounds next session.

*The next week, I switch the order of Bench Press and Strict Overhead Shoulder Press so you shoulder press twice and bench press once.

Resetting

You keep adding weight in linear progression until you can't complete the set and rep scheme. Usually I will give it two more tries (two more workout days of that particular weight) to make sure it simply wasn't a recovery issue and is a legitimate stall, before resetting. Shoulder press stalls especially hard because the shoulder muscles are smaller and take longer time to make progression. If you stall out on the shoulder press in the same spot over and over, don't be afraid to cheat some reps or even go heavier with a push-press (using your legs to add a little vertical momentum).

To reset, drop the weight 10% and start again. I like to then switch things up after the first reset and try and max out the number of reps on the last set, at least hitting five. That way, on any subsequent resets, even if you stall at the same weight again, you can see if you're getting stronger if you can grind out another rep or three on that last set compared to last time you saw that weight. This is the strategy of the Greyskull Linear Progression program (though Greyskull adds additional exercises to the mix than other LP programs).

Eventually, you'll end up stalling a few times at or near the same weight. One frequent reason this happens is you have issues with recovery such as not eating enough, not eating enough protein, not sleeping enough, high stress, or any other factors that contribute to the cocktail of recovery. Another reason is you've simply maxed out on linear progression. It happens. Now depending on your goals, you can search out and find other training programs that suit your needs. Ones that are solid for strength (not necessarily aesthetics) are Wendler's 5/3/1 or Louie Simmon's Westside Barbell programs, though there are as many other strength and conditioning programs to suit your needs depending what your goals are. Ones for long term looking good and getting strong are my Advanced Lifestyle Heavy Lift Rotation below (intended for the every-man or woman), or Layne Norton training series (basically a power/hypertrophy combo) for the motivated man. You can find more information on Layne Norton's program online for those interested.

The final program below is just trying to look good naked. It doesn't "reach for the stars" but is more sustainable and has a little more variety than the "by five" linear progression protocol and will at least allow you to maintain strength. It also shifts to a little more Sarcoplasmic hypertrophy meaning your smaller diameter, strong, dense muscles from linear progression will now grow a little larger due to the 10 rep range workouts. This can be the icing on the cake if you are mostly in this weightlifting thing to be strong and look better.

Advanced Lifestyle Heavy Lift Rotation

You certainly don't have to do a linear progression to start on this final program, but if you want to get strong quickly, linear progression is what I recommend. The tallest house has the strongest foundation, and linear progression builds a strong foundation to build upon. However, if you want to jump into this because this suits your style more, have at it. You'll still see some progress, and it has a nice mix of raw strength and body builder type hypertrophy, which generally means it compromises a bit on both.

If you haven't lifted much before, learn the lifts, just like in linear progression program since they are the same. If you haven't done a one rep maximum (1 RM) in a while or never, pick a 1 RM weight that you think would be challenging to start. Then, using a percentage of that weight, you'll cycle through the four exercises per week. The order that you cycle through the exercises is up to you and your schedule, but it is nice to keep each exercise on the same day of the week for planning purposes. If you are short on time and work in a home gym, you may end up doing one exercise four days a week. If you typically go to gym, perhaps doing two lifts per session is a better use of your time. If you combine lifts, do an upper/lower body combination. So Day #1 would be, say, bench press and back squat; and Day #2 would be shoulder press and deadlift. Try not to put two press or two leg days back to back if you are only doing one exercise in a four day cycle. One thing to consider is that every time you get to the gym, you get a boost of human growth hormone to aid in recovery, so in some ways frequency is important, though not as important as consistency and fitting it into your life.

The foundational exercises again are:

- strict overhead barbell shoulder press
- high bar back squat
- bench press
- deadlift
- accessories such as rows of some sort, pull-ups, chin-ups, ring dips

Week 1: Use 50% of your estimated 1 RM for each exercise, do 3 sets of 10 reps. Rest two to three minutes between sets.

Week 2: Using 70% of your estimated 1 RM, do 3 sets of 5 reps. Rest two to three minutes between sets.

Week 3: Using 85% of your estimated 1 RM, do 3 sets of 3 reps. Rest three minutes between sets.

All reps in the first three weeks of the cycle should be smooth and unbroken, meaning you move from rep to rep without a rest.

Week 4: Test out week – warm up well and work up to the heaviest single rep you can do using as much rest as you need, and use that as a 1 RM going forward. Use spotters, good form, be safe, but really challenge yourself. If you are still relatively new though, or didn't go through a full linear progression program, don't let your ego get you hurt as you likely don't have the long-term structural growth to really know how hard to push like those with more experience.

After establishing a new 1 RM, repeat weeks 1 through 4 indefinitely. You don't have to be rigid though. If you stall consistently and want to get stronger, add a little extra weight above the percentage next time or add another set. Play around a little to see what works best for you.

Now in many ways this Lifestyle Protocol will feel "easier" than the linear progression as those later weights in LP get really heavy after a while, but this is intended to be a long-term sustainable approach to lifting weights that should continue to leave you healthy and recovering well. If you really feel the need to challenge yourself, especially if your 1 RM stay relatively unchanged over time, is to do that last set with as many reps as you can do with good form at that weight instead of the rep scheme noted above. Always use a spotter for bench, and if you aren't comfortable dumping it from your back, back squat as well (you simply dump forward for front squat). Also, remember there are advantages to doing both front and back squats. You may want to cycle one month as a high bar back squat cycle and one month as a front squat cycle, but lean a little more heavily on the back squat if you had to choose just one.

Advanced Cardio Protocol

You've probably noticed that I haven't talked much about cardio or conditioning for these lifting programs. That's because the key to building and maintaining muscle is lifting heavy things. Those that think a lot cardio will enhance fat loss should reread the nutrition section again understand that so-called "chronic cardio" is detrimental to your fat loss and fitness goals. Fat loss is dictated by diet and nutrition. Some cardio is good, but in very small doses and at high intensity.

Dmitry Klokov, a very well-known Russian weightlifter, when asked if he did cardio responded, that "yeah, sometimes he squats in sets of 10." So your 10 rep workout (or more if you end up adding reps to that last set) is more muscular endurance than true strength workout, and is a cardio blaster when done right. The cardio we will incorporate should be between 5 and 12 minutes long and should complement the workout. If you are already walking regularly, lifting two to four days a week, then adding just two or three days with short high-intensity cardio thrown in is plenty and could even be too much for some people. I sort of make things up on this depending on what I'm feeling and what may supplement my key lifts but won't compromise my upcoming workout or strength gains. In general, the key movements I use for cardio purposes are:

- burpees (do a pushup, bring your legs into your hands stand and jump to full extension clapping your hands at the top)

- kettlebell swings (using a kettlebell, swing the kettlebell between legs with both hands holding the handle, raising it up to eye level [Russian swing style] – be sure to keep posterior chain tight and pop those hips as you bring it up)
- thrusters (barbell or dumbbell at shoulder level; squat down to parallel with weight still at shoulder level and as you come up out of your squat you thrust the weight overhead in a push-press motion)
- pull-ups
- pushups
- short run or rowing segments (up to two minutes in length – or roughly ¼ of a mile or less for running – sprints are good, rest shortly between sets)
- ring dips
- jumping rope
- tire flips (you can get large tractor tires for free from agricultural implement companies who have to pay to dispose of them otherwise – your main problem may be finding room to store these)
- prowler push (you are lucky if you can find a place with a prowler, basically, it's a metal sled you can load weights on and push around a parking lot – maybe the best cardio/strength workout there is)

I will take two or three complementary movements (say, swings and pull-ups, or running and thrusters) and put them together in a way that I can knock out a continuous workout in a set time. For example, I may do as many rounds as possible of 15 kettlebell swings plus 5 pull-ups in seven minutes. Or I may do 4 rounds of a 200 or 400 meter run (for me, partially around my neighborhood) coupled with 10 barbell thrusters with 95 pounds after each run segment.

Another workout which will increase your aerobic and anaerobic capacity with a very limited time commitment are called Tabata workouts after its inventor Izumi Tabata. After warming up with whatever workout you decide (burpees, pushups, air squats, rowing, biking, sprinting) you do eight rounds of the following: 20 seconds of as hard and as fast as you can possibly go, and then take 10 seconds of rest. You will most like slow down, not go as far and tire, but dig deep and give it your all for those eight work-sets. If done right, you should feel very, very wrecked after just 4 minutes of time (with less than three minutes of actual work). Compared to moderate intensity exercise, this increases both aerobic and anaerobic work capacity as well as fat loss, and at a very small time investment.

Notice I don't have many CrossFit favorites like box jumps, or handstand pushups, or high repetition Olympic weightlifting movements like snatch or clean and jerk on the list above. That's because those higher degree of technical movements as incorporated by CrossFit's way of high reps under fatigue are stupid and have a high degree of injury associated with them. We simply want to throw in a little icing on the cake, establish or maintain some cardiovascular fitness, and recover. Notice I keep stressing recovery. You gain muscle, lose fat and get healthy by proper recovery, not by beating yourself down and just barely holding it together. I've been there on numerous occasions and it is not healthy mentally or physically and leads often to burnout, injury, and elevated cortisol. Don't be afraid to take an extra day off if you got a poor night's sleep, your boss is riding you at work and you're simply not feeling it. Don't make it a habit though and try to stick consistently with a program.

Part of the problem with most programs is that for regular people, they can't do it consistently and recover properly. You and I are trying to cram 20 pounds of crap in our lives in a 10 pound sack, and it just doesn't fit very well. The younger athletes without kids usually have the advantage of less overall stress in their lives along with more time. We parents have to compromise, and usually sleep is one of the first things that gets reduced to fit in all the family stuff, work stuff, and fitness stuff that we should be doing. The more excessive exercise programs like many CrossFit or bootcamp coaches develop (5-6 days a week of heavy weights plus long high intensity cardio sessions) result in excessive stress on our bodies, large cortisol release, and can even lead to adrenal fatigue. Not good things. More is not always better. The short, high-intensity cardio I'm proposing is designed to supplement our heavy weight sessions which is the foundation. This approach for the average man is sustainable and can be recovered from much easier. You don't have to beat yourself up to be healthy and to look good naked. Better to work smarter, not harder.

These weight programs I presented here are scavenged, tested and modified from other well respected coaches and their clients without too much other stuff added to them, and there is no reason why they can't work for you too. Remember, abs are made in the kitchen, big muscles that make the wife get hot are made in the gym, and short cardio bursts benefit in the ability to jump in and have fun randomly in life, without huffing and puffing like a circus strongman who can't move efficiently outside of a gym.

As I alluded to, doing frequent runs or biking or elliptical 4 to 5 days a week is what is referred to as chronic cardio. You may get endorphin release and that "runners high" but this type of workout over the long-term is usually the opposite of fulfilling our goals. Running or excessive cardio from similar workouts tend to cannibalize our muscles for energy, which is the opposite of making them bigger, or you stronger and more attractive. And despite the fact that cardio does burn calories, it tends to increase cortisol production which, again, blunts testosterone and makes your body hold onto fat more. Look at many runners' bodies and you'll see many are skinny-fat. You are better off sprinting for eight rounds of 50-100 meters once a week than running 30 miles a week. Look at a sprinters body and a marathoner's body and tell me who you'd rather look like?

CHAPTER 3

Mental Health

W e've focused to this point on improving your body through healthy eating and exercise, but health and happiness is as much mental as it is physical. The physical body is a shell that often is a physical representation of how happy one is or is not. Take obese people for example. Their outward appearance is often a physical manifestation of something that is wrong inside. On the outside they may be the jolly fat guy, but more than likely inside they are hurting and likely know they have self-destructive tendencies. Both my brothers are obese and have struggled for years with their weight as well as alcohol abuse issues. They, like most obese people, are not happy. You can try and fool yourself and others, but we know that's not the case. Being fat is often shameful for the individual, whether they admit it to themselves or not. In the eyes of today's vain society, it is also very unattractive and instills guilt on top of whatever is the root cause of not being healthy. My point here isn't to make anyone feel bad, but to point out that being healthy needs to incorporate not just healthy physical living, but mental health as well. If you've seen the NBC show *The Biggest Loser*, you see that these people do an amazing job of going from obese to a much more healthy weight, nearly across the board. But if you've seen a "Where are they now?" type show, I'd say more than half have put a lot of the lost weight back on. They likely fell back into poor habits and I think likely still haven't addressed the underlying cause of their overeating.

We all carry various baggage from our past with us most days. Childhood experiences, broken relationships, mom or dad issues, day-to-day anxiety and stress. It all clouds our current mind and often feeds into how we behave on any given day. In today's society, there seems to be very little down-time, and any time that used to be spent on daydreaming or calming thoughts now seem to be taken up by entertaining electronic devices. If you watch any social session where there is down time (a kid's sporting event or practice, waiting at the mall, any sort of waiting in general) you'll observe first hand people face-first into their tablet or phone. You're likely one. I certainly don't care how you spend your time, but the constant stimulation and validation through texts, Facebook posts or Instagram, and the subsequent dopamine fix you get from those, is not doing your mental health much good.

Days where we would just chill and reflect internally on our life are drastically reduced. Even in times where we are perhaps driving and thinking of things, our mind is racing or we're listening to talk radio – external stimulation rather than internal reflection. Every second of every day seems to be filled with some sort of entertainment, usually electronic and visual. The results of these actions are multiple, but the worst impacts are that we don't interact as much with people we are with (we aren't mentally present), and we sacrifice our own mental wellbeing and tranquility with the lights, bells and whistles of constant entertainment. Being mentally present is especially critical if you have kids. They don't want to see your face lit up by your tablet. They want your attention and affection and don't want to have to compete with virtual reality for that. Your spouse may also feel disconnected with you for this, and iPad/iPhone addiction has, I'm sure, claimed a number of marriages.

Being mentally present is much more critical to happiness than being constantly entertained. In Eckhart Tolle's book *The Power of Now*, he talks about how homeless and practically penniless, he was filled with great happiness and contentment. He found joy in the amazing everyday things that we call life. Look up once in a while and accept the miracle that is the world. Instead of being unconscious and dysfunctional, which is normal behavior for most of us, pause and breathe in the world. Tolle's whole book focuses on being present and to calm your mind from all the internal chatter that usually prevents us from really enjoying life. We focus on the past, and the future, but often are so busy trapped in our own heads to truly appreciate the present. To do this, you need to calm your thinking mind and *just be*. This is very difficult to do since we are all so addicted to thinking, planning, projecting and wishing. By being present, this usually dissolves. Pain that creeps into our life (stress, anxiety, fear, sadness) usually will dissolve as well by staying present in the moment. Your egoic mind is calmed, and you can focus not on having things, or comparing yourself to others, but on simply being right here right now, of breathing and feeling the positive energy all around us. Yeah, I know how new-age hokey this all sounds, but give it a chance. Take five minutes in a quiet area, close your eyes and just try and calm your mind and be present.

I've found that by incorporating these types of activities, which in many ways are akin to meditation, I am much more aware of when I start to go off track with others and am not present. Additionally, I am much calmer and the anxiety and negativity that sometimes shows up usually can be dissipated if I refocus on the present and not the past or future. I am still using the present to improve the future (exercising, eating well, exercising leadership, providing structure, taking care of financial matters), but not as an end goal in itself. If I work out, I enjoy the endorphin rush, the feeling of lifting heavy things, of the satisfaction of testing the limits. When eating healthy, I enjoy the taste of the food and the satisfaction of enjoying a meal with friends and family. The long term benefits of consistently doing the right thing comes naturally. You can use this as a tool to let go of the past, of all the hurt that has built up over the years. The past does not define who we have to be today. You have a choice to be happy and have mental peace today, but you have to stay present to do so.

Some tricks that I employ to doing this is finding a quiet time once a day to exercise presence. You may or may not call it meditation as that is just a word. Most commonly, I do my mind calming at night in bed, before sleep. I focus on breathing, on calming my mind, and letting my relaxation state deepen. Letting go of anxieties and negativity, I instead focus on breathing in energy and peace. Sometimes I will fall asleep, if not, I try and remain in this state as long as I can. When I am out and about, especially in a nature setting such as hiking, I try to replicate this sense of presence. Breathing in peace, energy and joy, and enjoying the moments as we are currently in them.

Yoga has been another way to calm the inner mind, while at the same time bringing body awareness and improvement into the equation. It is practiced worldwide and is a Hindu spiritual discipline that brings simple meditation and body poses together for health and relaxation. If you haven't done it, you may get lost more in the physical aspect that yoga embodies, worrying about the poses and how hard they are. I encourage you to try to get past this and focus more on the mental aspect, relaxation and spiritual awareness it brings. Our busy lives don't allow my wife or me to take classes, or at least we haven't done more than a handful of classes over the last five years. What we have done though is watch led yoga sessions on DVD. If you are unsure of what this entails, you can likely check out various videos through your local library. Doing a quick search for "yoga" and "DVD" in our library system's catalog yielded over 450 results. Finding 30-45 minutes once or twice a week can yield some really nice results mentally as you unwind and relax, resulting in a peaceful energized feeling.

While this is only a brief description of the importance staying focused in the now, feeling spiritual energy and finding brief respites of inner peace, don't diminish the importance of doing these things. They can really go a long way towards letting go of pain and anger and finding harmony with your life, as it current exists. As Alice Morse Earle wrote in her 1902 book *Sun Dials and Roses of Yesterday: Garden Delights...*"The clock is running. Make the most of Today. Time waits for no man. Yesterday is history. Tomorrow a mystery. Today is a gift. That's why it is called the present." Don't let the clouds of yesterday and the haze of tomorrow impact the clarity of today.

Another way to deal with stress is through positive thinking and gratitude for what we *do* have. Researchers are finding many benefits exist through positive thinking and optimism. Those practicing these approaches are healthier, less stressed and have a greater sense of overall well-being. While we all suffer negative emotions and setbacks in various ways throughout our lives, if we are able to spin the challenge as a positive, we can make positive progress instead of getting mired in negativity. Optimists will focus on ways to resolve their situation instead of dwelling in their frustrations thinking "woe is me." They grasp that they control the situation, and are at least partially responsible for it, instead of the pessimist who assumes a victim mentality and that the situation is out of their control.

Physical health is also impacted by positive thinking and optimism. One study found that activation in brain areas associated with negative emotions led to weaker immune responses to the flu vaccine. Suzanne Segerstrom, a researcher in the Department of Psychology at the University of Kentucky, along with University of Louisville's Sandra Sephton, found that people that were specifically optimistic on a part of their life exhibited stronger immune responses compared to those with a negative view. Remember our old friend cortisol? This hormone is activated when stress is high, contributing to poorer sleep and possible weight gain. One reason why optimists may have better immune function is due to less cortisol secretion compared to pessimists. A 2005 British Journal of Health Psychology published a study that stated positive mental states contributed to positive physical well-being due to the reduced cortisol response.

While I don't necessarily believe positive thinking has a direct link with manifesting positive realities, I do think that with some follow through, correlation could exist. When you have a calm, open mind, and have a positive attitude, you tend to be happier and can surely see opportunities that you wouldn't have with a different mindset. Negativity tends to wrap yourself up in your own world, while being optimistic and opening your eyes (and closing your phone) you may very well see a chance to improve your situation. People often respond to energy in-kind, so if you have negative energy, that's what you'll find people interacting with you. If you radiate positive energy from your state of being, people will open up to you, and reflect that energy back to you. Life often takes some funny twists and turns, and you never know when an opportunity will arise that will change some part of your life, maybe for the positive. The funny thing about opportunity is that you have to be aware of it and ready to embrace it.

You manifest your own success by grabbing the opportunity and making it happen; you don't wish for your life to be better, you make it happen, usually one small almost imperceptible step at a time. An old saying is "if wishes were fishes, the sea would be full." Positive mental power and optimism can strengthen your resolve to start something new, at the risk of leaving poor habits and behaviors in the dust. Things like developing positive habits, using positive affirmations, embracing hard work and challenges in an opportunity and visualizing positive outcomes are all tools that can be used to change yourself one day at a time. These things may start out as more wish-like than reality, which is why you begin to support those through actual life changes. The "faking it, 'til you make it" is a good credo, but you can't wish you'll make it; you need to begin building the foundation. The earlier parts of the book on improving your physical self, and upcoming chapters on improving your marriage, all are part of the foundation of a happy life, but improving your mental self is just as critical.

Building on your interests, talents and hobbies are a great starting point. Leaving the beta-puppy dog approach of doing whatever your spouse wants to do, of leaving your hobbies and interests at the wayside after getting married or starting a family has *got* to be rectified. You build yourself up mentally by always continuing to learn. A Huffington Post/YouGov poll in September 2013 showed that 28% of adults hadn't read a book in the last year, while another 25% only read between one and five. Expanding your reading increases your depth of knowledge, expertise on a subject and vocabulary. Depending on the subject matter and reading material, reading also makes you a more interesting individual and perhaps a more articulate speaker. All positives in your personal and professional life.

Hobbies too contribute to increased mental fortitude, not to mention could provide that life mission thing that so many of us are struggling to find. Having key hobbies, where you are continually striving to improve or learn more, provide a positive mental (sometimes physical) outlet, and allows you to channel that mental energy into something creative or worthwhile. This is critical for a fulfilling and happy life. Having mental interaction with those on a similar path or with similar interests, especially other men, is important as well. Finding a destination outside the house has a way of relaxing us and allowing our true positive spirit to shine through. Those without these outlets tend to be more bored and depressed, have more cases of alcoholism or substance abuse and tend to have worse marriages to boot. Remember, familiarity breeds contempt, so if you never get out of the house to do your own thing, you stand a greater likelihood of being taken for granted. Instead, be awesome or do something awesome, and bring that feeling of positive energy back home to the family.

Remember that the inner side of you is just as important as what the world sees. Many shiny packages hide crappy insides, so try and work to get your inner side to shine in conjunction with your physical appearance. It takes time and effort to get out of the fast-lane that is day-to-day life. When you do, and take the time to be calm and clear your mind, you'll increase your mental energy and peace which translates into more patience, happiness and positive feelings. These then contribute to a better marriage, parenting and even work attitude.

Part 2: Marriage

CHAPTER 4

The Ghost of Marriage Past

T his chapter lays out some of the foundational definitions that play a role in upcoming sections. By better understanding the past and some of the false truths we've been fed growing up, we then will have the tools to improve the future.

The New Family Norm

As a married man, my life goals are pretty simple: live a healthy, fulfilling and satisfying life, love my children, raise them to be happy and productive members of society, and share my life with the woman I love while having a healthy sex life. I've come to realize that achieving these simple life goals is surprisingly complex. I had no idea why women behave the way they do, nor did I understand how the changing roles of men have impacted those fundamental goals (happy and healthy marriage, children). In fact, I never really gave much thought to feminism, gender roles, or divorce until recently. By then, certain things in my own life were getting stagnant, my brother was well on his way to divorce, and I basically had blinders on as to how both biology and societal changes had directly impacted my own marriage. What I discovered was the dominos started falling a long time ago, and that today's domino is leaning right up against your marriage, your wife, you, and your kids with a delicate balance that needs to be buttressed for long term success.

Society as a whole has changed so radically in the last 50 years that the environment in which we, and our kids, were/are raised in is entirely different than our grandparents. Today's typical man can't hold a candle to the men from 50 or 100 years ago. Using my grandparents as an example, the norm not too long ago was simply that men took care of the farm, were fed three hot meals a day, and the only expectations of them were to provide for their family and raise the children to learn and regard hard work as a reward in itself. Today's modern married father is usually still expected to be the primary breadwinner, but now is expected to share household responsibility equally, while at the same time has to make sure his wife and kids are happy. If extra resources remain, we may be allowed a small area of the house (the Man Cave) that we can call our own. We've been domesticized.

We've been fed the lie of "happy wife, happy life." Sacrificing our own hobbies and interests so that our wife and kids have constant entertainment is the new unspoken expectation for fathers. Households are now a democracy with both mom and dad being equal partners and wage earners across the board. Essentially, we traded a patriarchal society of hard work and men doing manly things for a more egalitarian (or even matriarchal) one. The dynamics of this change has resulted in an entire generation of men emasculated to the female's desire which continues to propagate itself in future generations.

I don't intend to get into a lengthy dissertation on feminism, today's modern woman, and the impact to family values, but a brief cause and effect relationship at least needs to be discussed to set the tone for why inter-gender relationships have become what they are in today's society. With the patriarchal structure, the father took care of providing a means for food, clothing and shelter while the mother was responsible for child rearing, cooking, cleaning, and maintaining the household. In this model, the father is the head of the family, the authority figure on all things including the wife, children and property.

In just the last 50 years, societal norms of gender dynamics have been extensively changed and we've seen the patriarchal structure that was once so prevalent turned on its head. Instead of doing what they want to do, men need to check in and get permission from their wives. The term "pussy whipped" is a common one used in describing the average married dad, but the irony is the most pussy whipped men lack sex within these marriages. Wives now, more often than not, wear the pants in the family and make most family decisions; much different than 50 years ago and opposite of what Christian doctrine teaches. The bible verse Ephesian 5: 22-24 states:

"Wives, submit to your husbands as to the Lord. For the husband is the head of the wife as Christ is the head of the church, his body, of which he is the Savior. Now as the church submits to Christ, so also wives should submit to their husbands in everything."

Increasingly, even in Christian homes, this patriarchal structure is the exception and not the norm. As a result, this change has played a huge role in how men like you and me, who've grown up in this post-transitional era, view and interact with women. Additionally, the adverse impacts resulting from the changed family dynamic continue to echo and reverberate through successive generations as they are passed down to our sons and daughters.

Rise of Modern Feminism and De-emphasis of Masculine Values

If you're a regular dude like me, you probably haven't thought much about the feminist movement, or had a Women's Studies class. As a fringe member (of sorts) in the men's rights side of things, I do see some of the media, on-line discussions and battles being fought with feminists, and have since learned more about it. While it doesn't have a large place here, I do think it does provide some valuable background into why women behave in the ways they do, the impacts of their behavior on themselves, and how it affects us as men and fathers. You may or may not find this information valuable or directly applicable to building a sexy marriage or healthy family life, but I believe having these small pieces contribute to the larger cause – another brick in the wall of knowledge. This knowledge can then be used to help us better understand what we are up against so our behaviors can be adjusted to maximize our life, family and marriage goals.

Today, the new modern feminist "norm," or ideal, is for women is to go to college, establish a career, climb the corporate ladder, embrace their sexuality, and have fun (e.g. be as promiscuous as they want) until their late twenties. At this point it becomes a priority to now settle down and try to start a family. As a result of this general behavior, the median age of first marriages increased from 20.3 years in 1960, to 26.5 years in 2010, and many adults are not marrying at all. According to Pew Research Center data, the percentage of married adults over 18 years old has declined from 72% in 1960, to 51% in 2010 (only 48% of American Households), an all-time low. Also, according to the research, only 20%

of households are "traditional" families (married couples with children), down from nearly a 25% in 2000, and 43% in 1950 (early in the baby boom generation births).

Recent data showed that for people aged 25 to 44 years the median number of lifetime sexual partners for men was six, and women four (data from 2006-2010, which was self-reported and therefore has a propensity to underreport due to societal pressures, especially on women and promiscuity). While I couldn't track down information on the sex partners in the Gen Y/Millennials demographic (birth year from early 1980's to early 2000's), I would expect to see those median sexual partner numbers continue to rise, as it logically makes sense that adding over 6 years to the median age of marriage in today's casual sex society will mean people will have higher partner counts. This means that both men and women are sleeping with more people prior to marriage than previous generations, and thus creating a casual sex environment that is today's norm.

The feminist movement provided much needed basic civil rights to women, but today's agenda often doesn't appear to be about basic rights since laws, and society, have secured most of those years ago. [Now, I refuse to be pulled into a debate on wage equality, or gender discrimination, or some other feminist argument along those lines, as I think some merit may exist in specific instances. I'm only stating here that the basic human and civil rights have been granted to women and are currently enforced by law.] However, in today's feminist society, the feminist movement has changed. Today, in the name of women's rights and equality, the feminist movement justifies the ability for women to do what they want, not for the betterment of society, but for the betterment of themselves. Subsequently, some of this "betterment" comes at the expense of men. Feminism has planted and cultivated the concepts that patriarchy, masculinity, and men are oppressive. This new doctrine has subsequently taken on a life of its own. It entitles women and shames masculine behaviors. Recognize I'm painting with a very broad brush here, and not all women think like this, but this thinking percolates down to the masses, despite being mostly pushed by the more extreme women thinkers.

Perhaps this wouldn't be that big of an issue if this thinking were buffered by male role models and masculine teachings. While those may occur by fathers and sports coaches in small doses on nights or weekends, the majority of time growing up today, as well as in previous generations, is spent with women. From infancy through their adolescence, children primarily interact with females: from day care providers to teachers and mothers. In the formative years of 4 years to 13 years, only 2.3% of men are preschool or kindergarten teachers, and only 18.3% elementary or middle school teachers, are men according to the 2011 United States Bureau of Labor Statistics. In my own children's kindergarten to fourth grade public elementary school, only one primary teacher out of twenty-six faculty is a man – the gym teacher.

What I think this means is that children are absorbing the modern feminism doctrine through osmosis, if not from direct teachings, from women raised under this very way of thinking themselves. Boys are expected to go against their natural inclinations of exploration and physical play during the classroom day, and conform to the expectations to sit still, listen and behave. If they behave, they are rewarded through feminine approvals that are in place through the educational system. Lessons such as "be a nice boy and girls will like you" is one such lesson taught very young, and as you'll see later, is detrimental contributor in inter-gender relationships.

The casual sex environment, the on-going erosion of marriage as an institution, and the de-emphasis of the traditional nuclear family has subsequently resulted in the growth of fatherless homes and single mothers. According to U.S. Census Bureau, approximately 25% of children in this country are being raised in single family homes. Of these nearly 14 million households, the mother's received primary custody nearly nine out of ten times. When you start to stack up the generations, you see more and more people were either raised in a single-mother environment themselves, or are finding their children being raised in that situation today. Adding in the expanding influence of generational feminist thinking on top of this woman-dominated life rearing, and it is no wonder that from young boys and girls to grown men and women all start to place a lower value on masculine thoughts – and men in general – than previous generations. This results in a society floundering with gender roles, and more importantly, boys and men struggling with their natural instincts in the face of a strong feminist headwind. At the same time, these same boys (and men young and old) are lacking masculine direction from the previous generation of fathers or mentors.

I was raised in this environment and you likely were too. It's also the environment most children are being raised today. Good behavior and acting nice was rewarded by teachers and women of influence; and typical boy instincts of wrestling, rough housing, getting dirty, and pushing the physical boundaries of play were discouraged or shamed. My father, who despite growing up on a farm with heavy masculine influences, did not impart on me too many masculine traditions or theories. Instead, he allowed my mother to lead the direction of our family with her naturally more dominant (or, as my wife observes, bullying nature). As such, I grew up to understand that the way to be successful in life was to be nice to women, to bend over backward to try and please them, while suppressing my own masculine needs or desires (or not being encouraged to explore them, since education was valued higher in my household than traditional masculine activities).

In this type of environment (common today as it was in my day), boys grow up rudderless without the understanding of how to be a strong man, and how to deal with people (men or women). As a result, those who find themselves in this situation know intuitively that something is missing from our core being. For most of my entire life, I've felt that I was missing some critical piece of thinking that other males inherently "had" as it related with dating, courtship and social/sexual interactions. In seeing other men I knew having the relationships I wanted, I wondered how they could be such jerks and always seem to have women throw themselves at them. Alternatively, my (forever failing) strategy with women was to shower attention and affection and show them how nice I was. I thought that because of my nice-guy behavior, they would reciprocate like the Disney movies have led us to believe, and I never understood why this wasn't the case.

Still, despite this "Nice Guy" approach to life, I had girlfriends throughout high school and college. I now see most of my behavior in these relationships as being utterly wimpy (or "Beta" in the vernacular I'll discuss in a bit), and it's no wonder things did not work out or I got cheated on. Eventually I met the woman who would become my wife, and early on my behavior continued to be "nice." I became a black-belt in conflict avoidance, and would bend over backward doing what I could to keep the relationship waters smooth. As a result, I thought things were generally pretty OK in our marriage. We didn't have any major issues, but things were on a treadmill. We were going through the motions without much passion most of the time. During a low point, I wanted to try to figure out how to improve things since I felt something was structurally wrong. I had decided I wasn't going to go through the next 40 years of my life without improvement in our relationship, despite how well my wife Holly and I got along as parents and roommates. I had to either fix myself to fix our relationship, or I had to give up and accept that this was as good as it was going to get. Divorce wasn't really an option in my mind.

Somehow I stumbled upon the loosely organized group of male-run websites commonly referred to as "the Manosphere" and it opened my eyes to another way of seeing things. This resonated and harmonized with my internal frequency, and I unlocked the key I was searching for all these years. As a result of these findings, I was able to begin the journey of becoming a better man.

The Manosphere essentially is the counterpoint to the feminist doctrine (that empowers women at the expense of men). It is a free form community consisting primarily of men on the internet sharing experiences and thoughts with the intention of educating, empowering, and improving the state of men and boys. These multiple websites, online forums, and blogs are updated with great regularity, and for the first time allow men to compare notes and share stories of various philosophical, political, economic, social, and scientific views primarily about how they impact men's lives. Through this open source, self-produced media with no real nucleus, masculine influence is again being provided to millions of men who have been lacking and who now choose to seek out these resources.

Be forewarned however, some of the Manosphere teachings are not for the faint of heart. Some who choose to contribute hold a bitter and jaded view on the world, or towards women in general, and like to paint with a large, broad brush. While a lot of truths can be found within their lessons and writings, if not careful the jaded view and bitterness can swallow you whole. Tread carefully, but the impacts apply to both young and old, single and married alike.

Game

To lay the foundation of what Game is and why it works I need to get into some basic biological and social-sexual background. All of us on this planet are reproductive machines, designed to survive long enough to pass on our genes. Prehistorically and historically, resources such as food that are necessary for survival were often times difficult to acquire or in short supply, thereby making them valuable. Those with the tools to acquire these resources thrived. Those with fewer tools or skills to compete died out.

For humans, reproductive strategies are pretty simple: males want to impregnate as many females as possible to further spread his genes while females want to be impregnated by male(s) whose genes have the highest value for the future generation (while simultaneously maintaining the necessary resources to provide for the offspring). These resource may or may not be provided for by the man who impregnated her. The largest, fastest, most dominant male (good genes) may impregnate a woman, but it doesn't matter if he sticks around or not if she's got the resources to raise the child by other means. This pursuit of good genes for women is what evolutionary psychologists refer to as **Hypergamy:** women want a man with a higher status, or value, compared to her own for the benefit of herself and their offspring. A demonstration of this is when you see younger women with successful, more established, older men. We would think women would always act in her own rational best, long-term self-interest when it comes to selecting or staying with a man, but this is far from true. Hypergamy is discussed in the context of all relationships (even short-term one-night stands) and I'll be applying this concept further to the marriage relationship.

In putting this evolutionary idea into modern terms, and applying it to modern female sexuality: women's base sexual desire is attracted to a man higher up in the social-sexual hierarchy compared to herself. Hypergamy is neither a positive or negative trait, it is simply a biological attraction mechanism. Therefore men who have an interest in attracting women (of equal or higher quality as themselves) have an incentive to acquire or maintain as high of level of social status as possible. Pretty straightforward and logical right? You don't often see a fat, slobby guy dating a hot girl at the start of a relationship. It may morph into that, but rarely is the hot girl attracted to the "big" guy at the start. Also notice that attracting women, or for that matter keeping your wife attracted to you, has nothing to do with "being nice," and everything to do with social status – which is a complex cocktail of physical appearance, societal success, and behavior.

Hundreds of Manosphere articles have been written about, or pertaining to, the hypergamy concept if you feel the desire to dig further. You need to understand hypergamy so you can recognize and stop some of the bad outcomes that can occur between your wife and other men. At a minimum, understanding hypergamy will allow you to see how your wife may view you, or the changes you make to better yourself. In doing so you'll better understand her reactions or possible outcomes born from your actions, or lack of action. You see, the new rules have changed how women view sex, and who they decide to share their bodies with.

The invention of the birth control pill, along with feminism and removal of the social stigma from women sleeping around, made casual sex more acceptable for men and women alike. For women, they could pursue their short-term hypergamous tendencies without fear of pregnancy. They could now pursue high social-sexual status men (who weren't necessarily the top economic provider) and not worry about how the child would be provided for – due to the fact the child could be prevented or terminated if desired, as well as the social programs available by the government to support a pregnancy did occur. So the dominant "bad boy" biker, or wanna-be rock star, who hold high social status (despite having poor income) are very attractive to females – while the good provider-boring, nice guy, professional type is nearly invisible (despite income and stability, this doesn't translate very highly on the social-sexual ladder).

The "bad boy", adventurous traits that show male dominant behavior are hereto referred to as Alpha traits, and are pervasive throughout media. Think Indiana Jones, Tyler Durden (*Fight Club*), Darth Vader (*Star Wars*), James Bond, and John McLane (*Die Hard*). Alpha gets its name from hominid or canid pack behavior where there is a single "top dog" in the pack. While in any pack there can only be one "Alpha" that dominates the rest of the pack. Behaviors that emulate the Alpha's are collectively known as such. Typical Alpha behavior in humans include confidence, dominance (in some arena), and the ability to inspire raw sexual attraction in at least some females. Usually these Alpha characteristics include humor, sense of adventure, risk taking, going against societal norms, physical dominance, and confident sexuality.

Women deciding to finally "settle down" in this new feminist world (usually after years of fun times and sex with various short-term partners), will often eschew their natural evolutionary tendencies (to pursue the dominant social male) and settle for a less dominant mate with better long-term qualities (e.g. steady paycheck, good provider of resources, less likely to stray) for the sake of her offspring. Going forward, we'll refer to the cooperative and compassionate behavioral traits of male providers as "Beta." To further define these terms in humans, they are traits designed to inspire comfort as opposed to attraction, and include having a good job, being "nice," being responsible, well-mannered, and intelligent.

The tendency for women to marry men with these primarily Beta traits, or who encourage the suppression of Alpha traits, obviously has a huge impact on the long-term viability of marriage. However, understand that while the biological nature of hypergamy will attract your wife to men with certain traits, how she controls her actions or reactions to this trigger is impacted by many other factors such as pair-bonded strength to her partner, moral compass, and her ability to rationalize or justify behavior that is goes against her social or moral beliefs. Understanding the evolutionary hardwiring of her hypergamous nature allows you (the husband or boyfriend) to adjust your own behaviors to elicit respect and admiration in the context of marriage.

Alpha and Beta behaviors are not static, and both are needed for a rock solid relationship. However, most married men have too much Beta behavior and not enough Alpha, so changes are often needed for a better balance. Think of it this way: Betas are comforters who tend to make excuses as to why they aren't getting the love the want, Alphas are trail blazers who do what they think is right and make no apologies for who they are or their lot in life. The bottom line is that you, like most men, are likely too damn nice and need to add some improvements in your life to create those tingles again. We've been brainwashed by the feminist magazine articles that trickle to our conscious (and subconscious) minds that helping with housework will make you attractive thereby leading to sex. Bullshit. Let me say that again. That type of Cosmopolitan or Beta-Men's-Health article is absolute bullshit. That cleaning and being nice stuff is not an Alpha behavior, so stop buying into that lie and start realizing you need more of something else to be a better man and to attract your wife. You'll see that Beta stuff is still good in some ways in keeping stress down and a tidy house, it's not what your wife is missing.

While the term Game isn't one I particularly care for, it is an easy way to wrap up this social behavior in a tidy package. Game, in its simplest definition, is a way for men to adopt attributes, behaviors, perspectives, strategies and tactics to create elevated social dominance with the general intention to increase their desire to women for the sake of increased sexual relations. Said simply – Game makes sex easier, even with your wife. Women's attraction toward men are based on any number of factors, including physical appearance, height, humor, coordination, intelligence, confidence, build, and dozens of other cues that feed into their conscious and subconscious.

Since many twentieth century men are typically weak, supplicative nice-guys (with a spare tire to boot), they need to unlearn their social norms that turned them into what the often referred to as Average Frustrated Chumps (AFC). Most of us, including me, were AFC's at one point, so don't let that be a roadblock from changing. It can be done! The AFC has many qualities including:

- (first and foremost) pedestalizing women, or a particular woman (that is, putting one woman, or the entire sex, as something to look up to – to worship, and whose happiness is more important than his own)
- Having little or no clue as to what qualities makes certain men attractive to women – and hence not having many of those attractive qualities
- fear of rejection and therefore fear of approaching women he is interested in (or fear of going after sex with his wife, if married, due to this fear of rejection)
- acting totally devoting and smothering when given the opportunity
- is generally insecure in who he is as a man, so makes up for it with compliments, gifts, and niceness.

The married AFC needs to ask himself a couple of questions. Does my behavior toward my wife resemble that between a man and a woman who desires him, or does it resemble a boy who is afraid of upsetting his mother? Do I avoid confrontation with my wife to avoid her emotional state? Am I an attractive individual, not just to my wife, but to other people and other women? Do I have hobbies that make me a better person, or do I waste my time doing things that don't benefit me? The "nice guy's" general approach towards inter-gender relationships, either romantic or platonic, is to attempt to gain the approval, or avoid the disapproval, of women.

While this individual can do some things to improve his likelihood of appealing to women, such as becoming more attractive by losing weight, working out (see Part 1), or dressing better, learning Game is arguably the most important. Game is a mixture of using confidence (real or perceived) along with applied knowledge of biology, social dynamics and female behavior theory in a way to improve your sexual/romantic attraction to women. While many think

Game is tricks and manipulation, at its core it is a mindset that destroys the myths and lies men have been taught and allows us to be the dominant, confident, and masculine being that is engraved in our XY chromosomes.

There are many, many facets of Game, from ways of dressing, to extensive behavior changes, to general banter tips with women. It is well beyond the scope of this book to get into the intricacies of Game, but in general key aspects that translate over to those of us in marriages include:

- Confidence, even at the risk of overconfidence
- Remove wimpy, Beta behaviors
- Stop putting women on a pedestal (eliminate supplication)
- Value yourself on your own merits and not based on what others, especially women or a particular woman, thinks of you
- Be more dominant in interactions with both men and women
- Be cocky and funny
- Be more sexually explicit or implicit with comments or jokes (embrace your sexual identity)
- Ignore her, or be more aloof
- Stop showering women (including your wife or girlfriend) with attention and niceness
- Stay emotionally calm in reactive situations (maintain "Frame") – you are a fucking rock
- Ignore what women say they want; listen instead to their behavior and body language (laughing and touching you at your dumb jokes, or doing what you request with no offer of reward are clears signs of attraction)
- Be outcome independent – do what you want to do with no outcome in mind; if said outcome is different than expected, no negative reaction

Game is really about improving social skills. You don't have to be the life-of-the-party-guy to have good Game, you really just need to be able to have mutually enjoyable conversations with people; young, old, men, women, customers, sales people, anyone. Holding eye-contact, removing social ticks, and generally being able to have an interesting conversation with no end result in mind is about 75% of the battle. Doing this consistently with anyone, over and over, and making them feel at ease, comfortable and laugh is the essence of Game. Moving the overall perspective to focus on women is what is considered the final piece. Looking at my bullet points above, they apply to most situations.

Now for single guys, Game is typically the effort it takes for a man to socialize himself into a woman's pants for a one or two time affair. That's the same goal for a married guy, except the woman is his wife and the frequency of the end-goal is multiplied a thousand-fold. For us married guys, Game isn't a one-time deal but one that we want to entice our wife into over and over again, so we must understand the sex side of the married game. For the wedded guy especially, one must realize the fallacy of the fairy tale romantic comedy as it relates to sex. In the bedroom, the largest lie that needs to be unlearned (by nice guys and AFCs all over the globe) is that women just want to "make love" in a tender, loving style, want to be treated like a "good girl" with respect, and need to give you permission before agreeing to your various sexual repertoires.

Understand, that the core of the AFC are primarily learned and developed in adolescence and early adulthood, and takes the childhood lessons of "if you are nice, you're a good boy" to the next level of life. Be it in the bedroom or outside, this mentality needs to be changed, and if I can do it, so can you.

The Red Pill

The Red Pill is a metaphor that has been adopted by the Manosphere from the movie *The Matrix*. In that movie, the main character Neo has felt that the world that he lives in is wrong somehow and he doesn't know why. Later, he is presented with a choice of a Red Pill or a Blue Pill. The Blue Pill will let him go back to the comforts of the false world as he's come to know it. By taking the Red Pill, the bitter reality of the world he lives in is revealed to him; that what he has taken for "real" in his past (Blue Pill days) is just an illusion, and most people simply follow the herd to their own detriment. These metaphors are used occasionally in this book, and represent knowledge and an alternative view point to how to view the world in which we live today.

For the purposes of this book, the Red Pill will generally focus on the social and cultural engineering of men's relationship dynamics with women, and how to break through those bonds to become masculine family leaders once again. Occasionally, the Red Pill may refer to our society's other deceptions that we are fed. The primary focus of this book is how we married men can benefit from Red

Pill thinking. That is, men improving marriage dynamics and sex, fathering and mental/physical health and fitness for a more fulfilling and happy life.

Alternatively though, the Blue Pill in *The Matrix* analogy is inherently unhealthy. Blue pill symptoms in real life can include:

- low self-esteem,
- passive aggressive behavior,
- sexless marriages,
- porn addiction as a coping mechanism for the lack of sex,
- hatred toward women,
- frustration,
- divorce,
- alcoholism or drugs as a coping method, and
- poor fathering as a result of being supplicating to the spouse, not disciplining or not being a family leader.

Swallowing the Red Pill is not always pretty. It is bitter as you take that "special butterfly" you've loved for so long off her pedestal you've put her on, and realize she's driven by biology and evolutionary principals just like every other women. Many men who aren't willing to truly swallow the Red Pill believe we're bitter misogynists who hate women, which is not the case for me, or most married men for that matter. We generally view women as better smelling but otherwise equal to ourselves. Many others who do swallow it, and begin reading up on Game, forums or divorce blogs get pretty bitter, jaded and cynical about the whole thing before eventually coming to peace about dealing with women. Many men that take the Red Pill go through the Kübler-Ross Five Stages of Grief, since it really is like part of us dying (or as I like to think of it metamorphosis like a pupa to a butterfly):

- **Denial** – "No way is this true. Red Pill is a lie told by jerks, being a Nice Guy is really the way to live life and get the love and sex I deserve."

- **Anger** – "This is total bullshit. Women are messed up. Why didn't anyone teach me these things? Why do I have to change, I thought I was doing everything right? You mean my wife isn't attracted enough to me to get turned on because I was TOO nice? Fuck that."

- **Bargaining** – "Maybe I'll just try some of the ideas a little and see if they work, I'm sure they won't though, and I can go back to Nice

Guy tactics, which just need more time to get the effect I'm looking for."

- **Depression** – "If this is the truth, this world is a sad place to be. I'm not sure I can ever look at or be with a woman the same way again. This sucks, I sort of wish I didn't unplug so I could keep pedestalizing women. What a messed up world..."
- **Acceptance** – "If I can't beat them, I'll join them. Good to at least know what I'm up against so I can play by the 'real' rules!"

If you come out the other side in one piece, you could still have a pretty cynical opinion of the whole situation, I know I did. However, I don't think you have to fall into that trap of being bitter, but it takes a lot of introspection and mental positivity as you shift focus from the mentality of working towards only sexual gratification to Inner Game, which is another way to say inner strength, inner peace and happiness with your own self. Advanced level Inner Game (where you are build your own abilities and self-confidence) will eventually make you a rock of a man that others, like your family, will come to depend and rely upon.

It's better to come late to the party and unplug from *The Matrix* than it is to remain plugged in to the drip feed of lies about how you should behave; it could mean the difference between putting your family life back on track and running it off the rails.

To summarize, yes many women do love jerks (Alpha), put nice guys (Beta's) into the friend zone, and do so because it is in their biological nature. Thus, to create attraction to women (and have more sex), men need to learn how to have, or pretend to have, those Alpha qualities. And you don't necessarily have to be jerk about it, you usually need to simply grow a backbone and be a better and stronger (literally and figuratively) version of yourself.

Love and Marriage

The first time I met my wife I threw rocks at her like a sixth grader to show I liked her. The problem was I was 22 years old. I like to think I was more like a caveman claiming his cave-woman but it was far from that. As the story goes, I was on a class field trip in college and had a hike related to the class. At the halfway point of the hike we took a break. I was goofing around with some friends, who were throwing pebbles at each other waiting for the rest of the class to catch up. A cute girl I hadn't yet met was sitting on a bench next to a friend so I started throwing rocks at her too. As my group started back up along our trek, I touched or patted yet-unknown or spoken-to girl on her head as I walked by, and that was all it took, despite the fact that we hadn't said a word. My heart was in my chest when later, Holly and I actually started talking, and spent the rest of the trip together. Despite having just met, we were instantly the focus of each other's world. She pretended to like *The Simpsons* and I pretended to care about her college sport just so we'd have excuses to hang out. We had a fun, frequent, and exciting early sex life and am sure we annoyed both her and my roommates with our frequent events. Even just thinking back to that time, my heart rate increases and I have feelings of euphoria.

In our current life stage, things aren't quite as heart-thumping. At the time of this writing we've been married for nearly 13 years, are raising two great kids, but most days are like the routine described in the Introduction. We have a really strong bond together, but it takes effort to recreate the feelings that came so easily those first 6 months. Like any married couple we've had our ups and downs, along with family issues, self-esteem issues, money issues, health issues, financial issues, sex issues, and children issues. In many ways we're no different than the other 58 million married couples in the U.S.

When we got married, I really gave no thought to the divorce statistics or laws as I "knew" we didn't have to worry about it. After all, my parents are now married 40 years and made it look relatively easy. Yet, I was in a real low spot after 9 years of marriage and two very young kids searching for answers. In my head, things were not aligning to where I thought things would be in our marriage. We were better than roommates as we got along – mostly – but only a touch above. Passionless and boring is another way to describe what we were going through. Perhaps it would have passed on its own, but felt I had to dig deeper and try to fix what, in my mind, was a problem. I stumbled upon this new way of seeing the world as described above and was subsequently determined to make sure we wouldn't become a marriage statistic. I wanted to make sure both us and our kids made it through their childhood as part of an intact family.

If you're an average married dad like me, you probably didn't realize some of the factors that influenced why you landed your wife; nor why after 5, 10, 15 years later she's not that into you most of the time (in that way). Nor do you likely realize what the statistics or impacts of divorce are. This next part will lay that all out, inevitably scaring the shit out of you, and perhaps convincing you to at least try and make it work. It will present some basic principles on how to prevent the bad stuff from happening.

Chemistry of Love

Harken back to that first kiss. It doesn't matter what first kiss, as most first kisses are the same. The desire. The anticipation. You wonder if it will be any good. Your heart is beating a million miles an hour. You feel as though you're on top of the world and bulletproof. Time seems to stop and the world seems to stand still as you picture the 360-degree camera spinning around your body capturing this moment forever... And don't get me started on a first sex experience. It's like the first kiss multiplied by a thousand. Body trembles, head in the clouds, eyes rolled back. You know what I mean. It's really, really sublime and it becomes imprinted in your brain for future reference.

This experience for some of us only happens once, twice, a handful of times. For others that go through this experience many more times (the "player" or the "slut") they may lose that excitement, which is really a shame since that feeling is pure electricity. It feels like taking a drug. The thing is, it is exactly like a drug and also activates the release of massive amounts of bodily chemicals into your bloodstream.

Doing something new and exciting or dangerous like riding a rollercoaster, getting chased by a lion, skydiving, or moving in for that first kiss gets your heart racing. In these instances, the brain sends a signal to the adrenal gland which secretes hormones and neurotransmitters such as epinephrine (widely referred to as adrenaline), norepinephrine, and endorphins as a response to stress. This gets your heart racing, increases attention and responsiveness, and prepares your body for its "fight or flight" response that stressful situations dictate.

Now pay attention, because this next part is important for later comprehension on life and marital aspects. Dopamine is another neurotransmitter, or a chemical released by nerve cells to other nerve cells. Dopamine is super-intense reward mechanism for the brain and rewards your brain and body for things that make you feel so good. The dopamine release from cocaine is the same one released from sexual gratification, both responses flooding the brain with pleasure sensors. It's the reason that people get hooked on cocaine (cocaine and crack cocaine is often referred to as the most addictive hard drug) and the euphoria of "falling madly in love." Dopamine is also tied to social interactions. Bipolar disorder manic subjects become hyper social or hypersexual as a result of dopamine (note the impact to sexual attraction here). This makes you feel "in love" and absolutely crazy for the new person, and applies to your "first" love, to your emotional affair with the secretary, as well as the way your wife may interact with her hot new coworker. I don't think I can overstate your body's reaction to this. Your body wants to keep chasing after the next fix (that super-intense reward feeling) at the expense of logical and rational thought, and is the chemical reason why people commit extramarital affairs despite "having it all" with their current spouse. The problem is their spouse doesn't make their life all that exciting. No excitement equals no dopamine.

Dopamine and serotonin are interrelated, and serotonin is one of the reasons you can't get your love interest out of your head. Like dopamine, serotonin is a neurotransmitter and regulates the perception of mood, sleep, pain, emotion, and appetite as well as social dominance. One of the primary purposes of typical pharmaceutical antidepressants (selective serotonin reuptake inhibitors – SSRIs) is to regulate the serotonin uptake at brain synapses. This can help treat social phobia, anxiety disorders, and depression. The downside is these drugs can also inhibit sexual desire. Alternatively, drugs like Ecstasy (MDMA) increases the activity of serotonin, dopamine, norepinephrine, and oxytocin (discussed next) and gives those using it energy, feelings of euphoria and intimacy with others along with reduced anxiety.

Oxytocin, or the "cuddle hormone", is a neuromodulator in the brain and responsible for pair bonding. It is enhance by estrogen and released in huge amounts during and after childbirth, creating the pair bond necessary for mother to bond with child, in addition to providing the "letdown reflex" for lactation. This hormone is also associated with feelings of contentment, reductions in anxiety and feeling of calmness and security around their mate. Related to the oxytocin hormone is vasopressin, a chemically similar structure which shares many of the same features along with impacting pair bonding behavior in males. Within men, vasopressin has been shown to counteract the desire to have sex with multiple partners and helps to put a woman into a "special" category and thus more attractive.

The release of all these hormones are highly complex and obviously not just involved with falling in love or pair bonding. They've been involved with the survival of our species in so many ways from appetite regulation, to promoting infant-mother interaction, to providing the attention, energy, and performance enhancer to survive against foes. However, falling in love involves the release of many of these chemicals in various doses depending on where you are in the timeline of the relationship:

- First kiss: epinephrine (adrenaline), norepinephrine, endorphins, dopamine
- On-going infatuation: dopamine, serotonin
- Early sexual experiences: epinephrine, dopamine, oxytocin, serotonin
- Long-term pair bonding: oxytocin

The problem is the brain and body is highly adaptable. Skydiving and public speaking is highly exciting or scary for the first time, resulting in adrenaline and dopamine release. Getting your 100th jump in or speaking in front of the 1,000th group, like you're the President, isn't likely to exhibit nearly the same response. As Dr. Greg Berns has stated in his book *Satisfaction*, your body gets used to the risk that is necessary to trigger reward. Just like drug addicts who need to take more and more of a substance to get back to the level of High they desire, so it goes the state of our marriage. Kissing your partner for the first time is exciting. For the 10,000th time, it's routine, thus eliciting no – or next to no – dopamine response especially for that morning peck out the door. The status quo needs to be raised to feel anything.

The movie *Crank* is about a hit man who is injected with a poison, must continually have adrenaline in his system to stay alive, and therefore needs increasingly more excitement and danger to live. Our marriages are a lot like that. To keep that dopamine fix going, we need more than a peck on the cheek before leaving for work or the butt-grab before bed. Most husbands have a lot shorter trigger on that dopamine fix, and much higher level of testosterone that triggers our sex drive, which makes it a lot easier to get that "fix." For women, having seen the same "show" day after day, week after week, the dopamine receptors are dulled. Unless she forces her brain to fantasize or actively engage in thinking about sex (not too many married women naturally do this), it takes more effort to take them out of the realm of "normal" and into the realm of excitement.

Which leads us into the most important hormone for men: testosterone. This plays the key role in the development of the testes, as well as muscle, bone mass, and hair during male puberty. This is *the* sex hormone for men, insomuch that men producing more testosterone than average are typically more likely to engage in extramarital sex. For women, higher testosterone increases the sex drive as well. In addition, ejaculated semen contains both testosterone and endorphins, and when absorbed within women's vagina, spike female testosterone, endorphin, and oxytocin levels, as well as creating a positive environment for conceiving. As men and women age, testosterone production starts to diminish which leads to everything from weight gain to reduced libido, which due to the importance as a men's hormone, more greatly impacts them compared to women.

The female equivalent of testosterone is estrogen. While present in both men and women, it is primarily associated with female sex hormones and is present within females of reproductive age at much higher levels as they are primarily produced in the ovaries. They promote secondary sexual characteristics such as breasts, are involved with regulating the menstrual cycle, and obviously reproduction, as well as being part of the puzzle for a healthy female libido. After menopause, women see a reduction in estrogen which can lead to hot flashes, vaginal dryness, irritability, and a decrease in bone density. Estrogen is also increased in men due to eating soy, which can make them have soft, fleshy man-boobs (or moobs as I call them), a notable decrease in testosterone, and subsequently a decrease sex drive. I don't believe any man should be eating soy (for a variety of reasons), nor do I think babies should be fed soy formula unless there are no other alternatives.

[Not to get side tracked here, but I see so many moms and dads going away from breast feeding early and trending toward non-milk formula. If that is you, please do your research. If that is your only alternative, then fine, but I've read that soy formula can contribute to ADD/ADHD and altered behavior due to higher levels of manganese; that it can interfere with proper reproductive development due to elevated isoflavone levels; and that soy-fed babies receive the weighted equivalent of five birth control pills of estrogen a day. I don't know enough to say one way or the other that these claims are true, but I have read enough about the impacts soy consumption in children and adults that concern me enough that our family doesn't eat any soy products in our house.]

The main thing to understand about these hormones and neurotransmitters is that they are the driving force in how we act and react to situations. You can't logically rationalize with these things; attraction is not negotiated. You can't compliment and cuddle, or logically argue, a woman into getting a dopamine response. Nor can you be all "bad boy" Alpha all the time if you want to maintain that bond. When the dopamine "high" (remember, it is a high just like cocaine) wears off, the woman will come at least partially to her senses about what a jerk you've been or how you don't do anything to comfort her (oxytocin– Beta). You need both sides of the equation to maintain a quality relationship long-term.

Marriage – Past, Present and Future

If you're like me, you've said something like this at some point in your life:

> I, Alex, take you Holly, to be my lawfully wedded wife; to have and to hold from this day forward, for better or for worse, for richer, for poorer, in sickness and in health, to love and to cherish until death do us part.

They're probably nearly identical to the marriage vows that my grandparents and parents said 65 and 40 years ago respectively. Marriage of my grandparents' generation was one where you expected to weather the ups and downs without complaint and understood that two people who bonded for life were a lot stronger than one. As religion was a major driving force in these marriages, the societal norms for divorce were much different than today. Basically, it was pretty taboo for couples to get divorced and you stayed married for life "until death do you part." Getting married young due to parental and societal expectations at the time, it wasn't ensured that you truly loved your spouse before you married, since teenage hormones, lust, and the opportunity for sex were often driving factors towards young marriages. This meant that after the bloom was off the rose, they had to learn to love each other *after* the wedding. These mating and marriage habits of old usually meant that these old timers didn't have sexual relations of any sort until they were married, which makes the long-lasting marriages of yore even more surprising. That they could find a way towards common ground and lifelong marriages as basically strangers is so foreign to most raised in today's premarital casual sex society.

Most marriage usually starts out pretty decent. We, as men, have "wife goggles" (similar to beer goggles) for our wives and both parties are on their best behavior. Though we're not exactly sure why, sometimes the sex has already dried up considerably, or has never really started, by the time we get married. The actual wedding night is usually a great experience! Tens of thousands of dollars spent for a grand party where the now-wife can look her absolute best. Hundreds of friends who will look upon this event with either jealously or inspiration (at least in our own minds), as we think we are sure to be one of the few that will make it through the divorce labyrinth and stay married.

The National Marriage Project is an initiative to provide research and analysis on the health of marriage in American and to identify strategies to increase marital quality and stability. It states:

> Marriage is a fundamental social institution. It is central to the nurture and raising of children. It is the "social glue" that reliably attaches fathers to children. It contributes to the physical, emotional and economic health of men, women and children, and thus to the nation as a whole. It is also one of the most highly prized of all human relationships and a central life goal of most Americans.

As the recently married, we want so hard to contribute to this subset of people and to provide a strong and stable foundation for raising a family, paying our taxes, and being productive members of society in the typical American Dream.

Soon after the honeymoon phase, the dopamine rush of the wedding and newlywed sex with the wife starts to wear off as a routine is established. Nothing is less romantic than dealing with the day-to-day interactions with essentially a roommate. Passionate sex is still an occurrence, though is typically less frequent than before, and the longer you are together, the less frequent sex often becomes. While sex is only one part of marriage, it is an important one, especially for men. We are hard-wired to need and want sexual interactions with women. It is the way that we feel love and feel connected to our wives. When we get married, our needs for spousal happiness are generally very simple: to be appreciated by our wives and to have sex with regular frequency with an enthusiastic partner. Read that sentence again if you're a woman. We men are simple creatures. Yeah, we often have great ambitions professionally, want to love and care for our off-spring, eat and be well. But with our wife the needs are more basic and primal. We're able to overlook a lot of poor wifely behavior if we're getting our physical needs met as described. In other words, our wives don't have to be even close to perfect if we're getting fucked properly.

What typically happens in a marriage is both parties tend to get complacent. They'll stop treating each other like boyfriend/girlfriend and begin treating each other more like roommates. For men, they are slowly and steadily being indoctrinated to be a cleaner, calmer version of themselves. If you've seen that part in the movie *Old School* where Will Farrell is acting excited to go shopping at *Bed, Bath and Beyond* as part of a fun Saturday, you know what I mean. We're basically being brainwashed to be more like women and less like the masculine man who attracted your wife in the first place. Both husband and wife are completely unaware this change is occurring. Think of it as someone slowly dimming the room – so slowly you don't even realize it is occurring – until all at once you notice it is darker than before. That is what is happening to men's masculinity and sharp edges as they become equal members of modern housekeeping brigade.

The irony is that the rough edges and raw masculinity is what attracted your wife in the first place, and neither of you realize a change has occurred. Eventually, the erosion of your manhood is so pronounced that you accept being a second class citizen status in your own house. Instead of getting the whole house to mark your territory, you are forced down into "the man cave" so she can get your beer and farts away from her delicate floral duvet in the living room. Or perhaps it was even your idea to get away from her henpecking. Either way, you're living on separate sides of the house, like some of our friends and neighbors.

Impact of Children on Marriage

Finally, we add the final nail in the coffin of killing the caveman within: kids. For those of us who genuinely want children, we hope to have the great experience of having lots and lots of sex for a few months trying to conceive. For me, my head was in the clouds (so was Holly's) when we went off birth control. We didn't really do any reading on ovulation or anything else that really matters in getting pregnant, and I figured it would take a while just banging away and having as much sex as I could stand before she would finally get pregnant without any worries.

What often happens though (and what happened with us too), after the excitement and exhilaration of unprotected sex wane, the baby-making activities start to become more clinical and sex becomes a little bit of a chore. You're not seen as a passionate man, but as a sperm donor with a responsibility to fertilize an egg. How romantic does that sound? The passion during this period is likely lacking, you're going through the motions with the express intent to bring little versions of yourselves into the world. Yeah, your wife loves you, but she's got a baby on her mind already, and you're simply a tool to her baby desires. Ideally she gets pregnant with no complications in short order, if not, other emotions start to creep in on both sides. Resentment, depression, blame. Perhaps you go through pregnancy drugs; testing your sperm (how does jacking off in the doctor's office sound?); in vitro fertilization; or even starting the adoption process. Whatever your experience, the focus very quickly changes from just the two of you to this theoretical "baby." It soon begins to be all you talk about, and then it finally happens: pregnancy.

Hormones are raging through your wife at this stage. She's likely a raging lunatic one moments and a crying baby the other. If you're one of the lucky ones, you can maintain a regular sex life through the pregnancy and your love strengthens in preparation to support this new baby. Many pregnancies result in issues that prevent comfortable or safe sex for the wife, though occasionally the husband will have issues with perceived hurting of the baby or not being attracted to their wife during this time. This is dangerous because how easy do you think reestablishing this connection will be if you cut out the physical aspect of sex for up to 9 months or longer? It will be like losing your virginity all over again, which is usually very awkward as you begin to feel each other out all over again well after the baby is born. In some ways this may even be weirder, and met with less success, than the initial sexual encounters.

Then the big day is here. Not to take anything away from my younger child, but for me, the birth of my first child was the most amazing experience of my life. It is one of the few magical days I remember most of the details. Holly did awesome despite having the baby facing backward, resulting in very painful back pain during labor and delivery (and no epidural for my stud wife), and I supported her as best as I could. She was so strong during the birthing process and I did my small part to help her. The young nurse who assisted the midwife was probably all of 22 years old, wide-eyed, and slightly overwhelmed. She may not have seen a lot of births yet in her career, but she basically said we were awesome as a couple during the process – something she likely hadn't seen much of.

Regardless of how the delivery went, you end up the day with a brand new baby that is entirely your responsibility. My only thought as we left the hospital and tried to figure out how to get my daughter into her car seat was "I can't believe they're letting us take this baby home... we don't know what the hell we're doing!"

A baby is a rude awakening for all parents, whether it's your first or fifth. It really does take a village to raise a child, and while parents or in-laws may help those first few weeks, pretty soon it's just you and your spouse taking care of the baby. You take turns waking up in the night, both exhausted, both cranky, trying to get through each day without any major issues. If you and your partner have a strong relationship then these sleepless night, back poops (how exactly does that happen anyway?), middle of the night feedings, cleaning up after being sick, and stress involved with the first year roll off your back and you generally stay happy together focusing on your new family member.

What happens in the husband is enlightening. Studies have shown that men's testosterone actually lowers during the birth of a child, and it's only natural for the dad to begin doing what he can to take care of and support the mom and baby. As a modern parent, men now share in the household and child rearing responsibilities. Dishes are done, meals are cooked, and houses are cleaned (at least some of the time) by men and fathers. In my case, when our kids were newborns, I was much less sleep deprived and more alert to the babies crying than my wife. If they weren't hungry for momma's milk, I took care of them, changed their diaper and comforted in the middle of the night while their mom slept. I believe this caretaking and overall household assistance is necessary for couples to get through this exciting and trying time, but it does redefine the relationship between husband and wife.

From the father's perspective though, our wives' needs are now nearly entirely focused on the child and not centered on us husbands as men. The emotional connection and needs that were previously fed by us are now being met by the baby. We're on the outside looking in and it can by really hard for us dads. I'm not sure the wives realize how difficult is for us to feel like we're the ones left out in the cold. Yeah, we love our kids more than anything despite not yet knowing them, but we love our wives in a way that can't be replicated by the love of a child. On a whole, men feel loved through physical touch and physical connection with our wives. It's inherent in our DNA: sex is to men what cuddling is to women. I read and hear about sexless marriages where sex gets totally cut off when the kids are young, sometimes for years.

No matter what your situation, raising young children is a really a stressful time for both parents, but for men, the best stress relief is to reconnect with the wife through loving marital sex. So when many wives put up walls of excuses, shut out their man, and expect him to live in a celibate life "for the good of the family," it kills him in many ways. When the child(ren) finally get slightly older (over two is a generally when things were a little better for us) things seem to settle into a rhythm once again. But how husbands and wives behave towards one another in that first year or two will often dictate the likelihood of long-term marriage viability. If you let things spiral during this time due to lack of attention toward your partner, you could find yourself with long-term lasting consequences to your marriage and subsequently your kids, your finances and your health.

CHAPTER 5

The Ghost of Marriage Future

T his chapter will continue to provide a description of the changing
marital picture in our society, notes what happens when things start to
fall apart for the couple, and how the impacts of divorce impacts
everyone in the family. It can be a little dark, but tough love and teaching this is
necessary to adequately appreciate the gravity of the marriage situation we find
ourselves in. Think of this section as laying further groundwork on the back story
so you can fully understand what you're up against and what we're trying to
prevent.

Marriage as an Institution is Crumbling

Usually the most critical stage of marriage is when the kids are fairly young.
The pressures of everyday life are often high, which starts the fracture of marital
disconnect. When sex dries up, it is the canary in the coal mine of marriage
viability. Despite what women say about sex being not that big of deal, when
gone it is a major sign things are going south as it is usually at the top of the list
for men's marital complaints. If any resentment from the lack of sex is there, it
needs to be addressed and dissolved. Wives need to realize a family isn't a family
without the dad, and dads need to let bygones be bygones, stop acting like the
wimpy caretaker that was necessary to help with the baby. Both sides simply need
to swallow their pride and reconnect. It's often a long and winding road to get
things back on track in the marriage, and if not done right, can eventually lead to
divorce. Again, I am not sure women understand the resentment that can be built

up within their husbands due to the constant excuses, rejections, and lack of sex. Eventually, if the sex elephant in the room doesn't get addressed and fixed, we really do become roommates and not spouses. It's all very sad.

Older married couples aren't immune from this disease either. My parents got married in the time of free love, sexual revolution, and lots of drugs. Many of their counterparts, upon reaching middle age and empty nests, found themselves with nothing in common. As may be expected, keeping families together for children can be a worthwhile and noble cause. However, if that is the primary reason the marriage is held together, then trying to reconnect with their spouse after the kids are grown up can be problematic to say the least. These baby boomers look at their spouse of 30-plus years and aren't sure they want to spend another 30 years together. The "I love you but I'm not in love with you" must have been coined by the baby boomers, who more than any other generation are looking out for themselves more than other generations (See: sense of entitlement for a generation as a whole, excessive borrowing and consumption, and key contributor of socio-economic conditions today). This has resulted in a 16 percent divorce growth rate from 1981 to 1991 for couples married 30 years or more, much higher than the general populace that has remained steady.

Today, two out of every three divorces in America are initiated by women. Coming at this new thinking with my head buried in the sand, I was startled when I first saw that statistic, thinking men were more likely to initiate divorce. Despite the *Mad Men* type media presentation of the businessman banging his secretary and then getting divorced from his wife to be with the secretary, it's really the opposite. Women are more likely to be the ones who are most unhappy (either legitimately or not), or are at least the first ones to say "Uncle" and want out. With that said, most men also realize the marriage may be over, but just choose to let the wife initiate the actual formal divorce process, sometimes simply to save face and not have the stigma of being the divorce initiator. Or maybe because he may hold out hope that they can reconcile. Both in statistics and in my personal experiences, if the man is not the initiator, divorce often apparently comes out of nowhere for the husband. Men may be thinking things are a little rocky, but not at a critical point. Meanwhile, the woman may feel at the end of her rope and that she's given him plenty of chances to fix his deficiencies. Maybe she's signaled and communicated in all the ways she knew to express her displeasure, but the man simply didn't appreciate or recognize the fact that things had gotten so bad until she physically separates from him. Or maybe it takes the divorce papers being served to wake him up, which by then is too late.

While book and movie *Eat, Pray, Love* wasn't about baby boomers per se, it both applies to them and our current generation. Author of the book Elizabeth Gilbert writes:

> "I don't want to be married anymore. In daylight hours, I refused that thought, but at night it would consume me. What a catastrophe. How could I be such a criminal jerk as to precede this deep into a marriage, only to leave it? …Why did I feel so overwhelmed with duty, tired of being the primary breadwinner and the housekeeper and the social coordinator and the dog walker and the wife and the soon-to-be-mother, and – somewhere in my stolen moments – a writer? I don't want to be married anymore."

Women, upon digesting the feminism doctrine or maybe seeing it for the first time without the obligations of raising children, are finally trying to get away from the "oppression" of their husband and seek adventure to "find themselves." Their parental duty is either now satisfied or never began, and the "death do us part" portion of the marital vows have since lost their taboo. Additionally, as I mentioned earlier, the demographics related to age and death statistics of previous generations don't apply today, meaning more wives are experiencing the 30- or 40-year "itch" to dump the stable suburban life for something more grandeur or exciting. In their mind's eye they see their future life like the movie *Under the Tuscan Sun,* with grand adventures, and all they need is a change of scenery (sans husband).

It's certainly these women's purgative to pursue "True Love," versus leaving a marriage due infidelity reasons, but in doing so I wonder how successful they really are. It's typically unlikely for these types of women to find fulfillment, though it usually isn't realized until six to eighteen months later when their fantasy is shattered. Their ex-husbands, on the other hand, have found that 45 or 55 year old men are highly attractive to women 10 to 20 years their junior (I like the formula of half your age plus seven for men – works well for most of our life – no joke). Studies have shown that men are more likely to remarry, and to remarry someone younger. Women, especially those with kids, remarry less frequently. It's not until these women shatter their "boring" marriages to search for the hidden Prince Charming's of the world do they come to realize that they've made a horrible mistake searching for the Alpha who needs taming. In their wake lies shattered families and their own lives condemned to be loveless, alone and bitter, with only their eight cats to keep them company. Yet despite this script being played out over and over again across America, women (young and old) bored with their nice, supplicated husbands will continue to want drama and excitement and are convinced there's more to life. This attitude can't even be classified as "first world problems", they're selfish delusional problems. Knowing that women want drama and excitement can be used to our advantage though, as you'll see in a bit.

Bringing us back to me and you today. My generation (Gen X – birth dates from early 1960's to early 1980's) and the one following (Gen Y or the Millennials) aren't dumb. They see their parents being divorced, feel the need to sew their wild oats, and are subsequently delaying marriage or not marrying at all. For those of us who did marry, and who continue to marry, we fall into two categories: those who grew up within intact families and those who grew up in single parent families, many as children of divorce. As the book *The Unexpected Legacy of Divorce*, by Judith Wallerstein, Julia Lewis and Sandra Blakeslee, notes: "Except for those raised in divorced families, few people realize the many way divorce shapes not only the child's life but also the child."

As one who grew up in an intact family, I honestly had no idea the negative impacts of divorce, despite being married to a child of divorce. I never researched marriage statistics, or the changing percentages of divorce, and basically got married because I thought it was the right thing to do when you loved someone. Society's general message is still to get married and procreate. This is covertly stated in every romantic comedy, children's fairy tale, and Disney movie. It is also a message echoing from both peers and parents, despite their own failures. As a man, we're still supposed to woo a woman to love us, marry her and have kids. It would take a strong man to not succumb to the pressure of marriage that is coming from a woman (and her family) after dating a couple of years. Even if there are questions or doubts that still may be rattling around in our heads it is hard to stop the machine once started.

I discussed this topic with a number of divorced men for this book, and found that many got married because "she's good enough." This to me is crazy. She wasn't "the love of his life" or "the perfect woman." No, she's simply "good enough" and was pressuring for marriage. Not exactly a ringing endorsement for lasting love and bliss. Another common theme in these crumbled marriages was that the wife was more interested in planning the "fairy tale" wedding than on laying the foundation for a successful marriage. Despite warning signs, the ball had begun to roll and calling off a wedding was akin to swimming against a riptide – something that can only be done if you are willing to fight for it and know what you're doing, but most either don't know how or care to fight. So these men ended up going with the flow, only to drown in divorce after the waters calmed.

Whether wives intentionally do it or not, often a large part of the cancer that starts the marriage falling apart is the withholding of sex. Sex in marriage is very important, and one even the bible recognizes as a key aspect of marriage. Corinthians 7:3-5 says:

> "The husband should fulfill his marital duty to his wife, and likewise the wife to her husband. The wife does not have authority over her own body but yields it to her husband. In the same way, the husband does not have authority over his own body but yields it to his wife. Do not deprive each other except perhaps by mutual consent and for a time, so that you may devote yourselves to prayer. Then come together again so that Satan will not tempt you because of your lack of self-control."

Christian women are often just as guilty as those secular types of depriving their husbands of this bond for any variety reasons, and I simply wanted to point out that neither party should hide behind the bible when making their excuses.

In the worst case, differing opinions on what makes a solid marriage will result in a couple that doesn't reconnect sexually or emotionally following children and can't reconcile their differences. The "I love you but am not 'in love' with you" gets dropped by someone and the process of divorce starts. Maybe the wife has found a new person that's exciting and tripping her dopamine trigger, or is ready to go the *Eat, Pray, Love* route and just "find herself". Or maybe the husband has finally had enough of being the second class citizen in his own house, unappreciated and unloved. Or maybe the wife's lack of sex makes him amenable to the flirtatious advances of the new girl at work. It's a complicated mess no matter how old the child, and both people are in for quite the ride.

Divorce

Divorce statistics in the U.S. are not pretty. Depending what source you use, 40- 50% of first marriages will end in divorce. But the good news is if you've made it 10 years together, the divorce rates drop to the low teens (percentage wise) or below according to a UK study. Still, if you're married, it's a flip of a coin if you'll stay married. Though my perspective is from growing up in an intact family, I realize half of you know firsthand what it's like growing up in this divorced environment. In various research conducted as part of this book, in a good number of divorces, it becomes apparent that after the luster of the wedding and honeymoon have worn off, the marriage is already on rocky footing. While the old adage of having more sex in that first year of marriage than the rest of the marriage combined may hold true for some, the fact that courtships are longer, premarital sex the norm and not the exception, and people getting married later all contribute to the fact that the best and most frequent sex usually occurs early on during the courtship period before marriage. I know that was the case for us. By the time my wife and I were engaged, and subsequently married, our sex lives had diminished significantly compared to the start of our relationship. Realistically signing that marriage license won't have any impact to the quality and quantity of sex compared to premarital sex. So if you were like me and thinking the sex would get better automatically, you were sadly mistaken.

Many men and women use marriage as an excuse to let themselves go since it's hard work to stay fit and healthy. Now that you've landed your mate, there's less incentive to keep the pressure on. For richer or poorer, for thinner or fatter, for frequent sex to sexless, 'til death do us part. The book *Evolution of Desire* by David Buss sited a Gallop poll that 80% of couples had sex once a week at age 30, but only 40% had that frequent marital relations by age 60, and I personally think that is generous for those older married couples. Kinsey Institute data presented in the Sex section in Chapter 6 shows a starker picture for most couples at these ages.

If you're on the path to divorce, there may still be time to right the ship and I'd urge you to try if you have children, as the impacts (below) are significant for how they develop as both children and adults.

The stereotypical 1950's and 1960's divorce were men having affairs and divorcing their poor stay at home wives. Today's version is where men dump their frumpy wives to trade her in for a newer model. While both are fallacies or caricatures anyway, they've been drastically reduced by men today with the advent of the no-fault divorce. Prior to no-fault divorce, if you got divorced, the judge would determine cause and men would pay alimony to the extent necessary to get the wife back on her feet as well as monetarily distribute portions of funds based on consideration who's "fault" it was based on factors such as physical abuse and infidelity. While not fully equitable, it allowed a lot of leeway for judgment and made an inherent incentive for people not to cheat. With the advent of the "No-Fault Divorce" this all changed.

No-Fault Divorce

The No-Fault divorce doesn't require any wrongdoing by either party. You can simply dissolve your marriage because you feel like it. First established in California in 1969, it has since been adopted by all states in America and many other countries such as Australia, Canada, China, Spain and Sweden. In this new paradigm of divorce, kids are usually the first consideration, and if primary caregiving is provided by the mother (90% of divorces), funds from the father are increased even further over any spousal benefits she may receive. The no-fault divorce then takes away incentives for women to stay married, especially if they are going to be bank-rolled by an ex-husband. As a result of this changed law, divorce rates increased nearly two-fold after being stable for over the 20 years prior.

These changed rules aren't lost on men either. These days, despite men complaining about their battle-axe wives, low or no sex marriages, and begging for permission to be a man, they rarely are the ones to file for divorce. As mentioned previously, nearly 70% of divorces are initiated by wives. The whole "I love you but am not IN love with you" (ILYBNILWY) statement is so common and provides the rationale for wives to be more open to the ideas of emotional or physical affairs, thus just checking out of the marriage. That's why it's so important to understand the full picture of hormones, rules of attraction, and how important it is to continue to work on yourself as a man. While the intention is to improve yourself for yourself, it will also change how you appear through the eyes of your wife. If left unchanged, you'll either continue to go forward in the marriage you've established as the "norm" (likely one not having your needs met), or one of you will decide to throw in the towel.

Divorce as a couple

Every divorce is different but usually both parties shoulder a fair amount of the blame. While many divorces are indeed initiated by, or the primary fault of the husband, the fact is that most divorces are initiated by women.

Though the long, slow decay of a marriage is often apparent to both parties, it is still usually one side that slaps the other with the surprise of divorce papers. For us men, we're sort of in our own little world, and the routine of our life provides comfort. Some of us who are more driven or curious are constantly learning or trying new things, but that takes effort. It's very easy to get into the role of employee, father, and husband, and spend any down time in front of the television winding down. It takes much more effort to invest in critical masculine hobbies. So while we may be completely satisfied in the world we created, unbeknownst to us, our wives are struggling. Her warning shots of needing more communication, nagging about how you could improve, or saying how unappreciated she feels for her efforts, all build up steam to the point of boiling over. For any women out there reading: a man's go-to complaint or warning shot is mentioning sex, or lack thereof. In both cases, resentment grows and even hatred can build where love was once the dominating emotion. When the pressure builds up internally to a critical level, either consciously or unconsciously, they'll at least be open to get their needs met by others, sometimes actively pursuing this feeling. Or they'll finally have had enough and initiate divorce proceedings.

If not a mutual decision, the one getting served papers is going to be hurt, confused, and have many conflicting emotions. They may try to buckle down and do whatever they can to make last ditch efforts to save the marriage. For men, that usually means acting super attentive, loving, and taking a much larger role cooking, cleaning, or child rearing, which ironically pushes wives away further as I'll discuss later. It usually takes some monumental effort to pull back from the brink since once the toothpaste is out of the tube, it's hard to put back in. Ego is invested in the decision. Stubbornness prevents putting in efforts, and by that point counseling is often too late or so pro-feminist/wife agenda that it does little good anyway. Stories abound of the marriage counselor finally taking the focus off the husband's faults (after beating them to death) and shining the light on the wife, only to find the wife goes all screechtard refusing to own responsibility of her issues. At this point, the wife will usually shut down counseling all together.

Ideally divorces are handled in a mature manner with finances split equitably and both sides just wanting a clean break. If you support a stay-at-home spouse, you are going to pay out the nose. Imagine building a nice nest egg (like in the Financial section in Part 3), and then having to give half of it away after you get the ILYBNILWY speech from your stay-at-home wife you supported because it was in the best interest of the family. Following the divorce, you will most likely still have money taken out of your paycheck to support this spouse. Don't let me paint the picture that this is easy for the wife either. Whether she stays at home, works part time, or works full time, she likely makes less than the husband. This means that it will be unlikely she'll equal the quality of life she had before. Despite this economic inequality their ex-wives may feel, many divorced men are still bitter having to help support them. That is especially true if she initiated the divorce or was fucking the tennis instructor you were paying for. In any instance, staying together has a large financial incentive for long term wealth accumulation for both parties.

As discussed next, add children to the equation and it's a whole different game. Even without kids though, women can take advantage of their former husbands and put them in a world of hurt with false rape or physical violence allegations, spousal alimony, and general craziness that could put his job in jeopardy. I personally think the actual instances of this type of behavior are pretty rare, but batshit crazy insane women (and men for that matter, this type of crazy ex-spouse behavior isn't sex specific) are out there, and hopefully you didn't marry one. In reality though, most divorces result in both husband and wife having immense feelings of sadness, hurt, betrayal, and depression that need to be worked through. Often both parties just want it to be over as quickly as possible to move on with the next chapter of their lives.

Health is often adversely impacted going through the process of divorce as well as during the initial mental adjustment period post-divorce. The stress is enormous, resulting in poor sleep, more frequent sickness, and often using drugs or alcohol as a coping mechanism. Divorced men have up to 250 percent higher mortality rates than married men, are more prone to disease, and have a 39 percent higher suicide rate than married men.

Impacts on Children of Divorce

My wife's biological parents got divorced when she was 9 years old and she still carries the scars of this action as a late-30's adult. Before the divorce, Holly and her two brothers lived in a traditional middle-class suburban environment with bountiful friends and neighbors close by, a large garden, dogs, cats, and playgrounds all contributing to the prototypical happy childhood. However, marital issues with her parents that couldn't be resolved resulted in her world being turned upside down. Her father moved to a different community about an hour away, and her older brother went to live with him. Meanwhile my wife and her younger brother stayed with her mom in an apartment. The financial security she once had was replaced with a much lower standard of living as her mother now had to go from homemaker to having an underpaying job. Even with ex-spousal support, Holly's mom had to find some income to support a modest apartment, food, and general provisions for her and the two kids who lived with her. They bounced from a number of different communities and were prone to believe their mother's propaganda against their father, which really caused a wedge in their relationship with their dad. Eventually, Holly's younger brother went to live with her dad as well since he was having disciplinary issues in school and was running with a rough crowd in their new location. This left Holly to spend a large portion of her remaining childhood years without her biological brothers.

This just illustrates one of the many scenarios that play out in families across the country. After divorce, kids often become one more bargaining chip in the game of money control. In an environment where the husband makes more money than the wife, if the wife has majority custody of the kids, she'll receive more child support money. Money she doesn't necessarily have to spend on the kids despite its designation. My wife recalls her mom having a closet full of designer clothes, while Holly had about two outfits. In today's world, the mother has majority custody 90% of the time. The interests of the children are sometimes less important than the lawyers fighting about money on behalf of their clients, and no matter what happens (even if the divorce was the right decision), children suffer.

The Unexpected Legacy of Divorce delves deeply into this subject matter. Some important points of this book are:

- Kids of divorced families say the divorce in many ways ended their childhood
- Kids of divorce perform poorer in school and get into more trouble
- Kids of divorce blame parents for not making it work; anger and relationship issues with both parents
- Divorce has adverse impacts to parents such as having to go back to school to get a better job that may take even more time away from kids. This additional pressure may make the parent more stressed and result in worse relationship with their kids
- Sports and social activities for the kids are difficult to manage if shuttling between different communities, even on weekends, further impacting kids

In the worst case horror stories, you hear false accusations of former wives against former husbands of abuse (both spousal and child) and a court system that is ill-equipped to get to the bottom of the situation. The mothers hold a much stronger position than the fathers, and are usually the ones given the larger share of custody regardless of how they are as a parent or person.

While I know I'm beating a dead horse at this point, and I don't mean to belabor a point, but we should be doing whatever we possibly can to avoid this outcome and make our marriages as strong as castles. While a large part of keeping our marriage strong is from making ourselves quality individuals and reengaging in the marriage (the next chapter), the other part of that is knowing what to look for with your spouse with regards to infidelity. And if any red flags are spotted, we need to address them immediately.

Infidelity

Two types of infidelity exist. The first usually precedes the second; emotional and physical affairs. Emotional infidelity can be as innocent about crushing on the new girl in Human Resources and not getting her out of your mind. But these innocent encounters can progresses to texting, calling, and Facebook messaging someone. This is exciting and intoxicating, and this person will dominate every waking thought of those involved. If you let an emotional affair go on too long, given the opportunity, it *will* turn into a physical affair. Both types of infidelity dump massive amounts of dopamine into the system, making that secret text session addictive, and subsequently the parties are addicted to that new individual. Again, it is not rational or logical because they aren't thinking at all. They are chasing that next drug fix and is therefore a biological response by the body.

If you have your radar up, you may start to see some common patterns emerge. She locks her phone when before she wouldn't. She is texting or Facebooking more than usual and has a handy excuse about who it is, and won't show you the texts. She is acting "not herself" – either happier, or sexier, or maybe with a shorter temper, or disappears for hours. She may all of a sudden take an intense interest in going to the gym. Or taking great care to look better, buy and wear new sexy underwear, and in general act like a school girl getting dolled up to impress the star football player every day. One of our friend's wife went pornstar sexy on him during the emotional affair stage, with wild sexual performances coming out of nowhere after being married for 14 years. After what we presume to be the start of the physical affair, she refused to sleep with him at all, going cold turkey after the intense sexually exciting time. He went from drinking water from a fire hose to living in the Sahara desert, just like that, and ended up separating with his wife six months later. Unsurprisingly they ended up getting divorced. That's how it goes people. Be very aware of this when she starts making broad, wholesale changes in herself for the better, even though you may be temporarily benefitting as you feed her turned-on libido.

So who is cheating with our spouse? It's almost always someone who they know; someone from work, or who they interact with during outside activities or hobbies; or perhaps an old boyfriend who resurrected contact with her through Facebook or text. Sometimes it's a vendor or sales person that while they don't see often, but they have a rapport with. Occasionally, physical affairs can be flat-out one night stands where you mix the combination of a marriage in the doldrums, a dissatisfied wife, an Alpha dude, alcohol and opportunity; could be either a stranger or someone she knows. These happen during girl's night outs (GNOs), weddings without you, work trips (very common), girls-only vacations with an exotic flair, and I've even heard of +hooking up while out of town for a funeral. Anywhere that they can conceivably have a cover story of why she was out late or didn't come home. It's sickening in my mind, but affairs are somewhat common occurrences; 22 percent of men and 14 percent of women have had affairs during their married lives according to statistics I've read. Of those, the married spouses did not find out most of the time (70 percent of married women and 54 percent of married men did not know of the affair). Cheaters are really, really sneaky and conniving.

Now you may think I've got some magical mind-reading skills because I know what you're thinking right now: "My wife would never cheat on me. She loves me and we have two great kids and a great thing going here." Am I right? This is the "not all women are like that" (NAWALT) argument. The hard part of this whole thing is realizing that your wife, and my wife, and your best friend's wife all have the same hypergamous tendencies inherent to being a woman. Now you may be a great guy, and your wife a very moral person, but you must realize that her little heart may very well go pitter patter as the good looking guy at church, the new guy at work, or the square-jawed guy at Girls' Night Out isolates and flirts with her. We're all human, so understand we all have the same human tendencies, including your special snowflake of a wife. This is the same fact that nearly universally men like young, long-haired, fit women with an hourglass figure. It doesn't mean that you would cheat on your wife with a woman like this, but you find them attractive, would appreciate her flirtations if the shoe were on the other foot, and if you were single you would totally hit that. Personal conviction and morals play a very important part in this, but the point is: we can't fight attraction, it simply happens.

You can't put your head in the sand and be blind to the fact that if you find your wife attractive, others likely do too, which means you need to continually be working to maintain your spousal attraction. Again, given enough time of not getting her needs met by a man that she may not find attractive (that means you. And not getting her needs met may be something as simple as excitement and the dopamine rush that comes with a more "exciting" marriage – God knows many men have been divorced by spouses despite being great providers, who did housework, and took care of the kids; prototypical "nice guys"), any wife could drop the ILYBNILWY speech. Do whatever you have to so you aren't the recipient of that, and simply being aware of these facts can go a long way towards prevention as you now aren't going through life floating on a raft as a passive participant – you have a destination in mind for you and your marriage. Chapter 6 lays this out in detail.

So what do you do if you think your spouse is cheating on you? First, ask for full transparency in seeing texts, Facebook messages, and e-mails. If they refuse they are most likely cheating, at least emotionally. If that is the case, the hammer

has to come down hard if you want to save the marriage. Rat out the other party to their spouse if they have one. Talk to the individual and tell them to back off with explicit ramifications (that doesn't put you in jail), such as you will tell their wife or even their employer. Now is not the time to lay in the weeds and pussy-foot around the issue. You need to be reactionary and attack with no holds barred if you have any chance of saving the marriage you built.

Gather enough data to know for sure, but once you know, come down hard if you really want to save your marriage. Your spouse and the other party are on a drug and will relapse if given the opportunity. Let me preface the following with the fact that I'm not a lawyer or private detective, so can't comment on the legality of these approaches, but they do work. Your wife and your wife's (potential) lover will make secret e-mail accounts and continue along that path if left unchecked. They'll buy a disposable phone you don't know about. Remember, they will be super sneaky ninjas about the affair and you cannot trust your wife during this time. Putting a keylogger program running in the background on your computer used to be a good idea, but more often than not a phone or tablet is the primary source of communication nowadays. You can purchase iPhone keyloggers that run in the background to accomplish this task. One I researched cost about $50 for a three-month license or $100 for a 12 month license (works on teenage kids too), so do a little research on this. However, one problem would be installing it without spouse knowing, but if there is a will there's a way, so keep trying to get evidence. If it doesn't help you with peace of mind, it may help you with ammunition. With no-fault divorce though, if she wants out, there's not much you can do to protect yourself or your money.

Another way to track infidelity is installation of a GPS tracking device in or on your spouse's vehicle (costs are around $100), or installation of a GPS application on the phone that also tracks them. *Consumer Reports* magazine had an article in July 2014 (check it out at your library) about tracking drivers with a GPS-enabled device that plugs into your car's diagnostic port under the dashboard. At a cost of $80-150 and approximately $20 a month subscription fee, it tracks every place they go and can even provide an alert to you if they cross a geo-fenced boundary that you can set.

If you're going this far, you likely won't like the answers you'll find, but at least you can know. Based on your findings, it will be up to you whether this is grounds for divorce, or if you'll work to keep the marriage and family together if

you reconcile and she casts off the interloper. Tough waters to wade if you find yourself at this point.

Some Final Words on Divorce

As part of writing this section, I wanted some additional perspective, so I took the opportunity to interview one of my good attorney friends whose caseload is up to 60 percent divorce related, and has been involved with over 500 divorce cases. As we discussed this topic, it became apparent that going through the divorce process is incredibly trying on all parties, from husband and wife to the kids. She described it as similar to dealing with a death, which is a surprisingly good analogy. She didn't have the same cynical perspective about women and their ability to vampire their former husbands, but noted that the courts are always looking out for the children first and will adjust things to best fit those goals. While divorce reasons weren't always known or shared, some common themes she saw were:

- The marriage between husband and wife often gets lost in the shuffle of day-to-day life and raising the kids. It takes a back seat and is hard to get back once relegated to this purgatory.
- Often emotional issues or trauma from childhood contributes in some way to how at least one partner deals with marital and communication issues. How you saw your parent(s) interact with each other, or with the kids, or dealt with stress, shapes a person's perspective. And let's be honest here: many people have really messed up childhoods.
- Substance abuse and depression issues are very frequent in divorce. People self-medicating to deal with life stresses, and then become addicted. Once this happens, everything from kids, to job, to husband or wife take a back seat and are often accompanied by depression.
- Infidelity does happen, but is a symptom of a weakened marriage, not the cause of one. I thought this was a very important point.

Additional information published in *The Journal of Family Issues* July 2003 on causes of divorce is noted below. Note the percentages sum to greater than 100 due to multiple causes sited.

Reported Cause of Divorce		
Category	% Men	% Women
Infidelity	15.6	25.2
Incompatible	19.5	19.1
Drinking or drug use	5.2	13.7
Grew apart	9.1	9.9
Personality problems	10.4	8.4
Lack of communication	13	6.1
Physical or mental abuse	0	9.2
Loss of love	6.5	3.1
Not meeting family obligations	1.3	4.6
Employment problems	2.6	3.8
Don't know	9.1	0
Unhappy in marriage	2.6	3.1
Financial problems	1.3	3.1
Physical or mental illness	1.3	3.1
Personal growth	3.8	1.5
Interference from family	2.6	2.3
Immature	2.6	1.5
Other	6.5	2.3

That chart on causes of divorce paints an interesting picture. I wanted to point out a couple of interesting things. First, many of these can be classified in the same soft category: incompatible, grew apart, loss of love, personality problems, or unhappy in marriage all sound similar to me. Second, we shouldn't be so quick to dismiss infidelity or substance abuse as a key contributor to divorce (per my attorney friend's experience). Infidelity could still be the straw-man for larger structural issues that drove the cheating, you just don't know with the data presented. Third, physical and mental abuse is a large cause, especially for women. Men also get physically or mentally abused by their wives, so I believe the *zero* percent (!!) admitting to that category as a sign of the stigma and embarrassment associated with having a wife abuse or assault them in this manner, as opposed to the idea that men don't get abused. Finally, look at the percent of men who stated they "Don't know" why they are getting divorced and contrast that with percent of women in the same category. Striking isn't it? These are dudes who probably thought things were pretty OK still and then got dropped the ILYBNILWT speech, and they are left scratching their heads thinking "what the fuck just happened here?"

In my attorney friend's experience, the average couple getting divorced is regular middle-class people, usually with dual incomes to support their average middleclass life. The divorce process is generally intended to provide a basic quality of life relatively equal to both parties, and especially the kids. But with nearly 90% of mothers getting primary custody of the kids, the ex-wife subsequently indirectly gets a larger cut of the pie when the courts start slicing and dicing the combined assets and incomes of the newly divorced couple.

This family law attorney's opinion is at odds against that painted among men's rights bloggers: that the family court system is designed to bleed the former husband dry. Often the former wife is often left in a poorer financial state than the husband due to the lower job quality – men still make more than women as a whole. I'd like to say I could agree with that statement (women end up with a lower quality of life post-divorce) with a giant caveat – that may well be true if the ex-wife actually uses the child support money for the kids and actually pays for the children's activities, clothes, food, recreation, and gifts. Often though, these deadbeat moms don't use this money for the kids nearly enough, and hence the ex-husband ends up paying both child support *and* basic necessities to support a halfway decent childhood life – a double-taxation if you will. But going back to the courts to reduce your payment, as was the strategy employed by my father-in-law when fighting against what he felt was in an unjust situation in child support payments, sometimes results in paying more child support (as my FIL can attest). And again, my mother-in-law used a good chunk of this money to increase her own wardrobe at the expense of adolescent-Holly's basic necessities (like clothes) or social activities (sports leagues) that most kids take for granted. No one is around to make sure the money actually is used for the kids, which like Harry Dunn (from *Dumb and Dumber*) really chaps my (and many other's) ass.

In our particular state, alimony isn't as common either, at least for two middle-class people just eking out a middleclass lifestyle. If you're a physician and your wife was a stay-at-home mom that now has to support herself, that is a different situation and suffice to say, the husband would be paying something significant to support his former wife. Divorce means splitting up both assets and liabilities, much to the chagrin of at least one party. Just because you feel entitled to the money you earned and don't want to share, doesn't mean the legal system will allow this to happen. Such is the reality of divorce on the financial side, and why staying together often means a better financial situation. Many men are very bitter about this situation – having to give up a large portion of their income to child support and possibly alimony – especially if they were the one that was cheated on. Such is the game of the no-fault divorce and the state looking out for the best interest of the children.

That doesn't mean you shouldn't get divorced though. Every situation and marriage is different, and we do owe it to ourselves to carve out a chance to be happy in our one chance at life. However, if you get divorced as a result of structural issues within yourself, you need to honestly evaluate how to address these. You don't want to carry this same baggage or life approach that contributed to your current divorce into future relationships. Please don't repeat the same mistake a second time. That's what I'm here to bring to light – how to be a husband your wife won't want to cheat on, and to create a marriage worth saving by improving yourself.

The Ghost of Marriage Present

Thank goodness we can put that dark cloud behind us. Even if you aren't on the path of divorce, and you and your spouse are in an OK place right now, there is still likely room for improvement. Here are the basics to strengthen yourself and your marriage. It may take some work to eventually get there, but you make it happen one day and one good decision at a time.

What your wife finds attractive

Marriage after kids is hard. Modern family and father roles have changed, where we're expected to provide emotional and kid support for our wives and to make everyone happy. The traits and qualities that originally attracted your wife (you were cocky, funny, put yourself out there to get her attention, and did exciting things on a regular basis in the courting rituals) have now gone into hibernation. They are replaced with helping with household chores, helping with child care, grocery shopping, and taking care of the cars and lawn, all while still bringing home the bacon... the softer side of marriage. The funny thing is, the more you try to be "nice" and help and make your wife feel like a princess, the more you spiral down and make things worse. Add to that the 5 lbs a year many people gain, and you're looking in the mirror at a dude 40 lbs overweight who is expecting or hoping to get laid by someone that you think is still attractive. You think you deserve it for all you do for the family. I mean why shouldn't she appreciate you man?

We're men, so let's put this simply as a logical theorem like we did back in high school (with the very large caveat that this assumes your wife's hormones are in order and that some medical issues aren't contributing to a zombie existence with no libido whatsoever):

1. Your wife will have sex with you when she is attracted to you

2. Your wife isn't having sex with you

3. Therefore, your wife isn't attracted to you

Now she may have sex with you to keep the fights down and gravy train rolling. She may even use you when her hormones are ramped up during ovulation, which is not a good indication of what she feels about you the rest of the month. Does this ring a bell in your life? The bottom line in most cases, and it is really fucking tough to hear: your wife does not find you attractive in your current state or with your current behaviors!

Enter Married Game, which is a concise way to roll up the ways you can change things structurally and mentally and approach your marriage in a totally different mindset and...wait for it....Have.More.Sex! And to top it off, it will be with a partner that is into you! As I discussed in Game in Chapter 4, these are basically techniques and attitudes designed to attract women to sleep with you, so married Game are ways to attract your wife again.

Remember the whole dopamine thing? Well Alpha aspects are exciting, and when experiencing these types of things release dopamine into our system. What usually happens is the Alpha qualities that made her vagina and mind tingle when you were dating get lost in the weeds, and what's left are the more Beta qualities that promote love and cuddles and bonding. A successful marriage needs both. Most of us end up like roommates with our spouses due to too much nice guy behavior and putting her on a pedestal, and not enough Alpha qualities. But how do you get to have these so-called Alpha qualities? Much of what attracts your wife is structural, the remaining part is sort of the missing pieces to take things to the next level...the subtle playful manipulation...the Game stuff if you will. The most important bullet list of structural things is below, but first realize you can only change your own behavior and attitudes, you can't change hers.

Leadership

Do you wear the pants in the family or does she? Does she make the major decisions and you acquiesce to her? Does she drive the family car with you in the passenger seat? Being a strong leader in your family is one of the core items in bringing back the attraction and an Alpha trait.

This will not come overnight and if you've handed over the keys to her leadership, she likely has gotten used to control and will test and fight you for it as you take this back. Leadership is setting the course for the family and having support from your wife to make things happen. Author Athol Kay (*Mindful Attraction Plan* and *Married Man Sex Life Primer*) calls this the "Captain-First Officer" model, which is a succinct description of what you're going after here. The Captain is the one piloting the plane, and the First Officer is a capable pilot in their own right, and takes control when the Captain can't. In addition, the First Officer can note conditions ahead that the Captain should be aware. Both work together as a team, but there is a clear hierarchy.

To be Captain, you need to make a habit of sound decisions for the betterment of the unit. How is your financial situation? Take charge, get it under control (Part 3). How is your ability to keep the house in order? You set the rules and expectations for everyone and follow through. This may mean delegating the cooking or kitchen work to your wife, having your kids take care of unloading the dishwasher, while you play your role doing other things. You have to lead by example. Work hard. Be ethical and fair. Keep calm in the face of adversity.

Unless you physically can't, due to exhaustion or having too much to drink, the man must be the driver of the family car. You are the head of the family and this is a very easy way to command subconscious respect. Does Jack Sparrow hand over the ship to the First Mate if he's able and capable of steering? Hell no! Same goes with sitting at the head of the table in your house. It's a position of power. Keep in mind these subconscious power positions and power plays, they do add to your leadership little by little, though your sound decisions trumps all.

A leader also does not shy away from tough decisions or conflict. These things may come from your wife, or it may come from outside sources. While I confer with Holly on big purchases and get her input, I ultimately make most of these decisions independently. This has come from years as being a trustworthy individual and having the best interest of everyone in mind. The last vehicle we bought was done entirely by me; Holly didn't see the car until I drove home with it. Now I got her input and thoughts before moving through the process, but I made the decision. When we bought our current house, Holly and the realtor (who has more of an interest in selling the house quickly) were trying to convince me of a higher offer. My wife deferred to me, and as a result, our offer of nearly $16,000 less that they wanted to propose was accepted. That's what you're going for. If you haven't built this trust, you need to do things to establish this in small ways.

A leader makes decisions. Choose where to go, what to do, what to make for dinner. Give direction. Kids like having a purpose, so set them to a task. So does your wife. Make them feel important, but set the course. No one likes the back and forth game of "What do you want for dinner? I don't know, what do *you* want for dinner?" Same with date night – find something interesting, or get some input, but make the decision and make it happen.

Physical Attraction

If you've let yourself go and put on some fat, why would your wife want to sleep with you? You may still be a nice guy, but that shit doesn't matter - you can't negotiate attraction. Get your diet in order, lose the fat, get some muscles, stop smoking, and cut down on the booze.

Depending on where you are starting from, this is going to take time and getting into shape may be the hardest structural area to get into order. In Part 1 in the Health section, I noted the key lifestyle changes in diet and options for fitness improvements to improve your physical attributes. If done right, these will likely have your wife telling her friends about her hot husband. As a leader, when you make the diet change, both she and the kids should be expected to fall in line, as it really is a big picture benefit to all. What happens here usually is that when you improve your physical attraction (combined with the other items in this section), she's going to feel consciously or subconsciously threatened. As in "Why is he trying to look so good? To replace me?" If she's dialed into you, and isn't just playing Candy Crush, the natural response will be to get her act together to keep up. Assuming she does, you are both going to be looking better naked, which can really be a springboard for getting the sex life back on track too. Do NOT underestimate the power of physical attraction even with someone you've been married to for 20 years.

Confidence

Displaying confidence in who you are and what you do goes hand in hand with being a leader and building attraction. Having that cocky, can-do attitude, and being funny about it, can be a learned trait. The fake it 'til you make it idea. But you need to have something to back it up. Why are you confident? As Napoleon Dynamite says, it's because you have some great skills. You've started doing Brazilian Jiu Jitsu, or can bench press your body weight, or are learning to rebuild engines or are doing improv at the local theater group. Expanding your horizons, or building on existing skills has a funny way of making you more confident... more so than watching television or saying witty things on Facebook. It usually isn't faked either. Confidence becomes a part of you as you're able to back up your talk and you simply are more at peace in your own skin having skills that not everyone else has.

Confidence is dealing with all people; men, women and children, in a way where they can almost feel your emotional strength backing it up. Walk tall and with good posture. Believe in yourself. Along with the losing weight and looking better, you're going to shed the negative self-thoughts and naturally become more confident. Compliment people genuinely, flirt with the waitress, be more outgoing (I know, it's hard for us on the more introverted side, but it can be pretty fun and exhilarating to get outside your comfort zone). Be the guy men want to be and women want to be with.

Cut the pussy behavior

Most of us have at one time begged or negotiated for sex because we "needed" it. This is low value and something that decreases attraction. Instead, going back to the confidence subject; confidently initiate relations with your wife. Period. That's the only way going forward. If you get shot down, don't whine, beg or be a little bitch about it, but laugh it off and do something else. When you apologize for something, do it with contrition and own it, but don't keep following her around saying you're sorry. That's not behavior you want to partake in. That's something a lesser man would do.

This also means not whining or complaining to your wife. She is your wife, not your friend. If you constantly use her to dump all your emotional problems on her, she's going to see that as a sign of weakness. What happens when she needs you as a rock to support her issues? Her perception may be that you're not capable of supporting them and your own baggage, and you may lose that opportunity to connect with her. It's like in the work place, always vent your frustrations up the ladder to your superiors, not down the ladder to your subordinates. Now certainly, talk about big picture stuff as it impacts things, but I can guarantee that your wife won't care that Bob in Accounting didn't get his TPS report completed in time, and you had to scramble in your meeting to cover for it. Boooorrring! I don't care who you vent to; your barber, your brother, your mistress (kidding), just don't do it to your wife unless it is important stuff that impacts her too.

Improve appearance

Learn a little bit of style, switch up your underwear (seriously, buy a bunch of new underwear – I like Lucky and Puma brand boxer-briefs – and throw out most of your old ones. When you do this, watch the wheels in your wife's head turn. When I did this, my wife outright asked me if I was cheating on her). Get a haircut. Maybe shave your well-worn goatee, or if you're clean shaven, grow some facial hair. There's always something to improve on here. It may cost a little money to buy some new clothes, but there are often gently used or even new designer clothes at local thrift stores, and Marshall's or TJ Maxx or similar stores offer some pretty good bargains as well. Be the best dressed in casual situations instead of the jeans and t-shirt guy. And lose the fucking Crocs Poindexter.

Stop Pedestalizing and Supplicating Behavior

This one is tricky for many men. They are seriously, truly, still in love with their wives. They put the pussy on a pedestal and have been conditioned to jump through hoops to try and please the master for "the precious" (say that in the Gollum voice). She says "jump" and he says "how high?" She makes unreasonable demands to see if he'll do them. Example: you are both sitting on the couch, she asks you to go get her something and you jump up like an errand boy. Stop that shit. In a cocky-funny way, make it known that she's got the ability to get her item, and she can get it herself; or if you're up next time for something you need, you'll grab it for her. Think Tai Chi, deflect and push back in a gentle way. She is testing you, and when you do these things you are failing as she realizes you value her more than yourself and hence, you aren't higher on the hypergamy status rank (remember, she wants someone higher than herself. This is subconscious, and by failing these small tests, you subconsciously show her she's of higher status than you which messes with the dynamic – whether she consciously realizes it or not).

Another point on the pedestalization topic (putting her up on a pedestal while you are beneath her – the whole treat her like a princess thing at your own expense): you likely see your wife as a very special snowflake, and you feel that there's not another in the world like her, who will love you like she does. And if you lose her or if she leaves you'll live a sad, pathetic life with a studio apartment eating cat food until the end of your days. You couldn't be further from the truth and that's maybe the bitterest pill to swallow. Now you obviously have a lot invested in the relationship, and it makes a lot of sense to figure out how to make it work because you do love each other and have a life together. But when you put her on a pedestal and bend to her will, she sees you as weak. She loses respect for you. It is the opposite of turning her on. Instead, get up on the pedestal with her, and be the leader she wants you to be.

She may not realize she wants you to lead her (remember all that feminist propaganda women are fed about not needing a man or that women can do anything a man can), but when you get there, she'll relax since that is the natural order between man and woman. Be the man she hopes you'll be. If the marriage really isn't meant to be and you end up losing her, there are many other women out there looking for a man who is a leader, confident, fit and dresses well. Don't be afraid that she's *"the* ONE"...that's just not true, there is no **The One**. That's a big mental hurdle for most. As Silent Bob said in *Clerks*: "There's a million fine looking women in the world dude. But they don't all bring you lasagna at work. Most of them just cheat on you." Find one that wants to be with YOU, isn't complacent on the deal, and keep her. I hope it is the one you married, but realize that even if it's not, you'll still be ok after the dust settles.

...

That is basically it on the structural side. In my opinion, this is 80% of the battle. Most of all, be patient, and remember, you can only control your own thoughts and behaviors. If you're overweight, recognize you likely put on that weight over a period of years and it will take some time to change your appearance for the better. If you're doing it right, being patient, slowly improving, and bumping back on unreasonable requests that she's unknowingly testing you, things in your relationship will likely improve. She'll subconsciously see the changes, and the foundation of comfort and beta pleasure she's become accustomed to will be slightly shaken. Think like a peacock showing off a little. You'll feel the shift. And expect some battles over the shift. Some fighting will be inevitable but don't budge.

You can't argue logically when she's emotionally struggling with these changes. The "Agree and Amplify" is one technique that you can use to deflect some of this emotional struggle a little, while still keeping her a little off balance. Example: she says "You're just going to the gym so you can get hot and then leave me!" You can respond with "Why would I leave you when all my girlfriends are OK with the current situation of me staying married," (you've agreed with her that you want to get hot, and then amplified it in a ridiculous, funny way) then slap her butt and give her a cocky smile. The nice guy in you will likely think this is a dick move, but if you respond with "I just really want to feel good about myself. I would never leave you. You're my super special snowflake that I love so much!" you are continuing to show that she is better than you, that she doesn't need to change her behavior, and that no matter what she does, you're going to stick around and lap dog her. However, if your wife is really struggling with this new you since you've really upped the Alpha behaviors, there can be a line you can walk in the middle to allow you to maintain your new status while preventing your wife from manifesting her fears and going into turtle-mode withdrawal. You can reassure her that you want a sexy marriage with her, and provided that happens to your expectations (respect, love, and frequent enough enthusiast sex) you aren't going anywhere.

On the other side, she could get very defensive, threatened, or angry at these changes. Don't fall into her irrational trap as she starts yelling about how you're spending too much time at the gym or how your new clothes make you like you're trying too hard. These are tests to see if you'll continue your improvement journey, since she has been used to having things her way and you're shaking that up a little. Don't just acquiesce on these points. Continue doing what you need to do to be the man you want to be. This takes practice, but can be done. You are an oak. A mountain of a man. Let the storm and waves of drama wash over you – calm in the face of adversity.

Again, be patient, and try to be Zen about the backsliding that will inevitably happen. You can't expect to respond in exactly the right way to every woman-crisis that she tests you with. Two steps forward, one step back is still progress. She may not trust that the change is going to stick, so be aware she may attempt to undermine or sabotage you in some of these regards to test your mental strength and fortitude in keeping with the program. At some point, after she mentally climbs the hill and sees you're in it for the long haul, things will get easier and will likely be better. When that occurs, don't back off – instead, keep doing what you're doing. Think tortoise and the hare. You are grinding through the tough spots when motivation is low, still getting out there. You aren't flaming out early. This time it is different. This time you are all in!

Other Alpha Qualities

- Put yourself first (have hobbies, do stuff; don't defer to her on her activities and have none of your own)
- Be the leader with your kids
- No matter what you do, do it 100% to the best of your ability
- Always be clear and direct
- Learn to say "No": a "Yes Man" is a weak man
- Have fun and be a fun person
- Always behave with personal integrity and honesty, including being brutally honest with yourself
- No matter what happens, you can deal with it and make it right
- Accept the consequences of your actions
- Never blame, especially shifting blame to your spouse. You are not a victim, and you have to understand that victims never succeed
- Stop making excuses
- If you find yourself in a bad situation, remove yourself from it. Don't wait for someone else to make it better or for change to happen on its own

Sex

Sex with our spouse is the perhaps the defining characteristic that makes being married different than any other relationship. When it is going well, you feel on top of the world. When it's not, it can undermine other aspects of your life, to the point that some men feel suicidal. When you've improved things structurally as noted above, you'll see it has a huge impact on your whole life. You may have started out "faking it 'til you make it," but eventually you actually will make it. People will start looking at you different and you'll really end up being a better version of yourself. Now I make general assumptions that you aren't having sex as much as you'd like, which may or may not be accurate. The weighted average for our demographic per the Kinsey Institute study is about once per week, though you can see below that many married men have even less frequency than that depending on their age.

Percentage of Married Men Reporting Frequency of Vaginal Sex							
Frequency/ Age	18-24	25-29	30-39	40-49	50-59	60-69	70+
Not in past year	4.2	1.6	4.5	9.1	20.6	33.9	54.2
A few times per year to monthly	12.5	9.3	15.6	16.2	25.0	21.2	24.2
A few times per month to weekly	16.7	46.3	47.3	51.0	38.3	35.4	15.0
2-3 times per week	45.8	37.1	26.8	19.9	15	9.5	5.8
4 or more times per week	20.8	5.9	5.8	3.7	1.1	0.0	0.8

Source: Kinsey Institute, data from NSSHB, 2010, excerpted from "Sexual Behaviors, Relationships, and Perceived Health Among Adult Men in the United States: Results from a National Probability Sample", Table 6

How frequently you and your wife have sex can be a complex issue and is impacted by stress, work schedules, travel, kids, health, state of exhaustion, and many other factors. However, under ideal circumstances for both, the quantity (and quality) of sex the Jones' down the street could vary a lot compared to the Thompsons' next door. It is really up to you and your spouse to find out what is right for the two of you.

Sex is a very taboo topic in our society and is a tough one even to discuss with our spouse. It is what makes a marriage different than any other relationship we have. We're expected to get that one need met through one person only, and when it doesn't happen to our satisfaction, it can be incredibly frustrating and lead to resentment in an otherwise "perfect" marriage. Add to the fact that many spouses don't often see eye-to-eye on what is the "right" amount of sex we should

CHAPTER 6: THE GHOST OF MARRIAGE PRESENT • 131

be having. Usually the one wanting it more frequently is the man (but not always), and this individual is often referred to as high desire (or HD), while the one wanting it less frequently is really the one with the power, and is the "low desire (LD) spouse. Whether fair or not, that's the nomenclature that has been accepted.

Now, as I mentioned above, there may very well be structural or medical issues that basically reduces desire for the LD spouse, so having a lower frequency of sex may not even really be the fault of that LD spouse. Hormonal issues with either the husband (low testosterone) or wife (estrogen imbalance) could also impact sexual desire and frequency. As those with young kids and busy lives know, life sometimes has a tendency to suck motivation to be intimate right out of us too. These things should not be an excuse to not have sex. Putting a sex discussion out there with our spouse as a circumstantial, neutral topic without blame can help jump-start talking about the "ideal" frequency for each partner; what should be a realistic frequency given life's conditions; and what each spouse's expectations are for their sexual relationship. Trust me, this isn't an easy conversation to have, but really is an important one.

I remember nervously sitting in our living room a few years ago with my wife Holly. I had made what I felt were rather large structural improvements as described above, and was in reality maybe a few months into the self-improvement journey, so I'm sure she thought my changes as temporary. It most definitely was not really enough time for Holly to buy into the new me 100%, but enough to see the glimpse of what things could be like. I was in the two steps forward, one back cycle, and our sex life followed suit.

That evening we had an intense emotional sit-down where I laid out the fact that she needed to get on board and come along with my leadership... that we had to improve our sex life...that I wasn't going to settle for being roommates. I remember asking her about what she thought of our life and of our relationship. While I don't remember her exact response, I remember her crying and saying she "just wanted to be madly in love," and I knew we weren't yet there. Now while I'm pretty sure talking was not the right thing to do at that point of my self-improvement process; and what I know now, a couple years later, would lead me to believe that shutting up and just keeping with the two-forward, one-back approach would have been best. Nonetheless, for us it was the crossing of the Rubicon. It made it very conscious in both our minds what the stakes were. We both then became present with each other's position for the first time, and it allowed us to heal and improve together.

For us, it took a fair amount of trial and error to finally settle into a groove that we can both be happy with where things are at with our sexual relationship. Things aren't perfect in our relationship by any means. I'd still like sex more frequently than my wife and she would like more excitement and putting her in the mood on my end. The quality of sex is generally good, but like everyone, there are some duds thrown in there and we still have a hard time talking about sex. Compared to before though, it's night and day. She recognizes where I'm coming from and I her, and it's not the sore point for both of us as it was before. But I'm not the needy dude I once was, nor am I the 135 pound skinny-fat weakling I once was either. For her part, she stopped being the guardian of Sexville and saw the benefits of connecting as a couple more frequently. It didn't happen overnight, but eventually, with patience things hit a groove that's pretty good. Like many men, one area I had to improve upon was the idea that women always want a man to "make love" to them tenderly and instead I had to develop more dominant behavior in this arena.

So here are some things to realize as you try to transfer your structural improvements into more or better sex with your spouse:

Always Be Initiating

The structural improvements above take time, but make your wife more attracted to you. This means your sexual advances will be met more favorably. Remember the "Don't be a Pussy" bullet above? That means you aren't going up to her and asking "Hey – you want sex tonight" or "I'm feeling horny, do you feel like getting down?" You don't ask, you do. It can be a subtle differentiation between passive and active initiation, and everyone's line is different, but basically, you are going into the sexual initiation with the expectation that she'll say yes. This is explicit initiation, versus the more passive "nice guy" initiation you likely did before which was: rub her back, maybe her leg, and see if she swats you away. Active, explicit initiation is what a man should do. You continue past the token resistance (there's almost always some of that, especially if this is relatively new to you), past the "I'm not really in the mood tonight", past the "I have to get up early tomorrow", past the "kids might hear us", until you either have her panties off or have a hard "NO!" And you will know when she means it and you need to respect that – no if, ands, or buts. You'll understandably be a little nervous as you are testing for this line, but often she'll be somewhat receptive to having sex, even if she's initially not into it. And sometimes it's a test to see how much you desire her, and will fight through her token resistance because you "had to have her." And sometimes she just isn't that into you or attracted to you. Respect that line of thinking as well.

The real facts about desire (below) indicates that in most, or sometimes all, instances men are the initiator of sex. I used to get upset that my wife never initiated (Beta) instead of simply accepting the fact that initiating was my job. I equated the lack of initiation on her part to be a lack of affection or love, which it wasn't. Like the Cheap Trick song "I want you to want me"; I too wanted to be desired, but some (most?) women are more submissive and often only respond when pursued. Them overtly pursuing us, the man, just isn't in their nature. So don't get all butt-hurt like I did if your wife won't overtly initiate herself but instead, will usually just go along with your initiation.

This type of woman will sometimes covertly initiate though. She may give you the coy look, or wear what she considers "sexy" pajamas (and it may not necessarily be the hot Victoria's Secret lingerie you bought her, but a silky something she got at Sears that she feels comfortable in), and rub your back or leg why you're watching *Game of Thrones.* That may be the extent of her initiating ability, so you need to be aware that you're not necessarily going to see her grab your cock when she wants sex. Instead, she will be very covert about it with signs you could easily miss if you aren't paying attention.

The bottom line is assume initiating is your responsibility and do so like a man should. Don't be afraid to romance her a little, but not in the wimpy sort of dipping the toe in the water. Do so with the understanding by both of you what the end game is. If she ends up saying no and shooting you down for the night, that's ok. Try not to let your hurt feelings show and instead accept it with a smile while finding something else to do. Creating a guilt trip will not endear you to your wife or make her more likely to be into you. It may cause dread and weird feelings about sex if this is a common occurrence.

Always be initiating and don't be afraid of being more sexual or showing your wife that sex is on your mind. I've seen some men say some very sexually forward things to women (not their wives) who should have been offended, only to have the woman smile and playfully punch their arm. That's the dynamic you're trying to build with our wives – cocky-funny appetizer at random times in pursuit of setting the table for a dinner of sexual initiation later. The serious stone-faced approach may have its moments, but a smile and a sexual innuendo at the right time usually has a better success rate with helping the initiation of sexy times.

Responsive Desire versus Spontaneous Desire

One big difference between men and women is our desires. Health educator and "Sex Nerd" author Emily Nagoski has written a number of articles that discuss how men have spontaneous desires and women have responsive desires. Spontaneous desire is the typical male response is "Bam! I just thought of sex and now I'd like to have sex!" Kenny Powers approach. Responsive desire is typically female where they don't even get "into" the act of sex mentally, or enjoy it physically, until they are actually having it, or are having hard precursors to it. Responsive desire also means that they respond to your desire. So if you go all Caveman on her, dominant and act like you have to have her...NOW, she may respond in kind. If you pussy-foot limp-dick your way all sweet, and give up at the first sign of token resistance, obviously she's not going to be turned on by that. This is important to realize, so that even if her mind and body aren't responsive at the end of your planned date night, she may still yet get turned on with appropriate stimuli and enjoy herself once you get in the moment. It's just that this moment may not be until you are actually having sex, which is hard for people to get their heads around.

So she may roll her eyes and accept that you want to have sex ("get it over with buddy"), but once you're in the moment, she may actually find herself happy and feeling good about it, full of desire after all. Yeah, women are very different from men, and I think both sides need to sometimes just "go with it" even if the wife isn't necessarily in the mood right at that exact moment. More often than not, she'll enjoy herself once in the act of sexual intercourse and even if she doesn't, you still have that sexual connection whose importance can't be overstated.

Ovulation

If you don't track your wife's cycle, it's about time to start. There a number of applications you can download to your phone, I use one called "My Days" and use it to track my wife's cycle as well as when we have sex since I'm a data geek. As you remember from 6th grade health class, when your wife is ovulating, her body is ready to make a baby, and therefore her hormones are much more likely to make her horny and her pussy wet. Knowing this isn't a big deal, but it does give you some idea of what your efforts may result in due to simply being in the right place at the right time. Some of the hottest sex I've had has coincided with my wife's ovulation window, and it may be worth initiating in this window if you realize you are in it, even in less than ideal circumstances.

Sex doesn't start in the bedroom

You can't expect your wife to get warmed up like you do. We men can go zero to 100 miles per hour in about two seconds. Women are like a diesel engine in the winter that needs to slowly get warmed up before she can shift into Drive. Passionate kisses with open mouth (not just a peck) when you leave or greet her, sexual innuendo jokes, comments on how her butt looks great in those pants, how sexy she looks in that skirt, butt grabs with a hug... that type of thing, done over time as part of your regular everyday routine, helps with connections. It doesn't have a finish time, but slowly marinates over the days and weeks. She may very well roll her eyes, but it gets her thinking about how (as a result of your comment) that sausage she's cooking for dinner *does* sort of look like your penis, at least for a second. And how having her butt grabbed maybe does feel good, and it felt good to be desired, at least for a second. Even if she's calling you a "perv." Listen, you are a man. We're crude, rude, disgusting pigs. Don't apologize so much for having sexual thoughts, nor filter them so much. Add a little edge to your "nice guy" routine if you get a chance. You will likely encounter resistance, especially at first. But as you improve structurally, her tolerance...nay, her embrace of your perv talk and butt grabs will likely increase. She may even smile and wink. But be patient and introduce these things slowly. And also recognize that you may be up against a lifetime of "good girl" indoctrination as a result of her upbringing – know this type of thing doesn't happen quickly (or at all) for some people. The past is a powerful kryptonite to our Superman, so go slow and expand that rubber band of sexuality slowly.

Not everything works in the bedroom

In attempts to keep thing spicy in the bedroom, you'll likely try new things. Maybe adult movies, maybe toys, maybe new positions or locations. Sometimes things are going to be a homerun and you'll both lie there in a puddle wondering what the fuck just happened. Other times things are going to fall flat on their face and you'll wonder how things with someone who've you've known so long could be so weird. Maybe you're so worked up by her new lingerie you come in about 15 seconds. Maybe the toy you bought sucks. And you'll both lie there dissatisfied …and hope it never happens again. Maybe that new metal cock ring you thought would be so great gets stuck around your balls, and you end up about 5 minutes away from calling the fire department. It's ok. We've all been there. We use the word "average" for a term to mean that sometimes things will be better than that, and sometimes worse, but we have to keep trying. Using the tried-and-true position you know to work every time may do the trick, but it's not exciting. Having a partner with you that is willing to explore those boundaries, even if those attempts fail, is something to cherish, even when things didn't go according to plan. Keep things fresh by adding variety.

Maintenance Sex is OK

Say that again: "Maintenance sex is ok!" Sometimes sex really isn't at the top of your wife's agenda, and if she's willing to give herself to you for your own pleasure, pound away and for heaven's sake, don't take offense. Sure, lying there and "Thinking of England" shouldn't be a frequent menu item, but on occasion, it's perfectly acceptable. If anything, it shows she's willing to be used as a tool for the sole purpose of your pleasure. Even if she mannequins it, pound away brother, it's all about you and does still play a part in your marital connection. Heck, she may even like it.

Use lube; consider coconut oil

You likely already use lube, if not, consider using coconut oil. Not all women have a lot of natural juices, and if she isn't adequately lubricated, may need a little help as you slide in. We've tried many types and products of lubricants, and our hands-down favorite is coconut oil; something we use in cooking and is in our kitchen anyway. It's solid below 76 degrees Fahrenheit, and liquid above that, so melts on touch to your skin. It's a natural, cheap, anti-fungal, and smells great. We've also used it on a variety of toys and it's not "oil" in the sense that petroleum products are (which are a big no-no when used with latex or silicone toys). You can also use it as a massage oil, and is a great alternative to silicone lube in pools, hot tub, or the shower where you need something that isn't water soluble. It only has a minor odor, and one that we like anyway.

Regardless of what you use, consider purchasing some decent lubrication to help with times when things aren't so moist or when things escalate quickly and she's a little behind you in the readiness department.

Your wife's birth control may adversely impact her desire

Based on a publication by the Guttmacher Institute, 36% of women in reproductive age rely on the pill, intrauterine devices (IUD), or other hormonal birth control. Sterilization makes up another 33% of birth control methods and are likely used by many of those who have already had kids. Compare that to condom use (14%), natural family planning (1%), other (like the sponge or diaphragm 5%), and no method (11%), and you see that many, many women are (or were in their pre-sterilization days) on hormonal birth control. One statistic I read was that the birth control pill has been used at some point by more than 80% of American women born after 1945.

First, I'm all for hormonal birth control in concept. Who doesn't like the idea of uninhibited anytime skin-on-skin sex with a trusted partner? This is especially true in the era of unplanned pregnancy and many kids born without fathers involved in their lives. This pill, device, or injection is designed to liberate women's sexuality through reduced anxiety from unintended pregnancy and let women have frequent sex on a whim. The irony is that often stunts the very desire to have it from messed up hormones that often reduce libido. Not having sex is a pretty good form of birth control, no?

Without even getting into the libido discussion (yet), there are many positives and negatives to hormonal birth control. It gives some women lighter, more regular, or reduced frequency periods; some seem to inhibit some types of cancers (endometrial and ovarian); reduce acne and anemia; while at the same increase the likelihood of other types of cancers (cervical, liver and breast). Hormonal birth control tries to balance between providing hormones to prevent pregnancy but not so many that it impacts their day-to-day lives or behaviors –

a very fine line to walk. The producers of these drugs are motivated by profits, and subsequently don't have a large incentive to research and present the findings of side effects beyond what is required by the FDA for approval. The companies like Ortho-McNeil Pharmaceutical, Merck, Bayer, Pfizer, and Warner Chilcott are the primary companies for hormonal birth control – all publically traded and answering to shareholders.

Now, millions of women likely have great success with these drugs, and for those women consider yourself lucky. However, the numbers I've seen for those women that may have sexual dysfunction related to their hormonal birth control seem to be in the neighborhood of 1 in 3. If you're happy and sane on your birth control, and are doing it like rabbits, don't change a thing. For many, the positives outweigh the negatives so staying on birth control may make sense for you.

Adverse side effects from these hormonal birth control can vary a lot. Some women get really, really loopy; or have major health issues with them. Some, like the IUD, have their own issues simply due to where they are installed (I remember feeling the wire from my wife's IUD poke my penis when we had sex – not sexy). While I'm sure Pfizer and the other drug companies will disagree (since their profits are at stake), there does seem to be some strong evidence of correlation between sexual dysfunction issues and hormonal birth control. I'll be perfectly honest: I was pretty naive and never even considered loss of libido a possible side effect of birth control. Women's issues are obviously not my specialty, and I'm guessing most men fall into this category. However, it's likely that some women are unaware of these side effects as well, and all parties engaging in sex should at least be aware of what can happen to a woman's body when they start to mess with the cocktail of their hormones.

Doing a Google search of "Hormonal Birth Control Sexual Dysfunction" yields over 1.5 million search results. Based on my very limited research (reading various studies as well as spending too much time on women's issues forums, where many share their own anecdotal experiences with all types of hormonal birth control), some of the most common alleged issues across the various forms include:

- lower desire and arousal compared to those on non-hormonal birth control methods
- reduction of testosterone (needed to stimulate sexual desire and regulate genital blood flow)

- decreased lubrication during sexual intercourse
- decrease of sexual enjoyment
- decreased sexual dreams
- lowered mood (more frequent depression)

This is a tricky situation for women, since the topic itself is one less frequently broached with a physician due to embarrassment or lack of knowledge of the potential for cause-effect relationship. Also, other aspects of the relationship also may be inhibiting libido (you may just not turn her on – as discussed earlier – or simply increased stress from life, not making time for each other, etc.), but checking blood hormone levels may be an option. There are many different hormonal birth control options and a different pill with different cocktail of hormones may be an option for some. Again, independent studies on this issue are lacking, and Big Pharma has an incentive to continue to keep women plugged into these long-term birth control options instead of educating them on the issues and alternatives.

In 2006, a study was published in the *Journal of Sexual Medicine* that showed that women using the birth control pill showed "markedly decreased" levels of sexual desire compared to those not on the pill. Even more, after stopping the pill, long-term adverse side effects were still noted. Androgens are sexual hormones produced in a woman's ovaries and have a direct impact on the pleasure women experience during intercourse. The birth control pill inhibits the production of these androgens and also increases the amount of sex-hormone binding globulin (SHBG), which is a protein that binds to testosterone and prevents it from being used in other beneficial ways. As you know, testosterone has huge impacts on libido in both men and women. Therefore, if you prevent a woman's body from effectively using it, you will decrease libido and sexual desire. This study showed pill users had four times the levels of SHBG in their system than women who never were on the pill, and after 120 days of stopping the medication, they still had twice the SHBG levels.

Keep in mind that while the hormonal IUD (Mirena) supposedly has decreased hormones compared to some birth control pills, it too has the same issues. While not scientific, I did some basic research on various women's forums related to the Mirena and found various anecdotal evidence that was similar to my wife's and mine experience. Namely a markedly decreased libido for some that used this birth control method.

If your wife (or you) decides to stop taking hormonal birth control, keep in mind it takes some time for things to get back to "normal." Some people on the pill say they're back to being their pre-hormonal-induced selves within 3 months, though many don't feel back to "normal" until up to 6 months after stopping.

Positive and negatives exist for all types of birth control, you'll just have to decide what is right for you.

Antidepressants also can inhibit desire

Selective serotonin reuptake inhibitors (SSRIs) are one type of anti-depressant commonly prescribed, and while they have plenty of potential side effects, the one I'll focus on pointing out is decreased libido. This family includes Prozac (Fluoxetine), Zoloft (Sertraline), Elexa, and Paxil (Paroxetine) among others; all documented as having sexual side effects. They cause a decrease in dopamine and norepinephrine (remember those important neurotransmitters from earlier?) in the brain impacting libido negatively. Alternatively, not all antidepressants impact libido. Wellbutrin has been shown to have zero, to a positive, impact on one's sex drive.

Depression is nothing to mess with, but can be a libido killer on its own. If you are concerned with the side effects of one, there may be other options; but please consult with your health care provider on treatment options.

Spicing Things Up

Sex is like food: you can be perfectly healthy if you have the same food every day as long as it gives you what you need, but it sure can be boring. Why not try different foods, different restaurants, and even totally different cuisines to change things up. The other thing is, sometimes – not all the time, but sometimes – your "good girl" wife wants to be the bad girl. She wants you to take advantage of her and be the "bad boy" instead of the normal, nice guy you are in day-to-day life. Sometimes, or maybe more often depending on the woman you married, you are better off throwing her around and using her like your own personal plaything. Regardless if you can get around that mental hurdle (for a lot of recovering nice guys), here are some ideas to grease the skids for some more exciting marital sexual action:

- **Change up when you have sex**. If you always do it at night, do it in the morning shower, or go to work a few minutes late and have a morning start. Or meet your spouse for a nooner under the guise of an appointment, something Holly and I will do occasionally.

- **Dominance/Submission**. *Fifty Shades of Grey* was a huge hit for married wives around the world for a reason, and probably bumped up sex numbers across the globe in the short term. Why? Dominance and submission. This seems to be missing from many married bedrooms around the world, and that is because of societal conditioning of men today. We have to unlearn this, and recognize that our wives aren't fragile porcelain dolls that will break (mentally or physically) if we are rougher with them. This is likely the biggest thing that we as married men can use to make our sex lives hot again. It can be a complex cocktail, but dominance can be as simple as holding down her wrists while kissing her forcefully, to full blown BDSM. I'm not going to get into this much here, but a couple of simple things that may work if you think you'd like to introduce your spouse to this area are 1) a blindfold and 2) scarves for tying up wrists (after you've tried the holding her down thing) 3) dirty talk 4) spanking and 5) hair pulling. Taking these one at a time. The blindfold takes one sense completely out of the picture thereby increasing her other senses and allows her to submit in a safe way. Scarves can be tied around her wrists in a way that, if she wants to, she can untie them, but at the same time relinquishes control to you. Dirty talk could be as simple as such as calling her "your bad, naughty girl," to pushing the envelope further with edgier talk. For example simply saying stuff like "pussy" and "cock" may be somewhat taboo or exciting to a vanilla housewife, and depending on her response maybe you can go further, even expressing fantasies. A woman's butt has a lot of fat and muscle, and many women like a good spanking by a dominant man they are attracted to. Some women really like hair pulling both due to the somewhat caveman dominant nature in addition to the plethora of nerve endings in your scalp. Some or all of these things may not work, but are things that many women think or fantasize about, hopefully your wife will be open to trying these things with you.

Tell her what you want her to do (don't ask) and direct her or position her. Dominance is way more about attitude (be a caveman and give into your raw, animalistic desires) than technique. Again, you need to be in a good place and structurally sound to make this work. But if everything else is in order, she's generally attracted to you, and your sex life is the only area that is really lacking, being more dominant will likely take things to another level. Remember responsive desire above? If your desire for her is so strong that you can't control yourself, her desire in return will be at a similar level. Be safe out there people.

- **Change of Venue**. If the bedroom is the only place you see your sexy lady, try this: after the kids are in bed, mess around on the couch, or move a blanket to the floor, or go into the laundry room and close the door, or go out into the garage and pretend you're teenagers and have sex in the backseat of one of your cars. Use your imagination and bring appropriate supplies such as lube, a blanket, and cleanup supplies.

- **Lingerie**. Duh, but it can be fun to shop for that together, rather than springing something on her. Don't be surprised that what she likes is different than what you like. I would rather my wife wear and be comfortable in something that isn't exactly my favorite than having it sit unworn in a drawer. She'll likely feel more comfortable and sexy in something she picks out than that leather studded thong and fishnet stockings you did. And don't forget some sexier man underwear for you – nice boxer briefs are a suggestion.

- **Toys**. There are tons of sex-toy shops, and can be perused online so you aren't embarrassed. My wife and I have picked out items together to try out, doing our online shopping on the couch after the kids went to bed. They don't all work, but can still be fun (or even funny when the FAIL is large), but at a minimum playing with bedroom toys usually result in a more interesting experience than plan old vanilla missionary sex.

- **Adult Movies.** A number of companies and types of movies are directed at couples. If you are new to this, I'd recommend Digital Playground's *Pirates* and *Pirates 2* as ones that are really well done and are two of the most expensive adult movies ever made. New Sensations Romance adult movie series is also geared toward couples, and are like drama, or romantic comedies... just with "romantic" hard-core sex. These movies generally have a story and the sex is more sensual than some crazy gang-bang or gonzo stuff. We occasionally dig one out to set the tone or add some spice for the evening, but admittedly isn't something we do that often. We've found some of the sexier HBO or Showtime series can go a long way towards getting us in the mood as well. Shows like *Spartacus* and *Game of Thrones* (which we can check out from the library) often have violence and nudity that tends to excite and thrill a little, so if hard-core isn't in your game deck, other alternatives may suffice.

- **Role Play.** Want to be star football player and cheerleader? Or doctor and nurse? All it takes is a little imagination and it can be totally hot. All you need is a pair of costume glasses, some cheap scrubs, a suit jacket, or any other prop along with a willing partner with some imagination to play along for some fun times.

- **Butt Play.** Yeah, it sounds maybe a little gross, or intimidating, or (GASP!) gay; but butt play can add a whole other layer of hot to your sex life if you can get into or around the idea. Anal beads, butt plugs, or fingers can be used to simply rub or to enter the rectum, which has many sensitive nerve endings. Butt play on men can be especially pleasurable due to prostate stimulation (the prostate has a plethora of nerve endings). For women, it may indirectly stimulate the G-spot, clitoral legs, or the cervix, and can be done during intercourse which can bring further pleasure. Remember, take it slow, use lots of lube, and you may be surprised at what you find. A little surprise, drunken balloon-knot massage may open the door to a whole new world... or not. But you won't know unless you try.

Physical and mental issues that may impact sex

I could expand this section considerably, but simply want to put the fact that health issues, either you or your wife's, can impact sex in many ways. Obesity obviously has considerable health impacts, and obese Americans are 25 percent more likely to report problems with their sex lives than normal weight people. Contributing factors are decreased sex drive, self-esteem issues, lethargy, performance anxiety, and making sex too strenuous. But there are a myriad of other health symptoms, diseases, or prescriptions that can impact how we respond to sexual contact. It is important to provide love and understanding to a spouse who is working around these issues, and be careful not to punish a spouse that is really trying to work with you on your sexual needs. That is what marriage is about when the sailing isn't smooth. At the same time though, don't accept or positively reinforce a spouse who is a "lazy bear" and is simply a fat sloth with no desire to change. Either shit or get off the pot. Put the pressure on them by improving yourself, though be warned, it may be a hormonal thing. If not, you'll need to decide how far you're willing to go being married to someone who doesn't love themselves (so why should you love them?).

Regarding hormonal imbalance and women: it is very common, especially as they get older and into the perimenopause or menopause stage of life. This is when menstrual periods start decreasing and essentially stopping. Most women start going through this phase in their late 40's with the average onset at age 51. For some though it could start as early as in their 30's or as late as the 60's. For the men who have no idea what this is: essentially, the ovaries, which are the main source of female hormones, ceases producing eggs. Women go through various mental, emotional, and physical changes, or show new life symptoms during this stage. These include fatigue, memory problems, mood changes, irritability, weight gain, or adult acne. Some women decide to have hormone therapy to address declining estrogen levels as they go through this period, but studies have shown that some of these hormone treatments increase other health risks such as cancer, heart attacks, or stroke. Related to sex, menopause means no more ovulation, so no more peaked sex drive around that time. Also, declining estrogen means less blood supply to the vagina, so lower vaginal lubrication. Like anything else though, experiences will vary, and some women report an increase in sex drive post-menopause.

Putting the lens back to men, we have a number of physical or health things that may need to be addressed to fully have a loving sexual relationship with our wives. These include premature ejaculation, erectile dysfunction, and low testosterone. What is common with all three of these is that they can mentally mess with our ability and desire to have sex.

Premature ejaculation and erectile dysfunction can fill a sufferer with performance anxiety and can become a self-fulfilling prophesy. You get anxious at the thought of underperforming or not getting it up, and because of that anxiety you are trapped in your head and underperform by ejaculating well before you'd like to, or have problems getting an erection. It becomes a vicious cycle.

Testosterone is THE hormone that makes us a man. It builds our muscles, deepens our voice, puts hair on our chest and maintains our interest in having sex. After age 30, most men begin a gradual decline in testosterone, sometimes resulting in decreased sex drive. It is common for many men to later recognize that low testosterone was their main issue, but other things could be contributing to a less than desired sex life.

A few notes on addressing those three items, though readers should research each of these more to better understand their options and potential solutions:

- **Premature ejaculation (PE)** – I suffer from PE occasionally so am intimately familiar with this physical issue. Relax and get out of your head. Take time to warm up with foreplay instead of jumping right in. When you masturbate, practice reaching the point of near ejaculation and backing off until you get comfortable with "the point of no return." When you get near that point with your partner stop, pull out, or change positions. The cowgirl position with the woman on top is often one to start with to get warmed up, as even those with PE tend to last longer as the woman does more of the work. With an understanding partner and working through similar exercises, you can start to address some of the things that make this one tough to handle. The biggest points being: relax, calm your mind, reduce excitement levels, and recognize sex isn't a finite resource to get so worked up about. If your PE stems from insecurity, tell that insecure being inside yourself to fuck off. You are an awesome person. Think positively about how long you'll last. Positive thinking and a mantra that you repeat to yourself have also been shown to have real results. Even repeating a phrase or song refrain have been shown to help by calming your conscious mind some (something along the lines of Monty Python's Life of Brian: "Always look on the bright side of life [doo doo, doo doo doo doo doo doop]").

- **Erectile Dysfunction** – It is estimated that 52% of men aged 40-70 suffer from ED according to author Jed Diamond in his book *Surviving Male Menopause*. Not being able to get or maintain an erection is a major psychological blow to a man. Any number of things may cause this: stress, alcohol, anxiety, performance anxiety, medication, and possibly even low testosterone (below). Communication on the issue with your spouse is very important as hurt feelings and blame can be common for both parties. Reassure your wife that not getting hard is no reflection on how you feel towards her. Talking with a medical professional, and possibly taking medication, could be a solution. As could implementing a healthier lifestyle with no smoking, more exercise, less stress, and a better diet. You can also still have sexual contact and relationship with your partner; oral, digitally, or toys could be a way to transition through this period while still having that sexual connection.

- **Low Testosterone** – First off, men begin losing approximately 1% of their testosterone (T) levels per year beginning at age 30 according to the book *Manopause: Your Guide to Surviving his Changing Life*. By age 50, an estimated 10% of U.S. men have "low" testosterone, which is probably underestimated in my opinion based on the current state of diet and obesity in our country, and anecdotal stories coming to light by men. If you do feel less motivation, lack aggression, lack passion, suffer from poor sleep, or have reduced libido, please get tested by a doctor who specializes in this sort of thing. Many aren't familiar with the intricacies of testing low testosterone so I would recommend finding a Hormone Replacement Therapy (HRT) doctor or specialist since they will know much more about this subject compared to a general practitioner. Second, start eating better and taking a few supplements. Things like B-complex vitamins, zinc, and fish oil all help to raise testosterone production along with cutting shitty processed foods including sugar and soy out of your diet. Lots of soy will make you soft, contribute to man boobs since it raises estrogen, and lowers testosterone. Do HEAVY compound weight movements like squats and deadlifts with most in the 5-10 rep range. This too promotes testosterone production, as does losing excess body fat, since that will also decrease estrogen and raises testosterone levels. Finally, as mentioned in Chapter 1 of the Health Section (Part 1), cortisol is a stress hormone and blocks the effects of testosterone. Chronic stress from whatever source (work, chronic cardio, a bad marriage, and alcohol) elevates cortisol and inhibits testosterone production and uptake. Reduce it if you want to bump T back up and be more of a man again.

Impact of porn

Using adult movies to spice things up with your wife notwithstanding, you should not be watching porn. It is a major cause of guilt and shame, erectile dysfunction, delayed ejaculations, and impacts your ability to be satisfied with your partner and your sex life. The website www.yourbrainonporn.com and TEDTalks "The Great Porn Experiment" (on YouTube) both have great summaries of what it does. High speed internet porn provides a massive amounts of novelty, thereby keeping the porn watcher entranced for longer and pumping out bucketloads of dopamine with each new video. This then results in more production of a chemical called Delta-FosB in the brain that promotes more binging, that then promotes structural changes in the brain.

These brain changes 1) numb pleasure responses 2) make the brain hyper reactive to porn (Caveman voice: "porn exciting, everything else boring") and subsequently 3) erodes willpower to stop this cycle. This then results in massive amounts of erectile dysfunction, and Viagra doesn't help since it's a brain change, not a physical change where Viagra can make your dick hard. Left untreated, eventually too much high-speed porn watching will make it impossible to get an erection. The good news is this brain change, and its symptoms, can be reversed. The other good news is that older men recover faster than younger men who were raised on this high-speed porn, since our brains were past the initial wiring stage when high-speed internet porn came into existence, which means unwiring it is easier. I'll discuss this topic more in Part 4: Parenting, because porn's devastating impact on children and teen's brains, and lives, can't be overstated.

To summarize: stop watching porn on the computer, it's bad for you!

The Softer Side of Marriage (Beta)

Up to this point, I've focused on the Alpha side of things and sex, since that's mostly where our generation of "nice guys" really are lacking or needing some work. However, you still need to understand what is important to our spouse on the emotional, or general life-support, side. In general, she wants someone for whom she can rely on when the shit hits the fan. That you're going to have a job, you're going to do your part to take care of the house, the kids, the cars, her. The prototypical asshole Alpha doesn't care about anything but himself, but you aren't like that, as you do care about all those other things. Remember, as you improve yourself, become higher status and more confident, you still have to play your own role internal to your relationship and family dynamics.

Perhaps household chores or responsibilities were skewed too far in your direction previously and you're working to correct that. That's fine, but that doesn't mean you overcorrect and don't help at all around the house, unless that is your agreement with say, a stay-at-home spouse. More than likely though, you may not be contributing enough. You have to find that equilibrium where everyone is contributing in an appropriate way. Some amount of trial and error may result, but you'll get into a rhythm where you are providing the right amount of Beta support in regards to keeping the household running smoothly. Finally, on this point, behave like a man and not a child. That means putting away your dishes into the sink or dishwasher, hanging up your coat, putting your dirty clothes into the hamper, and in general not act like you were born in a barn. Acting like the fourth child by being a selfish slob is a good way to create animosity.

Do you feel unappreciated by your spouse about the fact you work all day, help around the house, are in the New-Dad mold and generally kick ass? Many of us men feel this way. I can say that she does appreciate you, but is likely doing just as much crappy or mundane things to keep the household running smoothly as you. I recently read that you should get used to doing 70% of the household work, because likely at some point (or most times perhaps), she'll be feeling the exact same way. Regardless of how work is divided, understand that you are the man and the head of the house, and therefore you should do all of these things for your family without the expectation of "reward," even if that would be nice. Hopefully you both say nice things everyday showing your appreciation. "Thank you for making dinner tonight." "I really appreciate you cleaning up for my visiting parents." "I may not tell you often enough, but I really appreciate you taking care of the kids/adding to our household income/cooking Thanksgiving dinner for the large family – I really know it's a chore." These little things show emotional connection and can go a long way to building bridges with her, and hopefully she reciprocates.

You also need to understand how your wife connects with you, and with people she cares for. Gary Chapman wrote a great book called *The Five Love Languages* that does a good job of trying to identify which "language" most resonates with individuals, and subsequently how you can dial in your behavior to maximize this language, and perhaps minimizing the adverse effects of the other languages. These languages are Words of Affirmation, Acts of Service, Receiving Gifts, Quality Time, and Physical Touch. We all fall into one or two languages much more so than the others, and the book has exercises to narrow down which language you are. Many men identify with Physical Touch, meaning for them, touching their wife or having her touch him, carries a lot more weight than the other languages. Sex is a physical touch many men crave, desire, and equate with love and affection for their wife. My wife is a Words of Affirmation language, and subsequently really likes being complimented.

On the flip side of this Love Language thing is you can really do some damage if you do the opposite approach to a language, or the language goes unfulfilled. Holly takes insults and disparaging remarks very hard and we've had some big fights where I didn't filter myself or carefully make my point on something I was dissatisfied with. Likewise, if your wife is a Receiving Gifts language, and that doesn't even register on your radar so you never give gifts, she's going to feel unloved. This approach has at least helped us recognize how we receive and give love and has helped us connect on the emotional side.

Alternatively, there are some poisonous destructive things that you need to avoid. They can be cancerous and cause relationship erosion quickly. One of the foremost marriage researches, Dr. John Gottman, classifies these as "the Four

Deadly Sins of Marriage." They are: Criticism, Contempt, Defensiveness and Stonewalling.

- **Criticism** focuses on the person and not the person's behavior. I've told my wife she was the biggest slob I've ever met at one point. This was like a grenade for a "Words of Affirmation" language person, and full of criticism. I could have said instead, "I get really frustrated when you don't clean up after yourself." A similar message, but it would have been better received.

- **Contempt** is intended to humiliate or wound the person. Sarcastic biting remarks, name-calling, hostility, even eye rolls are contemptuous and likely to get responses in kind. This deadly sin is inexcusable and takes a long time to repair

- **Defensiveness** is the opposite of the Alpha behavior of owning up to mistakes and making things right. Your spouse is saying things to you and you use defensiveness as a self-preserving tactic. Use verbal judo to redirect that negative energy and owning at least part of the blame instead of letting it crash against your hard surface.

- **Stonewalling** is basically a passive aggressive way to put up emotional walls and keep people out. Another defense mechanism, they simply stand there and take whatever comes out without response. It can be infuriating to the person trying to resolve the situation.

Another one that should make this list, but doesn't, is gunnysacking. This is quietly accumulating grievances, slights, and hurts until you explode and unload on your partner in a massive avalanche. They likely didn't even know you were mad about something, but in your head you've been keeping a tab on all the shit they are doing to you. Instead of gunnysacking, be forthright and open in whatever your frustration may be and don't let it accumulate into a mountain.

How to Fight

Just because you fight with your husband or wife doesn't mean you have a bad marriage. We are all individuals with our own thoughts and agendas, and we simply aren't going to agree with any single person on everything. Depending on the level of conflict, your disagreement on any particular issue may result in a fight. Studies have shown that it's not *if* you fight that makes a difference in long term marital happiness, but *how* you fight. The biggest things couples fight about in marriage are sex, kids, and money (order depends if you're a man or woman), so you're not unique in your arguments with your spouse.

Here are some things to consider the next time you find yourself fighting:

1. **The first three minutes are critical**

   Studies have shown that if you are able to stay on task and not spiral down to mudslinging in that time frame, you have a good chance of making it into actual issue resolution.

2. **Deescalate**

   To get through past three minutes, usually de-escalation strategies need to be employed, especially if the fight starts ramping up to "Guns a'blazin'" zone. At least one person needs to try and deescalate things when they heat up. What usually happens when we fight is our ego takes a stance that we have to "win" the argument. So your partner's ego attacks, you naturally want to counterattack, back and forth that goes. Instead, change your mentality to not attack or react but to counter-steer the argument back to productive areas. During one of the training exercises I did in conflict resolution, we had a police officer come in and do some training drills he had learned that he called "Verbal Judo." Judo, if you don't know, is often called "the gentle way." This martial art uses your opponents force and redirects it to your advantage. One way to do this in a verbal altercation is to take a moment, let the argument or fight wash over you like a wave washes over a rock. Let the argument settle for a moment to clear your head, calm down for a moment and incorporate one of these strategies for de-escalation:

   A. **Affirmation** - affirm that your partner's argument has merit and you can see how he or she came to that conclusion. Then state your vantage point in a calm, rational manner. "I can see how you could think that, but here's what I meant when I said XYZ..."

   B. **Rephrase** - rephrase what your partner has stated "just so I can understand where you're coming from, you're saying that [REPHRASED STATEMENT]"

C. **Use Humor or Affection** - sometimes it gets hot and heavy so saying something disarming like "I hate it when we fight" can have a big impact on deescalating and getting to the root of the issue and calming both parties down.

D. **Take a time out** - Simply state that you some time to compose your thoughts and you aren't disengaging from the discussion; you just need a moment to calm down and think rationally.

Using some of these strategies will help to bring the overheating engine back down to an idle and give you an opportunity to discuss issues instead of just slinging arrows at each other.

3. **Know how to bring your issue to light - Complaint vs. Criticism (and Contempt)**

How you argue is very important. If you want the deflector shields to go up to Level 10, and for you to be rebuffed even in fair assessments, go into the discussion with a criticism. This is an attack on your partner. Compare that to a complaint - a more blameless approach to the same discussion point. The more general complaint (words like "I feel that..." can break the ice) will hopefully allow you to delve into salient viewpoints on the issue.

For example, a discussion on sex may go as follows. You may start the discussion with a complaint such as "I'm really disappointed we don't have sex more often," or "We should really find a way to improve our sex life." Now compare it to a criticism: "What is your problem? Why do you constantly shut down and rebuff my advances for sex?" Or "You're the reason our sex life sucks!" While those criticisms may be true, she'll always be on the defensive ready to attack back and her ego will try to fight hard against the more frontal assault.

Also, along with criticism is contempt. To snipe and say mean disgustful things to purposely hurt feelings is a way to escalate the fight, the opposite of being constructive. Even eye rolling is contemptful in that it shows disregard for your partner's viewpoint.

4. **Other things to consider**

One thing I've been guilty of is disengaging from battle when the heat is on. Rather than discuss things through to completion, you (I) throw my arms up and leave, or stonewall, and not respond. Holly is usually really good at getting me back into the ring despite my shitty behavior, but it shouldn't be on her to do that. Those are things that should be avoided when having a fight or discussion as it is not productive in the long term. At all. Also, when discussing things, try to be on the same physical level as your partner (both standing, both sitting), arms not crossed, making eye contact.

Take your share of the blame. If you didn't do anything "wrong," you should try and take your share of the blame without apologizing. But there's usually two sides to every argument or misunderstanding. Say things like "I should have been clearer in my expectations/my request/my communication and not have expected you to make the same assumptions/decisions I did. Next time I'll try and do a better job, but if you don't understand something or are unclear on it, please ask." Communication snafus is a common one for us. Hopefully, your spouse is big enough to behave in a similar fashion, but this isn't always the case.

One person has to bring the olive branch and make up. Being the one to reach out or hug the other and deescalate can go a long way to resolving the battle, maybe even resulting in some make-up sex. You can still agree to disagree, but can't let these hurt feelings linger. Try to resolve the issue before going to bed, and hopefully the carry over will be minimal. Also, try not to gunnysack and instead let out your thoughts in smaller bites or discussions.

Finally, during a fight we are all hurt, emotional, and have active egos. This is not the time to bring up the "D" word (Divorce) to hurt your partner. You may be seeing red, but no good can come from that in the middle of a figurative knock-out, throw-down fight. After nerves calm, and you can rationally think, you'll see that is probably not the road you want to go down, but if it is, it's better to start those discussions in a rationale frame of mind. More than likely, if you bring up divorce in a fight, you're just looking to hurt your partner and to show him how much they hurt you previously. Fight fair and don't go down to this level.

...

Hopefully this section gave you some new tools or insights you can use in your own marriage to improve your dynamics and hopefully lead to the marriage and sex life you want. Structural changes are hard and take some time, so be patient. When you do find yourselves in the weeds, use some of the conflict resolution tools above. Us married men can use the "real" rules of gender and social interactions (instead of the false teachings that we've been fed in our feminized culture) to our advantage and hopefully prevent infidelity and divorce. Knowing the rules of the game are absolutely necessary if we want to improve our chances of winning the game of marriage and life. In my own experience, I went from an average dude with my head in the sand on most of these issues to feeling enlightened. As a result, my whole life changed. Our marriage dynamic improved. Our communication improved. Our sex life improved. This knowledge has been the catalyst for a better life for me, and will be for you too if you take the next step.

Part 3: Financial Matters

Our Financial Beginning

The number one thing married couples fight about is money (number two is sex), so getting your financial house in order will likely automatically make your married life better. It seems like no matter how much we make, most of us could use more money for something. It really is a struggle to find enough money to just live, pay bills, keep the kids fed and clothed, save for retirement, maybe save for college, and have the things we feel we *should* have like cars, vacations, and iPads. Many have no clue how they took on the credit card debt they have, how to reshape their thinking to get out of debt, and how to tackle that 401(k) savings plan they are offered at work. If you have your personal finances in order, you're mostly ahead of the pack. The average 401(k) savings plan at the end of 2013 had a balance of approximately $100,000, which is a big improvement due in part to the bull market run of 2012 and 2013. However, this is very deceiving statistic since the median value was only about a quarter of this value, and continues to show that most (roughly 70 percent) of 401(k) assets are held by the richest 20 percent of Americans according to UC Berkeley Center for Labor Research and Education.

Getting out of debt and beginning to work towards positive net worth, hopefully being able to retire one day, doesn't have to be hard. Usually the hardest part is the change in mentality from consumer to saver. But that's exactly what needs to happen to change the norm. By making some basic (but challenging) changes, you can start to make progress and improve your situation. The security and mental peace you will have when you start to accomplish these goals can't be understated. Instead of anxiety about the bills, your mind can now relax allowing you happier times with your wife and children. See how it all fits together?

I've made tons of dumb financial decisions over the years. Tons! Some specific examples:

- **Collecting baseball cards** as an adolescent (using money from part time jobs) in the late 80's and early 90's when the market was absolutely saturated. All I have left for the thousands of dollars I sunk into this endeavor is some worthless thick-stock paper. I give them to my kids once in so that they can learn statistics and math, and teach them about baseball. Though these are all things I could have done for nearly free.

- **Started smoking** in college. While this habit only had legs for maybe 3 or 4 years, I probably dropped another several thousand dollars for the joy of having a smoke – and doing wonders to my lungs while I was at it. Thankfully, packs were only about $2 back then, so the damage is much less than it would be today.

- **Racking up credit card debt**. This one of which many of you are guilty, I'm sure. I graduated with credit card debt on top of student loans, and later used it as a crutch and excused my behavior because there were things I "couldn't afford to pass up." I rationalized purchases by saying I'd be making substantially more money in the future and would pay it down right away. Yeah right. It took a lot of time, missteps, many dollars in interest, and a lot of effort to finally dig out of that hole.

- **Buying a vehicle beyond my means**. I grew up of modest means, put myself through college (meaning I had to pay off all the loans, though I did pay mostly cash for room and board for the latter half of college, as I had from jobs throughout), and the car I drove in college through graduation was a POS 1985 Plymouth Horizon. I actually liked the car for what it was, but when I got into an accident with it, I was so ready to buy something "nice." I ended up buying a two year-old SUV that was way beyond my price range. I'm sure I got taken advantage of on the financing by the dealership, and due to my age, gender, and the fact I lived on the east coast, my car insurance premiums were high as well. I was spending about $600 a month on this monstrosity, right out of school. So dumb.

- **Having children**. Kidding! (not really). Ok, so kids may not be the best financial decision, but in my case they've been my best life decision. Thought I'd see if you were paying attention. Using a little calculator I found on www.babycenter.com/cost-of-raising-child-calculator, for my region, I can expect to spend just under $400,000 to raise each child from birth to 18. I think this is too high, in that they account for 33% of that amount as housing costs (living in your house), so taking that out brings me down to about $275,000, which is close to other numbers I've seen. So two kids and that's a cool half million bucks. Not a great financial decision. But that's not why we have kids, is it folks?

Even while making foolish decisions, at times living beyond our means, we still did some things right. We purchased a foreclosed home that needed mostly cosmetic repairs and lived there for 10 years building equity. Both my wife and I started contributing to our company provided retirement plan (401k) in our early 20's and at a fair amount (10% of our income to start and increasing over time). After selling the "new" SUV, we both drove older used cars well after they were paid off. We got married pretty cheaply by thinking outside the box, which meant we started to take on more "good" debt instead of bad debt.

Over the years, we got savvier, chipping away little by little on the debt side, while still being at least somewhat frugal and still spending money on things that made our lives better. Hobbies, legacy furniture, and a couple of major vacations (one was our honeymoon – to national parks in the southwest, and the other was a destination wedding for Holly's sister in Alaska) were some of the big dollar things we spent on before kids came. We eventually paid off our credit cards, and moved into a slightly larger home in a nicer neighborhood. This drastically reduced our commute and significantly increased our quality of life, primarily due to the new relationships made. At this stage of our life, we have a good positive net worth (take assets, such as investments or home value, and subtract liabilities, such as a home mortgage or car loans, and that's net worth in a nutshell) made up of some home equity, plus savings plus a good start to retirement accounts.

You probably haven't made it to 30 or 40 years old without learning some of this stuff out too, but these are good reminders for all of us. We're not being as maximally frugal or as smart as we could be, though we try to chip away where we can and make improvements in this arena little by little and year by year. For some people financial matters can be really intimidating. They are also something that we simply don't want to deal with, due to the frustration involved with managing bills, debt, and income. So instead of facing the challenge head on, we avoid it. Avoidance is human nature, and it causes anxiety and embarrassment to think about how far behind you are in debt management or in life. I'm here to tell you that you are not alone, and that the best way to add happiness to your life is get your financial matters in order and to focus on simplicity and relationships. That means personal finance, savings, retirement funds, life insurance and other savings methods. Today can be the first day you deal with your demons and improve your life.

CHAPTER 7

12 Pillars of Personal Finance

I.   Spend less than you earn

II.   Eliminate high interest debt

III.   Have an emergency fund

IV.   Buy items that will last a long time, at the best possible price

V.   If your employer matches retirement funds (401k or 403b), contribute at least up to the match

VI.   If a wife or kids depend on your income, purchase insurance

VII.   When investing, don't chase performance, chase a diversified portfolio with the lowest expense fees possible (index funds are your friends)

VIII.   Be open and honest with your spouse about all things money (debt, savings, spending)

IX.   Money is a tool to support your passions and relationships; it's about freedom, not riches

X.   Don't let "things" own you and stop worrying about others

XI.   Save until it hurts, using sneaky ways to protect *you* from yourself

XII.   You *can* make your way to your financial goals without a financial planner

Let's break these down a little, and then we'll get into much more detail on some of these.

I.   Spend less than you earn

"Annual income twenty pounds, annual expenditure nineteen pounds nineteen [shilling] and six [pence], result happiness. Annual income twenty pounds, annual expenditure twenty pounds ought and six, result misery." – Charles Dickens, *David Copperfield*

This is THE golden rule above all others. If you spend more than you earn, you will always have the cloud over your head as you wait for the other shoe to drop. You cannot begin to save if you spend every penny (or more) that you earn. This seems so simple, and yet is actually so hard to do with all the cool iPads, cars, fashions, music, televisions, purses, and phones out there. The easiest way to do this is to cut your spending. I would encourage you to look at your monthly bill list and itemized debit card receipts to see if you really need those services or items, and subsequently reduce or eliminate excess. Additionally, while the small things add up – a coffee here, a restaurant there, happy hour drinks on Thursday – the big-ticket items have the potential to really kill you. Buying a new car that is above what you need (and most cars are; we rationalize the quality, size or age of a car in most cases when an older, less expensive car would usually do fine). Living in a fancy McMansion when a similar quality of life could be found in something more modest in a nearby neighborhood. Big expenditures or small, nothing should be off the table as an option to reduce spending and grow the gap between income and spending in the right direction, and to the fullest extent possible. I'll have more thoughts on this topic later.

II.   Eliminate High Interest Debt

Notice that I said "high interest" debt. I mean credit cards, the bane of many people's financial existence, yet seemingly necessary at the same time. If you have the ability to stay on top of your finances, I have no issue with using credit cards, especially with so many offering great reward programs. But if you are carrying a balance, especially a balance that you can't pay off in a couple months, you should not be using a credit card. Period. There is nothing good about paying interest on a credit card. Typical cards in 2014 have interest rates between 15-20% annual percentage rate (APR) for a year. That means that carrying a $1,000 balance will cost you between $150 or $200 per year. Or more likely, that $10,000 balance will cost you $1,500 or $2,000. That's a mortgage payment (or more) for many of us. I'll outline a few ways to tackle that behemoth. Besides medical bills, credit cards are the leading cause of personal bankruptcy.

III.   Have an Emergency Fund

When the shit hits the fan it really hits the fan. Count on the fact that right when you put that vacation down on your credit card, getting close to maxing it out, is when you'll have a major car repair, or your furnace will go out, or you'll get injured and have to go on disability, or you'll lose your job. That's how it usually goes. If you don't have something to help buffer the financial hit, you could really be hurting financially; struggling to pay rent or your mortgage, struggling to get food on the table. Your emergency fund is a liquid (easily accessible for cash) account to help with this. Your income mix – i.e., one big income only, two medium-sized incomes, one big, one small income, etc., will dictate how much goes into this fund, but having one is worth the peace of mind.

IV.   Buy Items That Last a Long Time at the Best Possible Price

We have needs and wants; hobbies and passions. We aren't paupers and we enjoy life. One of my old bosses had a credo that was "maximize the amount of things that appreciate, and minimize the amount of things that depreciate." If you are going to buy an item that depreciates, make it a good one that lasts, while still performing in excellent fashion. Is it worth buying that $300 50" flatscreen by some Japanese company you've never heard of that breaks 6 months out of warranty and has no extra inputs? Or better to spend either a little more, or come down in size to get something from a company with a great reputation? We use *Consumer Reports* frequently to evaluate both consumables and big-ticket items, and find that this minimizes the number of times in which we're disappointed in a purchase. The more heavily used an item (cars, appliances, electronics) the more savvy it is to buy something reliable and energy efficient, even at a slightly higher price.

V. If your employer matches retirement funds (401k or 403b), contribute at least up to the match

This one is a real no-brainer, but in case people still don't realize what they are missing, it bears repeating. While some employers have eliminated matching fund programs, many still remain. While each company is different, in general it works like this: for every $1 the employee puts into a 401(k) retirement account, the employer will throw in a matching $1 (or $0.50 or some matching amount) up to a certain percent, usually 2-6%. So what I'm saying is YOUR COMPANY WILL GIVE YOU FREE MONEY, no strings attached. That's a 100% return on your investment immediately, which can continue to grow. Rarely do you see opportunities like this. All you have to do is take your *own* money and save it. I'll discuss my thoughts on the 401(k) as a retirement savings vehicle later, but even if your plan sucks, you still need to contribute at least to the match or you are nearly literally throwing money away.

VI. If a wife or kids depend on your income or contribution, purchase insurance

According to LIMRA's 2011 Life Insurance Ownership Study, only one in three Americans have individual insurance coverage. While many may have smallish policies with their employers (estimated at approximately 50% of people counted in this study, often covering a year's salary), if you are married and have kids, both you and your wife likely need additional life insurance policies. Whether you are the primary breadwinner or a stay-at-home parent, you both contribute resources to the family. In the event of an untimely death or accident, you need to ensure that your family is taken care of, that they don't need to worry about how they will pay the bills. Your wife should have life and disability insurance too, even if she is a stay at home mom (SAHM); if she were to die or become incapacitated, you would need to pay someone else to take care of childcare, and other household chores, to allow you to continue to work. The best financial move is to buy a Term policy for a fraction of the cost of a Whole or Universal Life policy.

I guarantee that when you bring up needing life insurance to an agency, the insurance agent will push Whole Life insurance. That's because they make a shit-ton of money over time on it. Whole or Universal life is sold as an investment, and your premiums are much higher for the same life insurance amount compared to Term insurance, but they will increase in value over time. However, you would be much better off taking the difference between a Whole and Term policy and investing into a mutual fund with a higher likelihood of improved financial returns. Insurance providers prey on the uninformed and those not savvy with investing, and on those who may not even need a life insurance policy (like those without dependents or with paid off homes and minimal debt). A term policy is essentially a life insurance policy that covers a set period of time, say 20 years. In the event of your death, the policy will pay out to your beneficiaries. Or clarity's sake, after those 20 years are up, if you don't die (the goal) you end up with nothing – term life insurance plans don't build equity. But the safety net knowing your kids and wife won't end up broke and homeless is worth the peace of mind for this relatively small price. The coverage is most crucial when your kids are younger. The need decreases drastically after the kids leave the nest and can support themselves, and maybe your spouse has an income as well. You may still want a policy if your wife stays at home with no income, or if you have a large mortgage or debts, but that will depend on your situation – and if you follow the pillars, you have a mountain of debt.

The amount of the policy is entirely up to you. As we joke in my house, I want to be insured enough so that if I die my wife and kids be comfortable and have their life necessities provided, but not so much that she's plotting my death. The more your policy is worth, the more you end up paying (and wasting) in the more-likely scenario that you don't die during the term insurance coverage period. A number of calculators exist online, but a general guideline is five to ten times your salary. Both Holly and I have policies that total slightly more than five times our salary (each), and that carry through to when our kids will be in their early 20's. After that point we don't plan on renewing as we still carry smaller policies from our employers at least equal to a year's salary. We also both make approximately the same income, so if one of us were to go down with the *Titanic*, the other could carry on following policy expiration with only minor financial inconvenience once the kid costs are self-supporting. We could have gone with a higher amount of coverage, and maybe should have with the rising cost of college, but if I were to die, maybe my kids go to the state school instead of Harvard, or have to take out more loans – not the end of the world. I can take the savings from purchasing less expensive coverage and do something else with it. The bottom line is I want my family to have a relatively normal life if my wife or I were to die (as normal as it could be, anyway, without a biological parent); to have food on the table, a house to live in, and the opportunity to attend college. The same opportunities I would hope to provide if I were alive.

Insurance of any kind is simply a risk management tool. It helps to reduce the likelihood of financial catastrophe should unlikely adverse events occur. Generally, if you are healthy and aren't covered by insurance through work or Obamacare (in which I am admittedly not well versed), self-insure at the highest deductible you can afford to lower your premiums, but still allow emergencies. In 2013 I contracted Methicillin-resistant Staphylococcus aureus (MRSA), a nasty, antibiotic-resistant staph infection that can kill you without hospital treatment. After having symptoms including a huge, puffy hand, and fever and getting various antibiotics (via injection and IV) that didn't make a dent, I was finally properly diagnosed. This finally happened at about 3 a.m. and I had to have emergency surgery on my hand in the middle of the night to remove an abscess that was causing this mess and attempting to take my life. Had I not had health insurance, this would have set me back almost $15,000 for my four day visit. Now, that is still relatively minor in the grand scheme of things, but what if you had contracted prostate cancer (very common for men) or had been in an accident of some sort? It helps to have the ability to pay but a fraction of what you would if you didn't have any insurance, even if that means carrying high-deductible insurance that is somewhat expensive.

I would also consider purchasing disability insurance, especially if it is not offered through work. If you become unable to work and earn an income, you not only incur medical bills but also lose the ability to work. This potentially cripples you on two fronts especially if you're the primary bread-winner. Check with your employer to see if they offer optional disability insurance and sign up. Usually, premiums are lower through work, but if you switch or lose your job, it expires. In that event, you may still consider purchasing private disability insurance, since if you are hurt doing a hobby or some random injury from an accident you may still be in a world of hurt.

Finally, without belaboring the insurance topic, consider a supplemental umbrella insurance policy to give you additional liability protection as a homeowner or auto policyholder. This provides additional coverage above your existing policy for medical bills, therapy, or loss wages in the event that you're deemed the person "at fault" in an incident. Let's say you end up in a car accident, or you have teenagers who are driving on your policy. Your "regular" insurance coverage may be around $500,000. Now if injury or death is involved (you cause a 10 car pileup with injuries in a foggy situation), you can easily exceed this policy leaving you liable for damages (including the potential for long-term lost wages of the impacted parties should they be disabled or die). I've recently seen umbrella coverage available for about $15 per month per person (in 2014) for a $1 million policy. This is cheap insurance to protect your assets (if you have any) and/or to prevent potential bankruptcy in that unlikely occurrence. Keep in mind though that too large of an umbrella policy may make it inviting for the lawyers to go after larger amounts should you ever find yourself in this situation, so you should try to strike a balance in cost and asset protection.

VII. When investing, don't chase performance, chase a diversified portfolio with the lowest expense fees possible (index funds are your friends)

While Jim Cramer and *Money Magazine* are talking about the latest hot sellers like gold, tech stocks or Bitcoins – or mutual funds that specialize in mining or energy or whatever – ignore them. You may be able to catch a rising star by following their advice if you're lucky, but you are much better off being a plodder. Think about the tortoise and the hare. By hare, I mean those that are chasing the next big thing, or trusting some hot shot money manager who runs the SuperAwesome Mutual Fund™ to continue to hit those 25% annual returns (that he's hit for two years) for your 2.7% expense fee. Meanwhile, the old plodding tortoise is investing in index funds with a 0.1% expense fee that mirrors some market index (don't worry if you don't know what these terms are yet, we'll delve much deeper later on). Over time, most (if not all) actively managed funds are a total crapshoot to match the performance of a similarly allocated market index. Sometimes beating the index's performance, but usually end up underperforming them. Even assuming they roughly match the performance of each other over time, you'll likely have much less significant funds in the SuperAwesome Mutual Fund™ at the end of the day due to the expense fee alone. The SuperAwesome Mutual Fund™ will need to beat the index by their fee (that 2.7%) year in and year out to beat the index funds with super low fees. Unless your fund advisor is the next Warren Buffett, that's unlikely to happen. It's like finding the needle in a haystack; better to buy the haystack.

Compound interest has crazy impact. So does having a diversified portfolio including a broad mix of stocks and bonds will lesson your risk for potentially slightly less returns, but that's a good thing. I'll show you some examples in Chapter 8-Asset Allocation.

VIII.   Be open and honest with your spouse about all things money (debt, savings, spending)

Much like hiding porn, hiding money issues is a bad thing, especially if those money issues are in rough shape. You two are a team in this life and, as such, each should insist on full transparency in both short-term (day-to-day, month-to-month) finances, and long-term (retirement planning or college funds) finances. She may know you're carrying credit card debt, but don't you think she'd respond differently if it were $1,000 versus $50,000? If that was the case, and you still let her shop designer purse stores because it makes her happy, don't you think she'd probably stop herself after she realized the extent of the thin ice you were on? It's a bitter pill to swallow when have to present bad financial news, so have a plan prepared on how you are going to present that information, and how you plan to correct the situation. You should also mention what she'll have to contribute or change for the situation will change. Expect turbulence. Deal with it.

Are you the one who doesn't know about your finances? Shame on you. Find out so you can be in the loop as the leader in the family. You can't direct the ship if you don't know how the tides and winds are behaving. I'm not saying you have to take over the management of the finances, but at least be knowledgeable of them. In our house, my wife manages all the day-to-day finances and monthly bills while I take care of all the long-term retirement, college funds, and emergency fund accounts. We give updates to each other on a regular basis on how things are doing, review checking balances, and compare notes on upcoming big-ticket expenditures, discuss where we need to pare back, and really just try to keep each other informed.

Discussing other money topics is something that you'll also need to do as both your kids and your parents get older. For your kids, have you talked about if and how you're paying for college? Or are they taking out loans? Or some combination thereof? Your kids should know, at the appropriate age, what the situation is before they start getting their hearts set on Stanford when you've only saved enough for the area technical college. For your parents, as they start to get a little older, have they established a will or a trust? Are they expecting you to pay for their retirement home, or buy the family home, or help them with the car repair when their own meager retirement funds or social security can't cover it? It's a good idea to not let the topic of money become taboo in your house since dealing with it head on can save a world of heartache later on.

IX.   Money is a tool to support your passions and relationships; it's about freedom, not about riches

Money is nothing more than a tool, one that allows us to experience life in the ways we want. Want to travel the world, or fix up a classic car, or build houses in third-world countries? Money will allow you to do those things. It also can allow you more time (the old adage "time equals money" has merit) to pursue the things you are passionate about. If you have money, you've got more freedom to do those things. If you have time, it also allows you freedom to pursue those things that aren't so money intensive. That's called balance. You can retire earlier if you have an inexpensive lifestyle focused more on nature or cheap hobbies and interests; or you can retire later if you need consumption and distant travel to make you happy – that's entirely your choice.

For us, it's not about accumulating a large bank account just to have a bigger number when we visit St. Peter. For those that truly value the relationship with money, and simply the tool it can be in life, it's about using it for good. A better way to approach your financial life is to improve yourself and your relationships and causes: to give back to others, or enjoy the finer things in life. As you go about your life journey and get your financial picture in better order, never forget what you're actually working toward. You may have this smoky image of what you think your retirement is about. Most simply focus on getting out of a job and not having to work without giving much thought of how they'll fill their days. Instead, a better approach for men our age is to start thinking about and developing outside interests and passions while we're saving toward these yet undefined retirement goals, but still remembering to enjoy and experience today. What's the fucking point of retiring at 49 if you have to live like a homeless guy on ramen who never took a vacation to make that happen? Or if you have no interests to make life fulfilling? If you make everyday life a fulfilling event, or at least make vacations part of every year, you may feel like stopping work early isn't necessary. Take the time to build, create and pursue passions and hobbies. In doing so you will be fulfilled both today and when you retire, when you simply have more time to pursue those passions. So many retirees have no passions, and really struggle when the socially and personally fulfilling aspects of work are taken from them. With a little thought, you can still set yourself up for a solid financial future and at the same time enjoy today.

X. Don't let "things" own you and stop worrying about others

So many people are beholden to the next great thing. The new 75 or 90 inch television. The great iPad for all the kids. New cars, jewelry, clothes, shoes, expensive kid items. Vacations! THINGS! Presents, not presence. The problem with this is we forget what is important to life. Here's a hint: it's not zoning out playing Angry Birds or Flappy Bird or whatever the next big mind-waster is. Life is connecting with people. It's improving yourself. It's about teaching and loving your kids. It's about calming the mind and appreciating the world that is around us. A hippy attitude, I know, but how many people on their final deathbed wish that they got to Level 200 on Candy Crush? How many wish they spent more time wrestling with their kids, playing card or board games with them, or spending time doing something cheap like camping?

The other side of this is that people worry so much what their *things* convey about themselves. They think that if they don't have the coolest phone, or have a million Christmas lights on their house, or brand name clothes, that people will think less of them. Let me let you in on a secret: most people have more than a touch of narcissism and mostly only care about themselves anyway. They're going to talk shit about you no matter what. If you dress nicely and are in great shape and have a hot wife and great kids, then you're a stuck up asshole (because they're jealous). If you wear last year's fashions, your kids do well at school, and you drive a (paid off) car that's 10 years old, they'll call you poor or a stingy bastard who must not have any fun. You can't win, so I highly recommend getting Zen and confident with your own awesomeness. Stop acting like a Junior High School girl worrying about what people think about your brown work shoes that are a little scuffed up.

XI.   Save until it hurts using sneaky ways to protect *you* from yourself

Many of us are our own worst enemies when it comes to saving. We get our paycheck, and psychologically we feel flush. The term "burning a hole in your pocket" is very true. I see many blue collar people who burn through a big part of their paycheck on payday doing really dumb things because they're "flush." Then they're depressed on Monday realizing they have to make it another 12 days until they get paid again. Then they go through this cycle again. Now I realize that's not most of you, but the psychology of having some money is the same – if we have it available, we spend it. Budgeting is very important, but you can do some pretty interesting things with automatic savings where the money is pulled away into appropriate savings devices before you even realize it. The result is that you learn to budget with much less money. By the time you get access to your spending money (for food, housing, bills, and entertainment) you've already paid yourself. I'll delve into this in much more detail.

XII.   You can make your way to your financial goals without a financial planner

I have nothing against financial planners (I have good friends who are in this line of work). They can really help those who need a lot of handholding and are overwhelmed or intimidated by investing or personal finance, but most of us don't really need them. While fee-based planners can be an asset in helping make sure you're on the right track, and certified planners are held to a code of conduct and ethics, most financial planners' businesses model runs off commissions. That business model is often at odds with what is really in our best interest. They will throw spreadsheets on top of charts and graphs to show that their recommended investment is in your best interest, or at a minimum, better than competitor's product or basic index funds. Many feel that they have to take these experts' advice (they are "experts" after all, and who are you but a regular dude who doesn't know an expense ratio from a dividend?) and unknowingly succumb to minor parasites known as fees that suck the blood of your portfolio a little at a time. It may not be that noticeable, but over time, you're left with a balance that's much less than what it could have been.

It may be a total information overload when you are just getting started, and when you have a million other things going on in your life, but educating yourself really isn't that hard. I'll show you the key things to look for and do to keep things simple – from your savings, to your 401(k), to an IRA, to maximizing an investment portfolio without high fees (that planners are likely to recommend). Finally, rolling over the 401(k) from your last job to an IRA (or your last two jobs for that matter), is most likely a really good idea and it is much easier than you think. Don't be afraid of the (small amount of) paperwork and (few) phone calls it takes to make it happen. It will likely leave you thousands, or more likely tens-of-thousands (or more), of dollars in your pocket long-term versus having them land in the pocket of your financial planner or 401(k) administrator.

CHAPTER 8

All About Money

Most of you reading this book work full time jobs. Maybe you're the sole breadwinner for a family of five. Maybe your wife works a full- or part-time job that is conducive to her being the primary caretaker of your house and children (a teacher, for example). Maybe your wife has a full-time job that is just as important and stressful as yours. No matter what your situation, you have set amount of income that must get you through all your living expenses and pay for all the things you should be saving for: emergency fund, college, retirement, maybe a dream vacation or a new car. Money causes a lot of stress in a lot of people because, let's face it: there never seems to be enough. So how do you even come up with any excess to tackle your debt load, let alone enough to save for *anything*? And when you do have that tiny bit of extra between expenditures and income, how do you prioritize your spending or allocations to best take you where you want to go? There are many great books, blogs and resources out there to help you navigate these waters once you want to wade in. If you're too intimidated to dive into outside sources, I'll lay out a variety of strategies to at least give you a basic framework you can to follow to meet your goals.

Again, we've made some financial missteps over the years, but with my lead, my wife and my family are accumulating positive wealth in a way consistent with the average lifestyle. Both Holly and I came from relatively humble beginnings. My dad grew up on a farm with five siblings and worked as a mailman for his career. My mom lived in a small home stacked to the brim with six brothers and sisters sharing only a couple of rooms. She regaled my brothers and me with stories of poverty. Things like where she had to hold up her socks with rubber bands after the elastic failed because they couldn't afford new ones, and the old-school Christmas with fruit and small trinkets. While we were growing up, she worked part time as a nurse and made sure we were out the door in the morning with a hot breakfast in our bellies, and a lunch to take to school. My wife was a middle-class happy kid and in a great place in life until her parents divorced. Besides the emotional damage this caused, financially her mom (with whom my wife lived) wasn't well off. Wearing the same clothes most days of the week wasn't that uncommon according to my wife, which is like a kiss of death as a pre-teen or teenager. Neither of us had any financial support from our parents as we put ourselves through college with a combination of loans, scholarships, student resident advisorships, and part time jobs.

We literally graduated college with a carload of belongings each (mostly paid for on credit cards, or found free or second hand). With nothing to hang our hats on other than hopes and dreams, we moved to the east coast. We had a mountain of student loans, were moving (together) to a very expensive part of the country, and Holly had no job in place and thus no known future income. While I had a job set to start when I got out there, she was going out to be with me, figuring things would work out. She worked in a hair salon for a while, before eventually using her degree in a role working... drum roll... at the same place I did. We lived briefly in a college shit-hole sublet with two random roommates, before moving into an apartment that was way too expensive. We lived on free "found" couches, camp chairs and air mattresses, and had a kitchen made up of thrift store cookware. Eventually we ended up purchasing a few necessities like a bed. I only mention these things to illustrate that we struggled as young adults. To say that we weren't exactly handed silver spoons is an understatement. But we loved each other and we persevered through this time.

We moved back to the Midwest a couple years later and we finally started to make financial traction. Once again, I had a job and my then-fianceé didn't. But we were still able to leverage our income, with the assistance of a small pre-wedding gift from my father-in-law, into owning a foreclosed house previously owned by a drug dealer. Despite our debts, I was able to contribute 10% of my income into my company's 401(k) retirement plan and we were able to work on home improvements over time. Holly of course found a good job, and then another, and she too dumped at least 10% into her 401(k). Later, we were able to leverage our home equity (after a number of years of projects) into paying off our credit cards, eventually having two kids, and bumping our contributions to our retirement accounts from 10%, then to 15%, then to 20%. These moves then allowed us to move to a home that increased the quality of life incredibly for our family. Our new home offered us better geography (a shorter commute), a safe and friendly neighborhood with many new friends and activities for the children, and a great school system. It also meant that while our house was only slightly larger than our old one, we took on a larger mortgage. But we still fell into the guidelines I recommend in "Evaluating the Larger Things" below. We were able to accumulate an emergency fund that supported a job loss with ease (one that occurred for us in 2013). We are now saving over 20% of our income, a figure which we still feel can be improved upon in the future.

That's our general story. While we don't have any real estate besides our primary residence, taxable accounts or any other investments to speak of at this time, we do have an Emergency Fund and fairly sizable start to our retirement accounts. These investments make us about $500k net positive on the net worth calculation, even despite our mortgage debt of relatively recently purchased house. I call this a start... but I know where we want to go and the specifics of how to get there, so each year we are improving.

Frugality

Remember my first pillar of personal finance? Spend less than you earn. This is THE golden rule. Earn more and keep expenditures the same, or spend less. Certainly gaining skills and taking classes is a great way to pull yourself up from your current job, as is putting in the time in your profession and paying your dues, but I am not going to focus on that in this book. Earning more however isn't the key to happiness though. Ally Bank recently did a study that showed that the more you save, the more likely you are to be happy and savings has a much more direct effect on happiness than what you earn. First, on the income side, there was *not* a significant difference in happiness between those households earning $50,000 to $75,000 per year and those earning over $150,000 per year. In fact, surveyors reported happiness declined 3% for those making over $150,000 per year compared to those in the $100,000-$150,000 income range. On the saving side, the less saved, the less happy people were. Only 34% of people with less than $20,000 in savings were "happy." The study didn't define if savings were from savings accounts alone or included retirement accounts or other savings. Regardless of their definition, of those with $20,000-$100,000 in savings, 42% were happy, an 8% increase over the previous category. When you reached over $100,000 in savings, 57% of those people considered themselves happy – a massive jump of 15% over the previous category.

Many people fall into a trap of spending more when they begin to earn more, saving about the same amounts (that is to say, not much). This is why, as income goes up, happiness stays relatively unchanged: consumption habits and what a person can purchase keep increasing just to maintain baseline happiness. The correlation between increased happiness and savings is due to the financial security you are gaining, and the ability to deal with unanticipated issues. Additionally, building up a savings nest egg provides peace of mind, pride, and allows people to be independent in the future without owing anyone or relying on anyone for their survival. And lest you think money is the source of happiness, of those surveyed, 91% say having good relationships with friends and family is more important to their happiness than savings is. So friendship and relationships trump saving; and saving trumps spending on the happiness continuum. You can be happy and poor if you have the right relationships around you.

So how do you maximize the amount to save? You become more frugal in your day to day life, making small changes that lead to the ability to make bigger changes over time. Big changes can also be made to expedite frugal living. Things such as moving to a smaller house or less expensive area, or getting rid of a car and taking the bus will all accelerate things tremendously in your goals, but those take much more willpower and effort. So let's start with the small stuff first.

Frugality does not mean cheap. It does not mean spending hours a weekend clipping coupons, or buying top ramen for your family to eat for the week, or driving a junker. It means being economical, prudently saving, and not being wasteful. Everyone is talking about programmable thermostats and compact fluorescents to save on long-term everyday costs, and those are great things that maybe you haven't incorporated yet, but are just the beginning. Keep in mind that if you can eliminate or minimize monthly or weekly expenses, you have a multiplier effect. For every $1 saved on a monthly expense, you save $12 on an annual basis; and for every $1 saved on a weekly expense saves $52. It adds up fast for those $5 and $50 per week or month bills. Here are some things you may want to consider, some things we've done, and some example dollar figures you may expect to see by incorporating some of these strategies into your own lives.

Get rid of cable television

Yes, you love the *Walking Dead* or whatever the hot show is on cable these days, but there is so much to gain by getting rid of cable, likely $100 a month or more. We were over $150 a month for what the cable companies like to call their bundle "deal," which was phone, internet and cable. We didn't need phones (we have cell phones), we *did* need cable internet, but decided we didn't need cable television. We could live without *Spartacus* and *Game of Thrones* on the premium channels (you'll see why). We didn't need to watch *House Hunters* or most of the other crap that populates everyday cable programming, and the kids didn't need to watch as much television, period. Advertising is the primary source of revenue for shows (beyond your subscription fees for cable channels at least), and seeing less of this shit is good for your kids; it means a reduction in pro-consumption brainwashing, with an added bonus of reducing sexual and violent messages.

With the prevalence of tablets and smart phones, there seems to be less need for the television as well. By leaving the very basic local channels (CBS, NBC, ABC, Fox), which you can get from an inexpensive internal or external antenna and keeping high speed internet, we saved approximately $100-120 per month, or $1,200-$1,400 a year. Instead of cable, we subscribe to Netflix streaming, which we use regularly. Movies, full seasons of television shows, TED Talks, standup comedy, and cartoons are what dominate our television these days when it is on (which isn't that frequently); not cable or even network TV. This means no commercials to damage the brain and that we have much more control over the content that gets watched. It has been one of the best financial and time-sink reductions we've made.

Use your local library system

Many local libraries have access to a vast volume of material, more than they can physically store on site, sharing books and media with other libraries in the area. What this means is that nearly any book you would want to read (and you've cut the cable now, so you're reading more right?) can be found at the library for free. Well not exactly free, your tax dollars go to support it. I just checked my library history, and in the last year, I've checked out 257 items. You'll be really surprised at what you can find there: Movies on Blu-ray disc™, DVDs, books on CDs, books on mini-audio players, music CDs, computer games, language CDs, videogames (XBOX, PS2, PS3, DS, DS3d, etc.), comics, magazines... oh, and books too. We've used the library for all of these things.

Ripping music to our iTunes library. Reading up on the latest tech or outdoors magazine. Checking out about a million kids' movies, games and books, as well as audiobooks for me while I'm on the road for work. Finding new grown-up movies, as well as full consecutive seasons of premium channel original shows from HBO, Cinemax, and Showtime. You just have to be willing to delay the impulsive response to see it now, so you can see it later for free. You can realize big cost savings from video game, TV show, movie and book borrowing instead of purchasing those items. For example, instead of paying $50 per game (or even $20 for used) we can get nearly any PS3 game for a couple weeks for free, and book rentals for free for a month or more with renewals. Without even counting the Looney Tunes™ cartoon DVDs (and where else are they going to see such classics since they don't show them often on television?) or kids' books, I'd say we probably save somewhere in the neighborhood of $1,200 to $1,500 a year by using the library.

Coffee

Both my wife and I are very regular, if not massive, coffee drinkers. But we rarely stop at a coffee shop like Starbucks unless someone else is paying. You can save a lot of money and make a damn fine cup of coffee at home, but you have to be willing to get rid of the bullshit drinks that take two minutes to even order. These foo-foo drinks are nothing but a milkshake anyway, so get a regular coffee and be a man. The darker the better, the stronger the better.

So here's what we do; most days we grind our own beans from Costco (about $4.50 a pound and still roasted by Starbucks, but sold under Costco's Kirkland brand, or some other premium brand at a similar price), and make a wicked pot of coffee that we finish in the morning and on our way to work. Two 2.5 pound bags lasts us over a month, which equates to $0.75 per pot of coffee over a month, each which yields four good cups. So we pay roughly $0.19 a cup for coffee. We did end up with a Keurig single-cup maker, and again, purchasing from Costco, we found individual cups to be between $0.35 to $0.50 a cup (or up to $0.65 a cup for a Starbucks House Blend). We use the Keurig when we're lazy or in a hurry, but it's still much less than the $2.10 average coffee price for Starbucks regular coffee and well below the $3-$ a specialty coffee drink costs. Take the extra 3 minutes a day and make a pot of coffee. If you are a regular drinker, the difference could be over $1,300 per year for a single person ($4 per day Starbucks specialty habit versus two regular cups of coffee at $0.19 a cup per day) so could be nearly $3,000 per year if you and dear spouse both skip this fiscally irresponsible habit. Oh, and the grocery stores usually have a bean grinder too, if you don't have one of your own (which is a great long-term investment for real java junkies).

Buy things in bulk

Whether you're a Costco or Sam's Club or BJ's Wholesale Club kind of person, they all allow you to buy staples at cheap prices. Paper towels, toilet paper, dishwasher tabs, laundry detergent, and things like ketchup are all significantly cheaper at the bulk club stores versus the other stores. Other things like berries, quality snacks such as nuts and many brands of alcohol make it totally worthwhile to find a club discount. However, every time you enter the store, you end up dropping $100 (at a minimum) so be careful on short-term versus long-term spending. We save enough money each time to well justify the visit, plus enough from the purchasing incentives to pay for the membership each year. I'd expect with a family, you'll do the same. However, stick with the key areas: staples, bulk fruits and vegetables, and food of which you eat a lot. Don't venture off into TV land, toyland or clothesland if you can help it (you have enough clothes already).

Credit card – Request for reduction

If you are a longtime good customer, or even if you're not, call each and every credit card company customer service number (on the back of the card) and see if they'll give you a rate reduction. If you're a longtime customer, tell them you're thinking of leaving and transferring the balance to a different company (beware the credit rating hit from actually closing accounts though - use this only as a bluffing tactic for now). Another method is to talk to the credit card representative about financial difficulties that will make it more beneficial for you to have a lower interest rate so that you can continue to make timely payments. That may or may not be true, and they may ask for documentation, so be prepared as to how you'll respond to that question. If the person you are speaking to can't make the decision or change your rate, ask to speak to their supervisor. If that doesn't work, try calling back and talking to a different customer service representative, sometimes just getting the right person is the key. If this approach works, ask for a confirmation letter. If they decline your offer, move on to writing a letter.

Take a few minutes to write to the "Supervisor of the customer service department." Include your account number and full name of account holder. Write why you are looking to reduce interest/rates or payment. Sign the letter and add your address, telephone number and e-mail. Enclose bank statements, income tax return, or other items as they may support your request (you don't HAVE to include *any* of these things, and if you do, black out sensitive personal information you feel is not pertinent). Follow-up by phone a week later if you don't receive a response. For all of this, the worst they can say is "no" so don't stress it too much. At best, they reduce your interest rate which could save you thousands of dollars over the life of the credit card if you carry a balance. These are thousands of dollars that could be used for savings, investing or college accounts, or that trip you've been planning. These small calls can save you tons!

Cell Phones

Consider going pre-paid on cell phones (even smart phones) or going on a family plan. In our area, we can get a basic smart phone plan with 500 minutes, unlimited texting and 200 MB of data (plus Wi-Fi) for $40/month on a prepaid plan. Other companies are popping up – such as Republic Wireless or Ting mobile – that are as low as $10 a month for phone and data after you own the phone (some utilizing WiFi for data and even voice to keep costs low, only using cellular technology if roaming). This is significant cost savings for those that mostly use their data in Wi-Fi friendly places. Usually, you can add phones to a family plan and share minutes and data. We can add an individual line for the cell phone plan we're on for $40 a month and split costs with my mother. That cuts per-unit costs for unlimited everything.

Also, try and fight the desire to upgrade your phone all the time. Realize that not having the latest version of the iPhone will not make your smart phone much less awesome. This consumer mentality adds up if you have say, three or four phones on your plan, and the cell company pressures you to upgrade every year or two. If all four plan holders upgrade every two years to the "best" phones (typically $100-$200 each), that may cost you up to $400 a year (average) just for new hardware. I may be an old curmudgeon, but I typically only upgrade every 3-4 years and will usually take an older "free" phone instead of paying an additional fee.

Cut or color your own hair

This is one of my favorites, though I'm sure some of you are shaking your head. I don't do it every month, but I do it frequently enough over the years to have saved a bundle (as have my brothers and brothers-in-law). Most times I do it myself, but occasionally ask my wife to trim up areas I have a hard time reaching. First, no one really cares about how your hair looks. Have you actually opened your eyes and seen how many bad hair days men have, especially men in their 30's and 40's? Trust me, you don't need to be spending $20 or $40 for a hair cut by a barber or stylist; you can replicate your basic "do" with a little effort and some hair product.

You can find a trimmer online for $20, which is instant payback – mine has lasted over three years thus far. If you feel the need, get two nice "style" $30 haircuts a year as a compromise. You'll still be spending $80 for a style/self-hybrid the first year, and $60 thereafter. Not bad. If you do every cut yourself, it's free after the initial investment of $20. If you currently get your hair cut for $30 each time (plus a $5 tip), once a month, that's over $400 a year, that drops right to your bottom line. For those whose wives color their hair, if you are able to convince your wife to talk her favorite stylist into giving her the high quality hair dye for cost (which may not be an option for some) you stand to save an additional $600 a year, assuming she's getting a coloring done every couple months. This isn't a huge amount, but if you add those savings up over a five year period and that's $5,000. That is enough for a semester's tuition at many in-state universities in 2014. Is it a little more effort? Yeah, but it can be a time saver too since you can do it on your own schedule. With a little effort and minimal cost, you'll both still end up with nice enough looking hair without having your wife compromise very much on her haircuts. If you encourage her to grow her hair long, and look more feminine in the process, you may even be able to reduce the costs more.

Bring your own lunch

This is an easy one, for you and your kids alike, plus it's likely better for you health-wise. Simply making extra food for dinner and bringing leftovers is probably the easiest way. Various personal finance bloggers have looked at this, and suggest that if you're paying $6 per day for a takeout lunch versus the homemade food cost of about $2 per lunch, this $4 a day difference over a work year (taking out vacation and holiday breaks) and is equivalent to nearly $1,000 saved on an annual basis per person. For kids' lunches, the savings may not be as dramatic, but feeding them food that is good for them instead of the standard school fare is worth it regardless of cost savings. So assuming a wash for the kids' lunches, you can still save nearly $2,000 per year for husband and wife by brown bagging it.

Eat dinner at home most meals

Similar to the eating homemade lunches, this savings is dramatic if you eat out, even at fast-ish semi-quality restaurants such as Chipotle or the local takeout restaurants. At these restaurants, we have a difficult time eating for less than $25 a meal for a family of four. For a typical homemade dinner, depending on what we're eating, we probably spend between $5 and $10 for ingredients. Let's compare two different busy families: The Jones and the Stevens. The Jones have a busy schedule, so end up getting pizza, take-out, or stop by the local fast-ish food place five days a week at $25 a pop, and cook at home twice a week. The Stevens also have a busy schedule, but take the time to do large meal preparations, throwing something in the crockpot in the morning, and freezing extra meals for cooking on busy nights. They also end up eating out once a week on the busiest day to save them some sanity. So assuming the average at-home meal costs $7.50, the Jones spend $140 a week for dinner and the Stevens spend $70 per week, half as much. So the Stevens end up saving over $3,600 a year compared to the Jones, a huge amount. On that note, if you're really trying to accelerate your financial goals, don't be afraid to have a homemade family dinner before a "date night" and stop in for a dessert and coffee while you're out instead of a full.

Swap babysitting

If you're lucky enough to live near some friends, or friendly neighbors that your kids already play with anyway, a great way to save money on "date night" or other times when you need to get away from the baby sharks, is to swap babysitting services. When we go out and hire the local teenage girls to watch our kids, we end up paying them $40 for an evening away. Your experience may be different, but if we can save that amount once per month by swapping with the Jones' (and taking their kids at another time for their date night), that's another $480 a year in each family's pockets.

Make the most of gym memberships – or build one at home

If you have a gym membership, use it, or lose it. Also, depending on your contract (if you have one), consider a cheaper gym that still meets your needs. Or better yet build one at home. We've built a home gym that is a hodge-podge of Craigslist buys, free stuff, home built stuff, and new equipment and have no membership fees. With our kids in grade school now, they don't need the constant supervision, so my wife and I are able to spend some quality time together exercising some mornings before work and on the weekends, which is an added benefit. For us, eliminating a $150 per month membership fee for a CrossFit gym meant that our equipment paid for itself in about four months, and every year thereafter saves us about $1,800 per year. Now I will say that if paying $30 or $60 or $150 per month makes it so you stay motivated and healthy, or if you need to get away from the family-brood for sanity purposes, then it may be worth it to pay that monthly expense. From the financial side though, the more fat you trim now (no pun intended) the more you can use to pay down debts or save.

Cheap alcohol

If you are going to imbibe in alcohol, the worst way to do it is at a bar or restaurant since there is a very, very steep markup. The better way is to have some at home, amongst friends and family of course. In our state, Costco sells liquor at great prices, and their Kirkland brand is pretty good and pretty cheap; not the best but definitely OK with light mixers. If you're so inclined, and patient, homebrewing can be fun and can result in cheap alcohol as well. I make my own fruit wines, and when I can get free fruit (fairly common as we have friends with a variety of fruit trees and berries) the small amount of ingredients probably result in a per bottle ingredient cost of $0.25-0.75. If I have to buy the fruit, it probably runs me $2-3 a bottle. It's something to think about at least. It's also worth mentioning that homebrewing requires an up-front investment for equipment, but if homebrewing is something that interests you, look used on Craigslist and hopefully you have a local homebrewing shop to guide you to resources and the necessary ingredients.

If you must join your friends out at the bars for a night on the town, do what I do. It's a secret passed down from father to son, and is as old school as it gets. Lean close now...bring a flask. That's right, take those cheap distilled spirits from home and order a club and lime, and dump in your booze on the sly like granddad did. It's sneaky and fun and feels like you're getting away with something. And you are, you're getting away with keeping $5 in your pocket each time you do this. Win.

Water, water, water

Order water when you go to eat. Not only is it more healthy for you, it is free. At home, utilize a filter pitcher, a filter off your faucet or refrigerator dispenser. This is one of the easiest and best alternatives to buying soft drinks or even juice. Buying a 12-pack of soda a week at $4.50 per unit costs $234 per year. And if you buy another can a day at work for $0.50 each, that's another $130 or more. Doesn't sound like much, but saving nearly $400 per year isn't anything to sniff at, and you should drink water for the health benefits alone. The savings is just a bonus. Utilize refillable water bottles and take them with you as often as you can so you don't have to purchase bottled water while out and about.

Stop collecting stuff, and get rid of the shit you have

In general, I am a minimalist. Despite my earlier baseball card collection in junior high, I've long been of the belief that collecting stuff is really a huge waste of money. I should expect some backlash on this topic, but I just don't understand paying money for things just to collect and *have* them. It's in the vein of acquiring for the sake of simply acquiring, of which I'm not a fan as it leads to clutter, the need for storage or display, which can all be another domino toward hoarding and surely a wasteful expense. For me, I measure the value of things by the utility they provide; collectable beanie babies, plates, dolls, figurines, thimbles, sports memorabilia, spoons, action figures, or beer cans have no use and simply take up space. Some may add some flavor to a home's appearance, and some may even gain value, but most are a money sink.

Additionally, most of us already have too much stuff to begin with. Remember when you were into hockey but now haven't played in 15 years? Time to sell your skates and equipment. Those old baby clothes? You can make some money off that. Those collectables? Some sucker will take those off your hands as you clean up your home of clutter. Videogames that you've beaten or don't play anymore? Get rid of them. Craigslist is my favorite way to conduct these transactions, though garage sales and eBay are also options.

Buy used if possible, or better yet, stop buying stuff

People shop just to feel good, to do something when they are bored. This is a bad habit and one that can be difficult to break. My wife is a fan of shopping, but usually spends most of her time shopping at the local charitable thrift store. She's cut her clothing budget considerably, and sells or donates her old clothes allowing us to recoup costs or at least write off these charitable donations, while at the same time keeping her clutter down. Yard sales, thrift stores and craigslist are great ways to save money on many consumables. A good part of my garage gym was purchased for pennies on the dollar off of craigslist. I purchased a nearly-new Nintendo DSi (with box, instructions and a couple of games) from some college kid for less than half-price off craigslist. You'll be surprised at how much you can save. Yeah, you're still consuming, but at least you're maximizing your money. There are hundreds or thousands of ways to start to find ways to reduce expenses. Trying to save and reach your financial goals without implementing some of these ideas, or other ones you can come up with, is like trying to fill a bucket with water that has many small holes in the sides and bottom. These little things slowly drain our money without us realizing it. We're fortunate enough to live in a society where so many great things are free and often underutilized. There should be no excuse why we can't cut back on things, refocus again on less expensive ways to pass the time and find peace with what we have. As the saying goes, "it's not having what you want, it's wanting what you've got." And most of us have got a lot to be thankful for already.

Evaluating the Larger Things

Just like you can lose out with many tiny holes in your bucket, you can lose out with several large holes, too. While tightening things up on the day-to-day expense side is often easier psychologically, you are likely to make faster and broader financial improvements to your life by making larger wholesale changes. These changes often require a "come to Jesus" moment after you've looked at your current situation: where you are and where you want or need to be.

Are you looking at or already living in a house that's too large or more expensive than what you really need? While a bank can use clever financing tricks to get you in a larger house, the general rule of thumb for fiscal responsibility has been 28% of gross income (pretax) as the limit you are paying for mortgage, insurance (homeowners or private mortgage insurance), homeowners fees and real estate taxes. For reference we're at about 20% and feel pretty OK with house costs as part of our overall budget. Another good recommendation related to home ownership is that the mortgage amount when you sign up should not be more than two-times gross income, which we are also below. You should be too.

If you have bitten off more than you can chew on the housing side, it may be worth the large hassle to try and sell your house and buy or rent something smaller. Be sure to factor in the costs for moving, packing, storage unit rental (if you have more "stuff" that you can't fit in a future home), commuting costs and other fees into the equation to make sure you are fully evaluating the switch. Many find that selling a home that is too expensive is removing an albatross from their neck. Saving $1,000 per month in downsizing drops $12,000 a year to your bottom line – leaving you to dig out of debt or, better, set you up for the future. Even if temporary, this could make a large dent in setting up a better foundation for the future. We're talking about short-term pain versus long-term gain.

For many who bought homes around the time of the peak market in 2007-2008, you may be underwater (owe more than what the house is worth) on your mortgage, which doesn't leave you as many options. If making larger payments is difficult for you on an underwater mortgage, reach out to your lender to see what options you may have. Some may include forbearance with reduced or delayed payments, instead of them having you simply walk away. While walking away in that situation certainly is a viable option, be very aware that defaulting on a mortgage is a big red flag and that doing so will impact your credit for a seven years, and will drop your FICO score 100-400 points. This means every other loan or line of credit you get will likely be at a much higher rate, meaning you pay more. Still, getting out of a toxic financial strain may still be worth it if you are struggling to simply survive, but the longer-term stress could be moderate to enormous depending on your situation.

Are you driving a car (a mode of transportation to get you from Point A to Point B) that is well beyond what you truly need? Yeah, you may need a minivan if you have four kids, but do you need a brand new tricked out one with leather heated seats, the navigation and entertainment package? Those add-ons don't really add that much value when you're trying to sell by the way. You may be able to sell or trade that vehicle in for a used, standard model with 60,000 miles for half the price (depreciation on vehicles is very front-end loaded). Instead of the entertainment package, buy a portable DVD player off craigslist or use your iPad to keep the rug rats entertained on trips. If you haven't yet purchased that car "you deserve," pause for a minute and think about what, after that thrill of purchase wears off, it really is: a mode of transportation. You are better off buying a reliable car with 150,000 miles on it for cash, than tying yourself to a five-year loan for a new car. In fact, I highly recommend avoiding loans longer than three years, and even then only if you plan to own the car until it becomes unreliable or dies. If you have to go to five years to afford it, you are buying too much car.

If you are sending your kids to private school, evaluate the financial aspects and the quality or benefit to their lives. Maybe the public school would be adequate. We live in a great school district, but some of our neighbors still send their kids to private schools for an additional cost. Meanwhile their wives will work a full time job they despise to be able to afford the so-called "finer things" including that private school education and after school childcare. When really evaluating the "big picture" things, be sure to include the full value of whatever you're buying. You may find more life value in having a spouse stay at home, homeschooling, and raising the family unit in the way you desire than in being the two-income family where the second income provides little financial or life value.

Everyone has their priorities, but changing up, or at least honestly looking at the big things, could potentially allow you to reach your financial and life goals more quickly.

Prioritizing Cash Excess

So after you've met your living expenses, and have implemented what reductions you think you can (they aren't enough, by the way), you have a little, or maybe a lot, of excess each month. What should you do now? Different financial experts will tell you different things, but all are generally in the same ballpark. Here is what I recommend in rough order:

If you have a 401(k) with an employer match, contribute up to the match. This is FREE money someone is giving you. You would be stupid to basically say "no" to some stranger who asked "Hey, you want $20? No strings?" So why would you do that to your employer on a much larger scale. You have to do this. It's a 100% return on investment in the short term. You can't find a better deal.

Pay into an emergency fund - beg, borrow, steal and sell so that as rapidly as you can, you accumulate $1,000 into this account. This account needs to be separate from your regular checking and savings accounts. I like to use an online bank as they offer much better interest rates than almost any bricks and mortar ones. Though the interest rate is still pretty poor, it still provides a more liquid location for getting cash out quickly. A number of online banks have interest rates between 0.75%-0.95% as of early 2014. Many will also allow you to set up sub-accounts for things like vacations or vehicles. This initial $1,000 emergency fund is for EMERGENCIES! It is so you don't use the credit card to pay for the huge car repair that impacts your livelihood. Most fail to reach their financial goals after starting out on the right track because they get hit with unexpected expenses, emergencies, or critical financial needs, and don't have the liquid capital to make it over the hump. Having this $1,000 buffer will allow you to weather a smallish size storm while doing the other key things below. Therefore, if you have some emergency home situation or car repairs you can overcome that with cash on-hand. Use the E-fund and not your credit card.

Eliminate high interest credit card debt. Now that you have a fund to get you through tight spots in cash (instead of resorting back to credit cards), pay every remaining dollar not assigned to 401(k), your other bill's minimum payments, or living expenses into your credit card(s). Most cards charge between 15-25% interest per year. This means that if you put that $1,000 television on a credit card with 20% interest, and just paid the minimum payment of 2% (or $10) per month, it would take 26 years to pay off and you'd pay over $4,000 in interest. When you think about it, the worst feeling is realizing those small purchases like coffee or opening a bar tab take years to pay off. You could conceivably be paying off that non-fat vanilla latte for the next 20 years. Talk about facepalm!

Two schools of thoughts exist on how to best attack credit card debt. One is to order your cards from smallest balance to largest, pay the minimum on all but the smallest balance, and maximize the payment on that one. So you have three cards with balances of $1,000, $2,000 and $3,000. The idea is to pay the minimum, on the $2,000 and $3,000 balances, and put your remaining amount, say $500, toward paying off the $1,000 balance. After that one is paid off, you pay the minimum on the $3,000 balance and now apply that $500, plus what you were paying before on the $2,000 balance, until that is paid off. It doesn't matter what the interest rates are, just start smallest to largest even if the largest has the highest interest rate and the smallest balance the smallest.

The other method is to order the cards by interest rate and start chipping away at the highest one first, before moving down. This way you pay the least amount of interest over the time it takes you to pay everything off.

Financial "expert" Dave Ramsey, and many others (including me) feel the first way is the best. Clearing debt is as much emotional and psychological as it is logical. If you have a large balance and are slowly chipping away at it, it is a total grind and things happen pretty slowly. People tend to get frustrated and give up when this occurs since progress can seem so small. However, when you have a small balance, and see it drop more quickly, eventually to the point of elimination relatively rapidly, you get that psychological boost knowing that you are really making progress. Remember, success begets success, and if you succeed early in eliminating any sort of debt, you're going to continue to make positive choices.

After credit cards are paid, bump up retirement savings in your own Roth IRA or 401(k) (or other employee-sponsored plan) to at least 10% (or to the maximum allowed). Even if you have other debts, establishing a baseline for retirement is very important. Compounding and market increases have the ability to help you make considerable growth if you invest early enough.

Like kids, there is never going to be a "perfect" time to start really socking away money for investing. You may still have other debts, but time is your friend (or enemy) in investing, as you'll see.

Build that Emergency Fund up to cover three to six months of living expenses. Now that your high-interest loans are paid, you have $1,000 to get over an "easy" emergency and you're up to a solid savings amount for retirement, it's now time to start building that emergency fund further. Depending on your situation, having three to six months of living expenses will help with a larger illness, a lost job, or other emergency that won't be covered by your initial savings. Having this liquidity provides a lot of peace of mind, which can be invaluable.

Continue paying down other debt you may have: car loans, personal loans, student loans and second mortgages are all important things to eventually pay off; try to prioritize higher-interest or lower-value loans, depending on your strategy. Keep in mind that some of those loans are tax deductible so it may make sense to pay off some loans like car loans before student loans depending on your interest rate, job stability, interest, and tax situation.

Further Savings and Investing. I think at this stage, savings should be spread a little, but definitely more weighted to retirement. Get your retirement savings eventually up to 15% of your gross income. Only after you're up to 15% retirement savings, with no debt other than your mortgage, and are building up a 3 to 6 month emergency fund should you begin socking away any significant money for college educations. Your kids can always borrow for tuition or utilize other strategies such as starting their higher education at technical colleges before transferring, or event go to trade school (another good choice). But you can't borrow or strategize from your future self for retirement funds. And finally, only those rare individuals who are maxing out all the above should consider taxable investing. But if you're one of those rare people, then you likely don't need my thoughts on the subject. If you do, more information is below.

What is a 401(k), 403(b), SEP or an IRA? What's the difference between a Roth and a regular IRA or 401(k)?

The 401(k), 403(b), 457(b), Savings Incentive Match Plan for Employees (SIMPLE) IRA, and Simplified Employee Pension Plan (SEP) are some of the employer-sponsored, tax advantaged retirement savings plans available to some employees. If you are one of the 14% that receive an employer pension consider yourself lucky but forewarned. Many private and public employers are so overdrawn due to past obligations that they are changing the rules even for those already retired. It may not be safe to count on these pensions, so contributing to an IRA account on your own, or putting money into other taxable investments may still be needed to reach your goals. That's a story for another day though.

A 403(b) plan is for public education or other non-profit employees, a 457(b) for government employees, and a 401(k) is for private companies that support these plans. The SIMPLE and SEP are individual retirement accounts (traditional) opened on behalf of the smaller employers, and even those self-employed are eligible to set up these types of accounts. Your company may decide to match a portion of your contribution (often a one-for-one match up to 6 percent, though some may go higher) in your account, essentially incentivizing their employees to save for retirement (and incentivize you to choose a job) by giving you free money. Often employers have a vesting plan for their matching funds, meaning that you need to stay employed with them for a certain number of years to take that free money with you. If you leave before that time to take other employment, they can take back some or all of the money that they put into your account. It's a way for companies to incentivize you to stay, since training and integrating an employee into a company culture is expensive.

A Roth option can be provided for both a 401(k) and 403(b) plan, as well as for an individual retirement account, or IRA. The difference between a Roth and traditional account is how their taxes are handled. A traditional 401(k), 403(b), 457(b), SIMPLE or SEP gets invested with pre-tax income that reduces your net income, and, subsequently, the taxes you pay in a given year. In a non-Roth scenario, when you retire and all your investments will have (hopefully) increased and made you a lot of money. You pay taxes on the value of your distributions at that time. But repeat the following investor's mantra after me:

"Past performance is no guarantee of future results." This means that investments can and will lose money, but over the long term, if history is any indication, we expect them to gain money. But it is not guaranteed. The Roth option is post-tax, meaning taxes taken are out in the current year before the funds are invested into your account, thereby reducing your take-home pay now. In this option, your investments increase tax-deferred, meaning that when you take your distributions out at retirement, you pay no additional taxes on them. Think about it. IF (and it's a big IF) the government decides to honor these rules, you will not have to pay any further taxes on future income.

So let's say you make $1,350, after taxes you end up with $1,000. That sucks, paying $350 of your hard-earned income to taxes. However, when you take that after-tax $1,000 and invest it in a Roth, and it grows to $10,000 30 years later, you withdraw without taking any taxes. If you had a similar tax burden, you save yourself over $2,000 in taxes not-paid, about six times as much as your original taxes to Uncle Sam. Hopefully, the government keeps this tax-free incentive for investing.

No one knows what the government is going to do regarding taxes in the future. Many experts believe tax rates will increase over time, so paying now would be a benefit if you expect to find yourself in a higher tax bracket at retirement. Alternatively, if you expect to be in a lower tax bracket at retirement versus now, perhaps you're better off deferring taxes through a traditional 401(k) and harvesting the tax benefits now. Additionally, while unlikely, the government may decide that the tax benefits given to Roth subscribers are too beneficial and decide to double tax you on the back end. However, reducing your taxes now and investing more (and having it grow) may have the same tax implications later. Whatever route you choose, I don't think you can really fool the Tax Man and likely it may be a wash. If the government ends up raising taxes, you could be better in a Roth. If not, and you're like me and expect to reduce your income needs as you get older, you may be better in a Traditional account. You just never know. We personally hedge our bets and have funds in both traditional and Roth IRAs, as well as both traditional and Roth 401(k)s.

Retirement Funding

If you have a 401(k) through work, you'll have to evaluate if that is your best option or if a Roth IRA would be a better option for you. While some 401(k) plan administrators are pretty efficient and don't charge high fees, others charge large administration fees. We want to maximize the amount of our contribution that actual works for us, versus what's being siphoned off due to fees or expenses. A percent or two of administration or expense fee makes a huge difference over a 20- or 30-year window. That's because investing takes advantage of the power of compounding. For example, if you invest $1,000 into a 401(k) account and are able to make 7% return on it, with the returns being reinvested back into the account, you'll end up with $4,038 after 20 years. But if you end up paying your administrator 1% and another 1% due to expenses from the managed fund you have selected, that return drops to $2,713, or over 30% less.

Many, or dare I say most, 401(k) or 403(b) plans have limited fund options, often with higher fees, than what you can buy in an open IRA fund through a brokerage firm where you can select your own funds. This is why many smart financial advisors recommend maximizing the free money from your employer match and then opening up an outside IRA account where you can select low-fee funds from anywhere. I have mixed thoughts on this. First, it is damn easy to simply have your 401(k) administrator take 10% of your salary before you even see it and automatically invest in the funds of your selections. With how busy life is, this is a real consideration for those pressed for time and those who simply don't have time to regularly log into their IRA account and manage their investments. However, the point of higher expenses in your 401(k) account has merit, and you likely can make broader and better fund selections with lower fees in your IRA than you can in your 401(k). If you think you've got the time and dedication to commit to staying on top of your own investments, you can usually set up an automatic withdrawal from your bank to dump funds into your IRA account(s).

Be aware that there are established maximum limits to what you can put into these accounts – and in the case of Roth IRA, income limits exist. In 2014, the maximum 401k contribution is $17,500, with an additional $5,500 allowed if you're over 50 years of age. For a Roth IRA, you can contribute up to $5,500 of after-tax income, with an additional $1,000 if you're over 50. On the Roth side, if you make $112,000 ($178,000 married, in 2014) there's a reduction in what you're allowed to contribute until you hit $127,000 ($188,000 married) per year. At that point, you aren't allowed to contribute at all. Note that these limits are based on Modified Adjusted Gross Income (so your income less deductions, exemptions, etc.) so talk to your tax advisor if you think you might be near or over these limits. At the time of this writing, President Obama was talking about setting up the MyRA funding system, intended for low- and middle-class citizens to start building up a nest egg. It is basically an IRA but with a focus on investment in safe (and lower-yielding) government bonds. While this approach is something, it will not likely grow aggressively enough for most investors.

A quick word on 403(b) funds. While I'm not that familiar with them and haven't worked anywhere where that this program was an option, my research tells me they are notorious for being poor investment choices (many offer a lot of annuities with high fees), high hidden plan administrator fees, and not matching any percent of your income. Like the 401(k) and IRA accounts, there are still tax advantages, but just be aware of what is out there and prioritize a Roth IRA account (maybe for both spouses) over a 403(b); especially, if the 403(b) options suck (high expense ratios, poor investment options, no match, high other fees), and if you don't need to harvest tax income now (versus later).

Opening up a Roth IRA

Establishing an account for your retirement funding may sound intimidating, but it's not. There are many online brokerage companies that will walk you through it. Scottrade, E-trade, Fidelity, Vanguard and Sharebuilder are a few examples. If you open a Roth IRA with a company who has their own funds, you may only have access to that funds' family, so if you think you may want to spread your investments to various other funds, you may consider a more open site like E-Trade, Scottrade or Sharebuilder, among others. Any of these firms should make representatives available to you to walk you through the process. It's hard to go wrong with the Vanguard family of funds, and going directly through Vanguard is what I would recommend to someone just starting up, or to someone doing a direct rollover (provided they meet Vanguard's minimum balance requirements). They have great customer service and make the process easy, and is something I can personally attest to.

Opening up an account is not very difficult. Log onto the website of your choosing. Most require a permanent U.S. address, a social security number, beneficiary's information including social security number, and likely employer information. Decide at what level you want to trade; this will set your fee schedule. The way most should invest is "buy and hold," so paying per trade may be the best option, but do be sure to read the fine print as to how each company handles their trading. If you decide to open a Roth IRA, and will be purchasing funds at regular intervals, maybe a package (an agreement of so many trades per month at so much dollars) could be better for you. Alternatively, many allow automatic reinvesting without this hassle.

Once you have the account open, you'll get an account number you can use to deposit funds into thorough your bank or writing a check to the company. Once funds are in the account you may purchase your investments, which is as easy as inputting the trading letters and clicking "buy." Make sure you double check those letters though, as it is very easy to transpose or mistype letters. I'll discuss asset allocation (or, how you distribute your funds amongst stocks, bonds, real estate, etc.) shortly, but here's a very important point: provided you're generally diversified, investing for retirement is much less about asset allocation than it is about A) starting early and B) maximizing the amount you invest. So give up that daily Starbucks, and start hiding money from yourself so that you can bump up the amount you invest.

Rolling over 401k

If you have a 401(k) from a prior employer, you should really look at rolling it into an IRA at one of the investment sites I mentioned above. Like setting up a Roth IRA, those companies can also set up a regular IRA account for the explicit purpose of rolling over. You want to move your old 401(k)s over for the same reasons your current 401(k) may not be the best idea – fees and expenses that siphon off your real returns. You can often select low-fee funds and in the long run, end up making a lot more money. I was intimidated by the thought of dealing with this hassle, and put off rolling over a couple of old 401(k)s for way too long. The process is actually relatively simple, let me lay it out for you:

- **Step 1:** Open up an IRA as described above for the purpose of rolling over a 401(k). This is done at any outside brokerage firm (such as E-

Trade, Sharebuilder and Scottrade), or at firms with their own family of funds such as Fidelity or Vanguard.

- **Step 2:** Contact the plan administrator for your old 401(k) and tell them that you want to move your 401(k) assets to an IRA through a direct rollover. They will send you a form to complete. It is very important that you go through this exact process, since if you instead cash out and then try to invest the funds, you will be paying taxes on this money. A direct rollover removes any tax implications until later. You can rollover a Roth 401(k) into a Roth IRA, but you'll have to make sure you set up the appropriate account prior to doing so, which is separate from a traditional IRA needed for a regular 401(k) rollover.

- **Step 3:** Fill out the form, exactly as they instruct. Remember: DIRECT ROLLOVER is what you want. Often your current 401(k) plan administrator will make the check out directly to the brokerage firm with you listed as beneficiary with your account number – don't be alarmed, this is standard practice. Send the form back to your 401(k) administrator.

- **Step 4:** You, or the new IRA firm, will receive a check made out to the new rollover financial institution with your name somewhere on the documentation. Make sure this check is deposited into the IRA fund within 60 days. Again, MAKE SURE THIS CHECK IS DEPOSITED IN YOUR ACCOUNT WITHIN 60 DAYS. Sometimes they will send it to you, for you to give to your broker, but this is less common. If this occurs, it is your responsibility to make sure it gets into the account.

- **Step 5:** Once the funds are in your account, purchase your new funds with your asset allocation strategy.

Asset Allocation

The decisions you make to select from the many funds your 401(k) administrator or IRA makes available is called Asset Allocation. Many 401(k) subscribers who don't know what they're doing just spread the percentages evenly across all of the funds, or put it all into one or two funds with no rhyme or reason. To select more effectively, you have to first determine your big picture strategy, age, and risk tolerance and then refine your specific selection based on what sort of funds you actually have access to within your plan. An open fund

IRA at a brokerage firm has a lot more options. Regardless of the asset allocation to which you have access, the best advice for those building up a long-term retirement nest egg is to buy and hold, with a quick rebalancing. Rebalancing is the process of selling "winners" that have run up in value and reallocate – buy more – of those assets that haven't kept pace. The idea behind this is, to keep your risk management strategy in line, and this process is usually done somewhere between twice a year and every other year. This is all the time you need to spend once your strategy is in place. If you are tracking it too closely, your emotions will mess with you, making you sell at the bottom and buy at the top, neither of which are very good ideas if you want to maximize your returns. By intermittent rebalancing, you can sell marginally closer to the top and buy marginally closer to the bottom, reducing risk and increasing your long-term returns. Slow and steady wins the race.

Here are some definitions of basic investing terms I'll be using, in case they aren't readily familiar. All of these have many nuances and there is many additional investing options but I'm leaving it at a high level, keeping them at a few sentences to give basic level of understanding:

- **Stock** – a share in the ownership of a corporation that represents a claim to the corporation's assets and earnings. These can be domestic (U.S.) or international and are often referred to as "equities." By owning stock, you share in a company's growth, but this comes at a greater risk than a bond.

- **Bond** – when a corporation, municipality or government borrows money for projects or activities, they pay interest on that money borrowed by packaging up this debt up and selling it as a bond. You are the lender in this borrower/lender relationship so like a bank, you receive debt payments from those borrowing the money. This is often referred to as "fixed income" investment. Different grades of bonds exist that represent a variety of risk and return options, but usually are less risky (and less return accordingly) than a stock.

- **Commodity** – A raw material that can be bought and sold. These are often packaged together and sold in a similar manner to stocks or bonds but on a different market system. Usually they are bought and sold "on paper" since taking physical ownership is cumbersome. Examples include grains, coffee, cocoa, oil, gold, copper, and beef.

- **REIT** – Real Estate Investment Trust – a corporation or trust that uses money to buy and manage income properties (office or commercial buildings) and/or mortgage loans. REITs are often classified in the "equity" class of investment, though they behave independently of the stock market (they don't go up or down in lockstep with stocks) since they are a form of real estate.

- **TIPS** – Treasury Inflation-Protected Security. A bond issued by the treasury that eliminates or hedges against the effects of future inflation. These are considered a very low-risk investment as the U.S government backs them. TIPs area a fixed income investment.

- **Inflation** – The upward pricing movement of goods and services in the economy that erodes the value of the currency. Inflation can fluctuate wildly, but historically 2-3% per year (though it has been, in various years, as high as 23% in the U.S. and as low as zero). Inflation erodes the "real" value of investment returns.

- **Mutual Fund** – An investment that combines a large group of stocks and/or bonds together. For the purpose of this book, and to keep the confusion to a minimum, we will assume mutual funds mean a stock mutual fund, though in reality, bond mutual funds are common. By grouping individual stocks together, you reduce risk (and reward) versus owning an individual stock.

- **Index Fund** – A mutual fund that tries to replicate a tracked index of a specific financial market such as the S&P 500; fees for Index Funds are usually very low due to lack of turnover (therefor taxes are minimized), lack of trading fees passed on to the customer, and their not being actively managed. One can also find bond index funds that utilize the same principles in keeping fees low while owning a class of bonds.

- **Equity Fund** – The same as a stock fund. For the purpose of the discussion below, assume the mutual funds and index funds I'm referring to are both equity funds.

- **Active Fund** – A mutual fund that is managed by a group of investors, trying to find the best group of investments that yield the greatest return. This process entails a lot of administrative costs to research, trade, take capital gain taxes, and time the market to find undervalued funds believed to have potential to increase in value. These administrative costs are passed on to the fund owners as a percentage of their holding, and are nearly always higher than Index Funds.

- **Capital Gains** – A profit from the sale of a stock or mutual fund which is taxable. A loss from a sale of a stock can balance out or reduce positive gains for tax purposes.

- **Dividend** – a distribution of a company's earnings to shareholders (stock owners), decided on by the company's board of directors. These are returned in stocks or mutual funds, and can be "rolled over," or, reinvested in the account so you can purchase additional shares, or can simply be taken as income depending how you set your account up.

- **ETF** – Exchange Traded Fund. Similar to a mutual fund in that it combines a large group of investments, but is sold like a stock in the form of shares. ETFs can be stocks, commodities or bonds. Many track an index or style of fund such as energy or pharmaceuticals. Similar to stocks, prices change throughout the day. If a mutual fund is a pie made up of a bunch of different stocks, an ETF is a small slice of that same pie. Fees are usually low for buy and hold investors, but frequent trading of ETFs like stocks (for those day traders) increase fees and erode returns.

- **Expense Ratio** – Ratio of total expenses to net assets of a fund. Expenses include management fees and other administrative expenses, which are listed in the fund's prospectus.

- **Load Fund** – a mutual fund that levies a sales charge. Front-load means the fee is levied when buying a share, back-load means fee is charged when selling a share. AVOID ANY LOAD FUNDS!! Many private brokers and financial advisors will put these into their recommendations for you to purchase as part of your portfolio. These are fees that you have to pay, reducing what goes into your pocket to benefit your financial advisor or fund managers for managing the fund's shares.

- **No-Load Fund**- alternatively to Load Funds, a No-Load mutual fund is one that is commission free. There are many high quality funds categorized as no-load.

All investments can lose or gain value, even those designated as "low risk." If a government collapses, those securities that are backed by that government are essentially worthless. Factors such as inflation erode the value of our money, so it is critical to find investments that at least meet, or ideally beat, inflation so that our money is not worth comparatively less in the future as it is now. If you hide money in a coffee can in the backyard because you are afraid of banks or bonds, when you dig it up five years from now, its purchasing power will be less than when you buried it.

Investment classes (for simplicity, we'll break them up as two different types: "equities" and "fixed income") all have risk, but each class has different levels. Equities (stocks, stock mutual funds, REITs) have much more risk. That means that they can potentially gain or lose a lot of their value more quickly as compared to other investment types. However, with that risk comes the possibility of greater returns. Over a 50 year period, the average return of equities has been between 5 and 7 percent *above* inflation. Over any 15 year period, to date, you wouldn't lose money invested in the stock market as a whole. It doesn't mean it won't happen in the future, but the likelihood is very, very small. In the short term though, equities can be very volatile.

Some people believe that stocks today are artificially buttressed by low interest rates and the fact that many Baby Boomers are heavily invested in the market. When they sell stocks to rebalance or maintain their lifestyle, or when interest rates finally go up, some investors feel that the law of supply and demand will glut the market with equities. As supply goes up, demand goes down, along with prices, causing the stock market to fall. At a minimum, these investors feel that under that scenario there is higher likelihood that the returns of equities would be lower than historical averages over longer periods of time. I only state this to say that anything is possible with the return of investments – again, past performance is not indicative of future returns.

In any given a one year historical period, stocks have lost as much as 43% of their value and have gained as much as 54%. For similar five year periods, they've lost as much as 12% and have gained as much as 29%; and you have a 40% chance of the stock market being down in any 5-year window. For a 10 year period, they've lost up to 1% and have gained as much as 20%. If you are counting on a steady income in the short term (and depending how you define "short term"), having too many stocks is a very, very bad idea.

Stocks should further be broken down into domestic (U.S.) and international. With either U.S. or international funds you can "tilt" your portfolio to Value Stocks, Growth Stocks, Small-Cap Stocks (stocks of smaller companies that are traded in the U.S. Stock Exchange or NASDAQ), Mid-Cap Stocks or Large Cap Stocks. You can index part or all of the U.S. stock market if you desire. It is interesting to note that the largest U.S. 500 stocks (which make up the S&P 500 Index) make up 80% of the overall value of the U.S. stock index. So if given the choice of various stock funds with higher expenses in your 401(k), versus an index fund that tracks only the S&P 500 Index, if it falls into your asset allocation strategy you're probably better off with the 500 index fund as you'll still get a very broad exposure while reducing your risk and giving you weighted ownership of most of the market at lower expenses.

Many, if not most, of the larger U.S. stocks have international exposure, but true international stocks are much more heavily invested in holdings specific to international companies, international currencies, and international economic markets. While the U.S. has been very stable as a whole in the last 100+ years, anything can happen. Japan had a huge economic boom in the late 1980's, which was basically the end of a three decade long economic increase, culminating in the Japanese Nikkei Stock Index (similar to the S&P index) peak of nearly 40,000 in 1989. The bubble popped and the index crashed to under 20,000 (a 50% reduction in value) by 1992 and was under 10,000 (a 75% reduction from its 1989 peak) by 2003. As of 2013, the index is currently at around 15,000. Realize that market forces can compromise any single nation's companies and overall economy (the U.S. isn't immune from this either), so it is good to be diversified between international and domestic funds. If you want to read a contrarian view of the U.S. (and world) economy, selling essentially doomsday predictions, check out *End of the Road: How Money Becomes Worthless* – a documentary you may find on Netflix. It paints the picture that U.S. treasury bonds, which many countries invest in, are a Ponzi scheme, and that it is only a matter of time before the dollar collapses. Could this happen? Sure, it has happened to other empires and countries. Is it likely? Hard to say, but I personally feel the risk of not investing due to a potential full-scale economic collapse is foolish as well.

Coming back to today's economic climate and risk balancing in your asset allocation: there is no hard and fast rule, but the general consensus here in the U.S. is to own 20-50% of your equity portfolio in international index funds, depending on your risk tolerance, since there is a higher risk associated with international funds. Some investors decide to own zero international funds, some take nearly the opposite approach. As with anything, you have to decide your own risk/reward in terms of your portfolio balance.

Alternatively, bonds have less associated risk and often track differently than stocks. While I am not going to discuss bonds extensively, there are multiple types, all of which behave differently: High Yield, Corporate, Global, Municipal, Government, Short-Term, Intermediate-Term, International, Long-term or Junk. Note that different bonds types have different yields, different structures, and different risks. They also have different tax implications whether you hang on to them in a taxable account or tax-advantaged retirement account, or if you get taxed at the local level or not, but that's beyond the scope of this book. Like stocks, they are often grouped together and are available as both mutual funds and ETFs. In general, a broad bond fund or ETF has exposure to U.S. investment grade bonds that include a mix of corporate and U.S. government bonds of short, intermediate- and long-term issues. They usually have less theoretical and historical risk compared to stocks, and thus, less theoretical (and historic) return than do equities. They typically lose 3% of their value (sometimes less), in the worst years, and have average returns that are 3% less (and in many cases more than 3%) than equities. To illustrate this point, equities earned an average of about 10% from 1989-2008 and a U.S. aggregate bond index earned about 7% for the same period. In bull runs, they can earn much less return than stocks; and in bear times be comparable. As buy-and-hold investors, historical long-term averages are as good of a guess as any as how the two will behave comparatively. It's good to have both in your portfolio, as you'll see.

The best mix of equities and fixed income in any investment portfolio (retirement or taxable) will be based on risk tolerance, age, job security, and other investments. In general, though, most experts recommend that you increase your percentage in fixed income investments, and decrease your percentage of equities as you get closer to retirement. Basically, as you get older, you have less time to overcome a financial downturn if the shit hits the fan, so you need to reduce your risk by reducing your holding in equities. If you are a young buy-and-hold investor, you can have more substantial holdings in equities, as, even if there is a downturn in the stock market (even a long term one), you have a long time to gain that back. And historically (remember that equities have been greater than inflation by 5 to 7 percent over the last 50 years), returns have always shown that long-term investment in a broad holding of stocks will be positive. That being said, anything can happen, so even a 30 or 50 year positive return isn't guaranteed. Though if history is any indication, it's as close to a surefire bet there is in this day and age if the timeframe is long enough and the world economic structure remains.

Asset allocation strategies vary even among industry experts. *Money Magazine* did a brief article with an info graphic in its January/February 2014 Investor's Guide showing different asset allocation strategies based on age and retirement age. One allocation showed Jack Bogle's (founder of the Vanguard Group) way of "owning your age in bonds." Another allocation showed a single balanced fund approach from the start of investing to retirement age, with 60% stocks and 40% bonds for the entire duration. Additional allocations compared a couple of "Target Date" funds that automatically adjust equity-bond ratio based on the age of the investor. What is interesting about the target date funds is that they are more aggressive in the amount of stocks held than most other methods. Depending on your Target Date fund, you may hold as much as 84% in stocks as late as age 50. Compare that the Jack Bogle (who is admittedly conservative) way of holding only 50% stocks at that same age. It is really your choice as to what your allocation is, but don't blindly assume the Target Date type funds in your 401(k) package represent a level of risk you are comfortable with.

If you are a slightly more aggressive-than-average to average investor, and are psychologically OK with receiving no return (or worse, losses) in the shorter term, then I'd recommend a rule of thumb of owning your age minus 10 to 20 as a percent in fixed incomes. If you are very risk-adverse, and have a tough time mentally with seeing short- to mid-term negative returns in your portfolio, then owning your age plus 10 in fixed income (bonds) is probably a better mix. The Boglehead way of owning-your-age in bonds is generally considered conservative today, but is not a bad investing strategy for some.

While not absolutely necessary, on the equity side, adding real estate (such as REIT funds, or even self-owned rental property) will contribute to additional diversification as it does not go up or down with either bonds or stocks. On the fixed-income side, TIPS are a low risk addition to bonds that will keep pace with inflation but often return less than typical bond funds for that reduced risk. Some feel that owning stocks are inherently a hedge against inflation and feel TIPS typical modest return for that inflation hedge isn't worth it. Neither REITs nor TIPS need to be very big holdings as part of your portfolio, or even in your portfolio at all. Diversification of any type can reduce your long-term peak yield, but should soften the downturns and reduce risk, which for most is a small price to pay for the slightly reduced maximum potential.

To illustrate what an average portfolio may look like, I'll use ours as an example of a self-directed asset allocation. Our married portfolio (each age 38) looks like the following: 75% stocks, 5% REIT, 20% bonds – so we own roughly our age minus eighteen in fixed income. Of the stocks, we're about 35% international, 65% domestic. All of our holdings are currently in tax-advantaged retirement accounts and a higher percentage is outside our 401(k) (they are in our IRA accounts, both roll-over and actively deposited) and are held within ultra-low expense index mutual funds, mostly from Vanguard.

We invest entirely in mutual funds. Due to the higher risk (as well as potential reward) of owning individual stocks, mutual funds invest in a much broader group of stocks so that the risk is lower.

When choosing our actual 401(k) funds, like many, we have to pick from a less-than ideal selection. I don't have access to Vanguard funds or any other ultra-low expense fee investment options, and it's unlikely that you do either. What I do is look at my fund options and what the expense fees are. The lowest fees are usually with something like an S&P 500 index fund, which by its definition has a large group of stocks, and is designed to mimic the returns of that index. I evaluate other low fee funds and make a compromise to try and replicate the rough equity/fixed income mix I want with the lower fee accounts. Usually I have two to four individual holdings total in my or Holly's 401(k) fund mixes, with the majority made up of lower fee funds. You can also tweak your 401(k) holdings with your other IRA or investment fund holdings to get the mix of low fee funds with the diversification you desire between your different accounts. This is big-picture management of your funds. If you have weak fund options in your 401(k) and any fund option in a brokerage IRA, take the best of the worst in your 401(k) and then adjust your holdings in your IRA to meet your overall asset allocation strategy.

When assigning your asset allocation mix for newly created, or for that matter existing, IRA accounts held outside your 401k, you have a number of ways to go about it. You could simply purchase a Target Date fund, which does all the work for you at very low expense fee. For example, the Vanguard Target Retirement 2040 Fund (VFORX), has a fee percent of 0.18%, and the fund is comprised (as of 2014) of 63% total stock market index, 27% international stock market index, 8% total bond market index and 2% international bond market index. However, this may be too aggressive (or too conservative) for some investors. The advantage of a target date fund is that it automatically rebalances over time, meaning as you get closer to the target date, it will hold fewer equities and more fixed income assets. To compare, Vanguard Target Retirement 2020 Fund (VTWNX) – for those intending to retire in about 5-6 years - holds 26% fixed income (versus 10% in the 2040 Target Date fund) in roughly the same ratio between domestic and international equities and bonds as the 2040 version.

If you'd like to build your own portfolio, there are a number of other resources that are designed to perform reasonably well in most market conditions over a long time horizon. In general, they include just a few low-cost (low expense) funds that are easy to rebalance. Some examples of similar stock/bond ratio long-term "lazy portfolios," where you simply buy and hold (and rebalance occasionally) for the life of your investing career include:

- **Basic Two Fund Portfolio** – 40% Total Bond Market Index Fund, 60% Total World Stock Index Fund
- **Basic Three Fund Portfolio A** – 33% Total Bond Market Index Fund, 34% Total Stock Market Index Fund, 33% Total International Stock Index Fund
- **Basic Three Fund Portfolio B** - 40% Total Bond Market Index Fund, 40% Total Stock Market Index Fund, 20% Total International Stock Index Fund

There are other lazy portfolios with four, or more, funds giving exposure to other segments such as real estate, but you can easily see that with just a few funds, you can assemble something with very-low expenses that mirrors broad market indexes and has decent balance between long-term risk and potential gains.

One thing to note when purchasing mutual funds through an IRA or taxable account is that there is usually a minimum investment amount required to start the fund. For example, Vanguard requires a minimum $3,000 investment for an individual fund purchase. If you don't have that much to start a fund, you could meet similar allocations by purchasing individual shares of ETFs until you hit minimum levels, at which point you can sell the ETFs and buy mutual funds. Both have low fees, and in all honestly, similar returns for the buy-and-hold investor except that when purchasing smaller amounts of the pie, you'll likely incur more standard trade fees ($5-10 each at many of the discount brokerages that I mentioned earlier).

College and other Savings

After you've got your credit cards paid off, bumped up your retirement savings to 15% of your total gross income, and you've got a three to six month emergency fund (which should be based on job stability and/or other factors of risk you decide upon), you should be using that online savings account to continue siphoning funds out of your paycheck towards cash accounts – for vacation savings, Christmas gifts, car repairs, home maintenance, or other big ticket items. I don't think the online account we use even has a limit to the number of sub-account types we can have. So you may decide to drop $100 per month into vacation, $50 for the Christmas account, $100 per month into a car fund, and another $100 for home maintenance. You've saved that much from cutting cable and daily Starbucks, remember. See how easy that was? And at the same time you're saving for every day "things," you should consider saving for college for children.

Before I discuss the actual process of saving for college, I'm going to get up on my soapbox for a bit to discuss college in general, so bear with me. College right now can either be a stepping-stone to life fulfillment, or a slippery slope into a life of debt. Aaron Clarey's *Worthless: The Young Person's Indispensable Guide to Choosing the Right Major* cautions against using college as anything other than an actual vocational school. His point is that an English major isn't getting a vocation in speaking English, so people who want to actually have a job should not be majoring in areas with limited job choices. I agree that majoring in history, or the arts, or creative writing is not something that typically leads to financial viability long-term, and that you as a parent probably shouldn't support that endeavor. If your child's thirst for this type of knowledge is so strong, there are many free resources out there to give them the enrichment they so desire. Or, as another option, instead of signing up for a BA program with limited job options, there also exist very inexpensive options to enroll in not-for-credit classes, or classes at the community college. For those interested in pursuing the arts or music, building a portfolio for their graphic designs, recordings of their music, and pursuing fine arts training without paying for a degree, are all much better use of their money and are just as likely to yield job prospects.

With that said, the science, technology, engineering and math (STEM) fields still have pretty reliable long-term job prospects, prospects that can even conquer the mountain of debt while accelerating adulthood. Or you could be like many of the soft parents today, afraid of telling it like it is, and encourage young Johnny and Jill to "follow their dream." This will likely yield the unsurprising result of having your child as a long-term roommate, living in your house for the next 15 years, trying to find a job with which to pay back debt from that worthless degree. If your kids have shown strong aptitude, have a vision for education, a work ethic, and a passion, it is possible they could succeed in other endeavors. But music, women's studies, and fine arts will always face an uphill battle towards financial success in this life. This is especially true when factoring in the high cost of college today.

Other post-high school options are vocational and technical schools that teach jobs which will continually be in demand. The "hard trades" – plumbing, electrical, carpentry, controls, and mechanics – aren't going anywhere. These trades are hard work, but are specialized, and ones you can make a solid living without spending a fortune getting trained. My two brother-in-laws are electricians, and they got paid for classes to become Master Electricians while working full-time. These trades can then lead to specialty jobs such as transmission line worker or large diesel mechanic, which pay many times more than even white-collar workers in other fields. Fields such as IT, nursing, radiation therapy, or funeral services can also be fully completed, or at least started, at technical schools and can lead to higher-paying career options without a mountain of college loans.

If you do decide that little Sally and Johnny have to go to college, you had better have started saving yesterday. A number of options exist for paying for it, but the most common now is the 529 College Savings Plan. This is named after Section 529 of the Internal Revenue Code, plans which the IRS created in 1996.

Basically, it allows your college investment to increase tax free (federally) in a way similar to your 401(k), which are only tax deferred. You can select any state's 529 Plan (they all vary somewhat in terms of investment choices and fees, which we all know by now impact our returns). However, if you select your in-state 529 plan, you may be able to deduct the contribution from your state income tax return up to a certain amount, provided you meet certain qualifications, thereby increasing state money in your pocket.

In the 529 Plan, unlike some earlier designed college savings plans, you'll stay in control of the account. So if Sally doesn't want to go to college, you can reallocate those funds to other family members, like her brother, who decides he wants to go to medical school. Additionally, you can have funds automatically withdrawn from your bank accounts similarly to the other automatic savings devices. Any money you utilize in these accounts should be money above and beyond all of the other retirement and emergency funds you have going. This comes back to the original Golden Rule of Frugality. The goal is to balance a reduction in living expenses to best provide for ourselves, and give our offspring a great chance of success, while still balancing happiness of today. This is a tough task, but forgoing an extra beer at happy hour to put $10 every other week into a college account is a start. Slow and steady and step-by-step you can reach your goals, $5 and $10 at a time.

We've been very successful with "paying ourselves first" using these sneaky saving methods to allocate money to various accounts – an online emergency fund, college savings and IRA – so that it's gone before we even realize we had it. We're forced to live off a smaller amount, which forces budgeting and good financial decisions.

Attacking Other Debt

Paying off other types of loans (car, student, mortgage) may not be advantageous long-term. It depends on a number of factors including the interest rate of the loan, your job volatility, your ability to defer loan in troubled times, and the opportunity cost of paying off that loan. I'm in favor of paying off personal property like a car, RV, or boat sooner since that property depreciates fairly rapidly and you may end up underwater if you don't get it paid off (remember that being underwater is holding an asset that is not worth as much as the loan). This is very problematic if your asset gets into an accident since regardless of its worth, you owe the balance of the loan.

If you have an adequate emergency fund, your car loan is, say, at 2% interest and your car is worth roughly what your loan is, I believe you would be better off throwing more money into your retirement accounts. The historical return of stocks over 10 year rolling periods averaged 7.4% real returns (though returns ranged from -5% to +20%). It would make sense then if you were a little more aggressive, and rather than paying off your loan, to invest and potentially make a 5% return over the period of your interest note by hitting those average returns. On the flip side, if stocks go down 5% over that five year period, you would have been better off paying off your loan. Think of paying off any loan as being a risk-free return at the rate of interest of the loan. Paying off a 4% student loan early is essentially a risk-free 4% return on your money. Contrast that with a potential riskier return by investing elsewhere, such as in mutual funds within your IRA or other retirement or investment accounts. The best allocation of your funds once again comes down to risk tolerance and your personal view of debt.

Other loans such as your home mortgage (a different animal which I'll talk about later), home equity loans, and student loans do offer you some tax advantages, as you're able to write off the interest you pay and reduce your taxable income. Now it might not be much, but coupled with lower interest rates and the potential to build up my nest egg, I'm willing to take the chance of extending out those payments. Additionally, student loans (depending on the source) often offer you the opportunity to defer payments in times of financial hardship, though interest does accumulate and you will have more to pay off if you do this. Finally, if you were ever to declare bankruptcy, you will still be on the hook for student loans, so there is some incentive to get those taken care of.

I am basically taking a slightly different stance than Dave Ramsey who says to pay off all debts (except the mortgage) and then funnel money into investments or retirement. I say invest early for retirement, invest often, and deal with the debts accordingly. We were hitting 10% 401(k) contribution amounts while we were still paying off high-interest credit card debt. Tweaking how you distribute your funds toward debt reduction, retirement, and savings will ultimately be up to you. There is no right answer since no one knows how the stock market, interest rates, or income will behave in the future. But it is better to plot a course and be slightly wrong, than to not plot a course at all.

The Automobile

Besides your house, your car is likely the biggest purchase you make... again and again and again. In Thomas Stanley's book *The Millionaire Next Door*, he devotes 36 pages to buying cars and generally beats on the point that cars are depreciating assets and you're better off buying used. Author Dave Ramsey also advocates buying used. He states you should start out with a $4,000 car paid for entirely with savings, continue to save your $400 car payment and upgrade to an $8,000 car in 10 months and so forth, until you are driving what you want.

I think both Stanley and Ramsey's points are well-made, though most millionaires (two out of three) buy new cars, but they drive them awhile, that is the reason why they don't, by definition, drive "new" cars. A recent review of financially conservative Boglehead's forum took a survey of members and how long they drove cars. Nearly 50% drove them 10 to14 years. Sounds about right. A quick aside: billionaire Warren Buffett advises young people:

- Stay away from credit cards and invest in yourself.
- Money doesn't create man, it is the man who created the money.
- Live your life as simply as you can.
- Don't do what others say, listen to them, but then do what you feel is the right thing to do.
- Don't buy brand names; instead just wear those things in that make you feel comfortable.
- Don't waste your money on unnecessary things; rather spend it on those who are really in need.

Profiles of Mr. Buffett describe him as owning and driving a 6-7 year old car. We personally try to drive our vehicles at least 10 years past their "born on" date, and buy cars with good to great reliability ratings that meet our family's long term needs.

Some respected financial experts recommend only buying a vehicle worth 1/10 of your gross income, which is actually pretty good advice if you want to end up living a financially viable life. When you spend a lot on a car, the opportunity cost is the ability to dig yourself out of debt, to invest in your retirement, and to create a wealth snowball. This is, not to mention, having the additional worry about not being able to make your car payments. Now Ramsey recommends paying cash, but I'm not sure that's realistic for many people just starting out on the financially viable journey. What I will recommend is that you never take on a loan with a term longer than 3 years. That is the maximum. If you can only afford payments by extending the term to five years, you are buying too much car. I've done it. It sucks to pay for five years, though if you plan to own it for 15, it does tend to justify such a purchase. But most people simply purchase another new car after their last is paid off, so perpetually have payments. Using this three year payback (or less) method is a good starting point from which to transition to Ramsey's cash payment plan, and is far better than the financially-bleeding 5 year car purchase plan most people take. Worse yet is leasing a car. You may be able to get "more" car by doing this, but you forever have a car payment, which is very financially irresponsible if you want to be financially independent instead of just appearing to be rich.

Part of the problem that occurs is that when you finance a car for longer than 3 years, most cars depreciate at a rate faster than you're paying it off. Meaning: it is often worth less than what you owe. Your car is underwater. So what happens if your car gets totaled, and the insurance company gives a check for what your car is worth, but it still doesn't pay off the remaining car loan balance? You are left owing the difference. For example, you owe $9,000 on your car but it is only worth $6,000. If totaled you'd get at $6,000 check for the value of your car, but you still owe the bank $3,000. That sucks, and without an emergency fund of adequate size, many would be in trouble. With a shorter loan, or by getting a less expensive car (used cars usually depreciate less quickly than a new car), your loan-to-car value will be much more likely to be equivalent. When that accident does happen, you can at least pay off your loan.

Taxable Investing and Paying Off Your Mortgage

Let's say you are one of the few that are really on top of your finances, or want some long-term stretch goals for when you finally are. After maxing out 401(k) and Roth IRA tax advantaged accounts, investing in your kids' 529 accounts (or maybe they're out of school), saving for your next vehicle(s) and vacation(s), you still have money left over, you'll be deciding on how to best spend your funds. For regular people, the decision will likely be between buying taxable investments and paying down your mortgage to be totally debt free. Both have their advantages. If you have a low-interest fixed rate mortgage, you may make a better return by purchasing taxable funds in a brokerage account. On the other hand, many people feel a total feeling of elation and freedom owning their home free and clear and have no regrets from paying it off early, even at the expense of more wealth. Maybe you're more like me and can see both sides. So you to apply some more money to your mortgage payment to apply to the principal balance (accelerating the pay-off date) while at the same time investing in a tax-efficient portfolio outside of retirement accounts.

Investing does require that you take into account tax implications, which erode returns. Most of us we won't need to worry too much about this in the short-term, since funds in retirement accounts don't have too many tax ramifications from fund turnover (buying or selling), taxable gains or dividends paid. But once you take those same mutual funds, stocks or bonds out of those accounts, they are treated very differently by the IRS. As such, you have to look at your big picture and allocate investments in taxable accounts a little differently, and may need to subsequently reallocate your retirement investments to maintain the overall portfolio distribution you desire while minimizing taxes. How you manage your investing in taxable accounts will need to be managed carefully if you are looking to keep as much as possible in your pocket, and out of Uncle Sam's.

Without getting into too much detail: those funds which have a lot of turnover, have dividends that aren't reinvested, and which realize regular capital gains, almost always carry higher taxes that eat into your return. In taxable accounts, we want "tax efficient" investment offerings. These offerings can still be diverse to a large degree, and complement those other holdings that aren't tax efficient. You place those tax inefficient funds in your 401(k), 403(b), Roth IRA, SIMPLE, SEP, or whatever tax-protected account that you may have.

The hierarchy of tax efficiency – with efficient at the top and very inefficient at the bottom – ranked in order is:

1. Low yield money market, cash, short-term bond funds
2. Tax-managed stock funds
3. Large-cap and total market stock index funds
4. Balanced index funds
5. Small- or mid-cap index funds
6. Value index funds
7. Moderate-yield money market, bond funds

8. Total-market bond funds
9. Active stock funds
10. REIT funds
11. High-turnover active funds
12. High-yield corporate bonds

To clarify: with taxable accounts, you should own more or only the higher ranking items above, and few to none of those on the bottom, unless you have no other choices on diversification or fund options.

Basically, when in doubt, hold bond funds in tax-advantaged accounts and stocks (especially tax managed stock funds) in taxable accounts, and still manage both to your desired asset allocation. There are many books and articles available for those who want to learn more on this topic, or any of the topics in this section. It's worth mentioning that many other factors complicate this depending on your exact situation, including income limitations on certain accounts. I would recommend consulting a financial advisor or tax professional if you find yourself with questions that you can't answer.

...

If you take anything away of this section, understand that while finances can be very complex, for most of us, they don't have to be. If you implement the following rules, and start early (don't fret if you haven't started yet, but now is better than later), you'll end up in pretty good shape:

1. Live below your means
2. Eliminate high interest debt (CREDIT CARD DEBT IS BAD!)
3. Save early, save often
4. Diversify your investments based on your risk tolerance – you don't want all your eggs in one basket
5. Have an emergency fund to handle "real" emergencies
6. Remove lower interest debt, leaving the mortgage for last
7. Find something that gives you passion, since money isn't everything

The next step, beyond what I've laid out here, piggybacks on building a large enough nest egg to let it do the work for you. To let the interest, dividends, or rent pay you passive income where working isn't necessary and you have the freedom to pursue your passion. But that's a story for another day. My 12 Pillars and 7 items above will get you 90% of the way there. The last 10% will be on you.

Part 4: Parenting

CHAPTER 9

Parenting Today

Being a parent is hard, often unappreciated work. While parenting may not have received title billing on the cover, it is still a key component that needs to be discussed as part of this book. At its inception, most of us felt completely unqualified for something with such large ramifications on redefining family. The rewards of being a parent are immeasurable as we watch our offspring grow, learn, and experience life. While any two dummies can make a baby, being a good parent and imparting love, wisdom, and discipline doesn't come naturally for most. This, and subsequent chapters, will discuss the Cult of Child, what we can do to provide love, discipline and structure for our children, the importance of fathers, and key life perspective that will help set up your son or daughter for success in the real world.

The Cult of Child

Family roles have changed significantly from the more traditional patriarchal structure that historically existed, as I discussed earlier in this book. Instead of being husband-wife centric, most families today are child centric. Thomas De Zengotita, author of *Mediated: How the Media Shapes Our World and the Way we Live in It*, stated "No society in history has ever sanctified children the way we do." Children in my father's generation, and specifically in my father's family, were not coddled; they were used as a supplemental labor force for the family farm. They were given freedom to explore and get in trouble on the farm, but were expected to contribute to the family work, keep their mouths closed and were just a part of the overall family structure. Even my generation were allowed great freedoms in playing and activities with very limited oversight. We made it home by dinner, went back out to play until dark, with mom and dad enjoying the time without kids to work on their own projects and interests, as well as to stay on top the housework. Allowing this type of freedom to kids today is rare.

Many, many families today make most of their decisions based on what is good for the child(ren) versus what is in the best interest of the family unit. They make sure kids are in various activities, are constantly entertained by the parents or with the parents' involvement, and subsequently the children are at the top of the food chain at the expense of the parents. Parents often sacrifice exercise, date nights, hobbies, friendships and weekends for the "betterment" of the kids. This in turn sacrifices their own happiness and well-being as well as the solidarity of the marriage itself. Comfort and happiness of the kids trump anything else, meaning mom and dad clean up after them, provide them any toy, let them get away with excessive electronic device use, and center their weekend activities on the kids. How many times have you had to go to some playmate's or classmate's birthday party on a perfectly good Saturday instead of doing something more worthwhile for either yourself or the full family?

Most of us need to get back to having the kids be a role player in the family unit, supporting the bigger picture. That means allowing the kids to be temporarily unhappy or bored. That means having them do chores and help with cleaning up, cooking, cleaning, setting the table. Instead of growing entitled children, we need to be growing self-sufficient children that understand the world doesn't revolve around them. The new child-centered structure leaves children dependent on mom and dad for everything, which in turn unwittingly sacrifices life skills for alleged safety reasons and short-term happiness. This is learned helplessness that needs to be corrected on a societal basis, but since we can't fix all of society's ills, is something that can at least be addressed within our own individual families.

Being a father and a parent, I know it's easy to fall into this trap. After a long day of work, we are often too energy-zapped to want to go head-to-head with children on conflicts, teaching them life's lessons and forcing them to follow through on self-sufficient tasks...but in our family, we do this despite our fatigue. It's not easy fighting against the tide, to discipline kids or be "the bad guy", but it's the right thing to do.

As noted in the Marriage section of this book, making children the center of the family also can make the marriage take a backseat, upsetting the order of the family universe. How can a child respect mom and dad as a unit when mom and dad let them get away with anything, and subsequently the kids are the boss? Husbands resent being a secondary citizen (those men that allow this to happen anyway), and for letting the family structure get this far in the wrong direction. If your house is like that, you need to work on being a leader and reestablishing a family centric unit with you as the head. Your marriage needs this. Your kids need this. You need this. It is best for all parties, and will allow you to raise more independent kids with a good work ethic, patience and problem solving skills especially compared to their entitled peers and their compliant parents. Don't forget that kids often model their own behaviors (and future marriages) after their parents. If they don't sense that their parents' relationship is at the center of the family, your grown children will also have a hard time making their own marriage a rock that it needs to be. The rock that is key to a successful and fulfilling marriage in which to raise children.

Father versus Mother

Fathers approach raising children differently than mothers, and both approaches are needed– more so needed today than yesteryear – to counteract the feminist dominated culture that kids are inherently raised in today. Schools and teachers are designed to stifle boys' adventurous and boisterous nature, and discourage their natural roughhousing type of play. So much stress is put on test scores and achievement, that anything that gets in the way of this is discouraged and controlled. It's no wonder why girls tend to do better in this environment than boys. Mothers often are overly protective of playtime activities to ensure that little Johnny or Sally doesn't get hurt, while fathers allow much more freedom. Kids are allowed to take more risks under dad's watch, allowed to be pushed higher on the swings, and learn through their father's examples and longer leash.

Fathers tend to encourage challenging activities for both boys and girls, let the child take charge, and then allow them to proceed at their pace. Physical play is also more encouraged, including roughhousing, wrestling, running, climbing higher, and going faster. We also tend to be more lesson-oriented after failure, versus immediately providing emotional support in the case of minor injuries or children's frustration; allowing them to deal with the problem and their emotions differently than the intervening mother. While the empathetic mother is important in making kids feel good about themselves, the father's approach also has a lot of merits. Unfortunately the men's benefits are often dismissed due to the mother's "take charge" parenting style so prevalent today.

I certainly acknowledge that both styles of parenting are needed, but when the emotional, nurturing boo-boo-kissing style dominates over physical, challenging and risk-taking styles, problems can arise. Kids need discipline and structure, adventure and exploration, and when these are stifled by deferring to a more nurturing and accommodating style, certain life lessons are muted. Parents both need to be on the same page on how much freedom is allowed, acknowledge that structure and discipline are important, and be a team by not undermining the other when a parenting decision comes down. Husband and wife should talk later about the decision if there is a disagreement. Discussions of parenting stylistic differences in a reactionary way where the kids can observe is detrimental to both parents, but especially the father. A simple "we can talk about this later" will suffice if your wife wants to press the issue. Better to lose a battle on parenting with your wife later, but maintain your kids' respect now.

As a husband and father you sometimes have to fight to establish or incorporate your parenting style, especially in the case of a wife and mother who has worn the proverbial pants in the family for years. As you remake yourself into the leader, and take back a more patriarchal structure, this will become easier. Regardless of where you are in your marriage, incorporating a masculine parenting style is important for both sons and daughters.

Discipline and Structure

Pushing back on the Cult of Child is the structure I'm proposing here – Dad as the leader of the family, Mom as the second in command (Queen to dad's King) and kids far below on the ladder. This power dynamic lends itself to a solid family structure with the ability to establish routines and incorporate the much needed ability to discipline.

Lack of structure and being "buddy-buddy" with your kids is a more common problem today. Men are raised in the Sensitive Man Movement to parent more like women and to stifle their natural authority and masculinity, along with curtail discipline...to "talk it out" instead of punishing kids. That is absolutely the PC bullshit that needs to be fixed. Entitlement is much more of an issue than ever, and kids run amok over their wimpy parents. They want and need structure, authority, and discipline from birth to teenage years. Without these things, they feel a little out of control. Sometimes they don't have the strength to stand up to peer pressure, so this also provides them an "out" against poor decisions. "My dad says I can't do XYZ" lets them save face and makes you the bad guy.

Kids need to know that mom and dad are going to consistently behave in certain ways at certain times. This calms anxiety and sets their mind at ease. However, establishing and enforcing routines aren't always easy, as anyone who has tried to get a kid to bed knows. For our children, they often seem surprised every night at 8 pm that they have to get ready for bed, but they start the routine of brushing their teeth, going to the bathroom, and settling in before we come up to say goodnight.

Typical routines revolve around waking up, meals, getting ready for school, and going to bed, though you'll find many other routines you can incorporate if you desire. Homework time, chore time, reading time, and cleanup are all other good routines to reinforce. You can assign one parent, both parents, or rotate parents during the routine, but have it generally be the same each time, and at the same time of day. Set clear expectations of what part the child is supposed to play in the routine (wash your hands, set the table, get dressed before coming down for breakfast, pack your backpack, etc.). We've found a chore list with clear expectations set them to task and they like checking off the list.

Positive attention is a good way to reinforce good behavior, and should be given immediately upon completion of good behavior to make a connection between expectations and their follow-through on those expectations. A reward chart on a dry erase board, bulletin board, piece of paper, or refrigerator is a common method employed. They do something good: they get a sticker or magnet or smiley-face placed in the box. Do something bad: remove the sticker or mark. Tell them why they both get one or have one removed. After five or ten stickers, reward the child with an outing to a local park, some treat (hopefully not crappy foods), or activity that fits in your budget and acts a motivating force.

My six year old loves stuffed animals, and we let him pick one out at the thrift store for fifty-cents or a dollar as a reward for good behavior.

Kids also need discipline starting at a young age. Not just discipline, but consistent discipline. Many parents are all bark and no bite, using threats and yelling without follow-through, which in many ways is worse than no barking at all. Kids learn this quickly, and realize that they hold the power. They learn that if they just keep whining and grinding on you, you'll cave. Empty threats need to be removed from your vocabulary and replaced with discipline or loss of privileges. If you say you'll do something, follow through. That means you'll likely need to modify your threats. They know you won't leave them at the store, but if your threaten loss of television or electronic device privilege, that may get their attention. If it doesn't, at least follow through on the punishment.

One of the things we implemented into our discipline arsenal early on was the three count and the use of "The Naughty Chair," which incidentally we learned about not from a parenting book, but from the television show *Supernanny*. This is a technique for younger kids, one which we've used for years and works very well. The premise is simple; state your expectations to modify the behavior you want changed, count to three, and if the behavior hasn't changed, the child goes onto "The Naughty Chair." This doesn't have to be a chair at all, but simply a spot to cool off. We've used a designated spot in the hallway away from distractions, as well as the top of the staircase, or laundry room, or anywhere close by free from distractions.

When using this method, especially at first, the child may rebel. This is especially true when the child has been getting their way for most of their lives. You need to harden your resolve a little in the early stages of establishing discipline, since it may take a while to "break" the child. They'll get up, you simply put them back, picking them up if necessary. Don't respond to their whines, cries or tantrums, and do this wordlessly. It is unlikely that they will quit after a single round. They will test your resolve by playing this "game" until one of you finally gives in. You must not give in. You must not give the child attention when they are on the naughty chair or while moving them there. On *Supernanny*, sometimes the child would test for an hour or more. No one said instilling discipline and structure was going to be easy.

Consistency is the key to discipline. They may very well repeat poor behavior multiple times, but you need to understand that until routines and expectations are established, and then reinforced, discipline will be necessary. When they misbehave in surroundings away from home, you can still usually employ this technique by taking them to a quiet spot in a store, restaurant, or someone else's home depending where you are Yeah, you may be embarrassed. And it is not that fun to do this, but it is something that most other parents will at least understand and empathize with. A rule of thumb to employ is have them spend one minute per years of age on the naughty spot. You can use this technique through maybe 7 or 8 years old, after that, a chill-out spot like their room may need to be used to let them calm down (and for you to likely calm down too), and have them think about their actions.

Basic rules must first be established and disciplined consistently. Rules must be clear and consistent; "don't make a mess" is not as specific as "put away toys at the end of the play session." The few basic rules we have in our house are: no slamming doors, food must be eaten in the kitchen (except for special circumstances such as popcorn on movie night), treat the dog well, no jumping or walking on the furniture, no talking back, and treat parents and siblings with respect We expect some loud talking, sibling disagreements, and some minor running in the house (though we warn about getting hurt with running – love and logic – more on that later), but you may decide to make those rules for your children.

Physical discipline like spanking is a controversial topic. Both my wife and I were spanked at various times in our childhood, and it can be an effective discipline tool when incorporated without emotion and as part of a specific cause-effect discipline threat. For us, this was sort of an "In Event of Emergency Break Glass" type weapon. It has been used probably a handful of times total on each of our children when other methods didn't work. Use of it as a more frequent discipline technique is not recommended as the child may start to see this as a fear and intimidation tactic and thus, under these circumstances, can cause more harm than good. As part of a loving and caring overall relationship with your children, spanking can be an effective tool. I certainly understand alternative views to spanking, and I certainly don't advocate a paddle or other instrument. Nor do I support any other sort of hitting. But a spank on the rear with your hand may very well curb behavior and make them think twice about repeating said behavior, especially for egregious or dangerous actions.

Another effective discipline technique is grounding when the child gets to be around 7 or 8. This works especially well if there are activities they like to do, or kids they normally play with frequently in the neighborhood. Again, effective communication is key: "If this happens again, you will be grounded for X days." For example, daughter Birdsnest left her swimming suit in the pool locker room after practice. We told her if that happened again, she would be grounded on a Saturday, which meant she couldn't play outside with her friends. When she left it again at the pool, she was very upset about being unable to play with her neighborhood best friend. Since then (nearly a year later) she hasn't made the same mistake. Now Love and Logic parenting (below) disagrees that parents should ground children, instead believing that the consequences of their action will be enough to curb behavior. I contend that when used correctly, in addition to allowing the other consequences to happen (in the swimming suit case, having to purchase a new suit with her money if it couldn't have been found), grounding has the intended effect in accelerating learning.

Parenting with Love and Logic

Holly and I want our kids to grow up and make sound decisions on their own, eventually graduating to being capable and productive teenagers and adults who can take care of themselves. This requires letting go to a large degree, unlike helicopter parenting where the parents protect the child from making mistakes by making all the decisions for them. These types of parents, who dive in and fight back against teachers (or coaches or anyone else who may have "harmed" little Johnny's ego or didn't give him the highest marks), are doing their children a great disservice by not letting them make mistakes at all. Another poor parenting technique is drill sergeant parenting where the parent (usually the dad) dictate all decisions to the child, and are often very critical of their child's ability to complete the tasks properly. A better parenting approach is to allow children to make small decisions. Then larger and larger ones, subsequently allowing them to make mistakes in the same scale as well. This allows the child to see the ramifications of their decisions, and thereby learn from their mistakes. Parents who coddle and protect their children (helicopters), or make all the decisions for them (drill sergeants), don't allow them to make these valuable life lessons.

These are some of the key concepts in *Parenting with Love and Logic*, by Jim Fay and Foster Cline. While I don't agree with some of their hardline, passive aggressive approaches they state in their books (which I think would breed anger and abandonment in some of the situations they site), if you curtail it to your own beliefs while still giving freedom of choice to your kids, you'll be much better than the typical helicopter or drill sergeant parent. Let the child stretch that rubber band of life experience in a safe and effective way, using clear communication and potential consequences of their actions drive their decisions. Let them succeed or fail on their own and not because of your interference. However, notice I said "safe." In some areas we need to especially keep an eye on them where they could come to dangerous, physical harm by their actions.

We employ these very concepts with our kids, and here are some real examples. LoudBoy didn't want to eat dinner, or eat it to completion. Holly and I note that he may be hungry later but that is his choice. The result is that he's hungry later, and has to learn from his decision as he goes to bed whining about how hungry he is. Birdsnest loses her new, nice winter gloves at school. She's advised that she should check lost and found, and if she can't find them at home or at school, she'll have to spend her own money on another pair, approximately $15. "But I only have $20 saved!" she says, to which we respond with empathy ("That must really suck!"). We are hoping that this natural consequence will be that next time she'll take better care of her items. Things like letting the kids dress themselves, including deciding on outdoor gear, is common in our house. We'll make recommendations on modifications to their choices based on weather, but ultimately they have to live with their decisions. There have been sometimes they've regretted their decisions, being way to cold or hot for the environment. Bummer.

The key to this Love and Logic approach is choice, and not get into telling them what to do, which turns into a power struggle. Instead, you give them two choices that you can live with. Perhaps you have issues with bedtime since they don't want to settle in or go to sleep, which was an issue with us. The kids would test us, and argue and whine. It seemed like a battle every night. Eventually, our expectations were laid out, giving them the power of choice. We told them that mom and dad needed time alone, beginning at about 8:15 pm. They were expected to brush their teeth and get in bad at 8:00 pm, at which point we would say goodnight. The only expectation then after that was they were to stay in their rooms, and we would wake them up every morning at 6:15 am to get ready for school. If they stayed up late, they would have to live with their consequences of being tired, which has happened more than a few times and they are always struggling the next day. Most nights though, they may stay up a little while reading a book, but then put themselves to bed. As a result of this good choice, most mornings the kids are pretty awake and chirpy.

When they do make poor choices, you allow them to live with those decisions. And when they do, give them empathy. "That must really suck that you didn't get your homework done. What are you going to do about it?" Or, "That's a real bummer that you don't have any clean clothes because you forgot to do your laundry." Without saying "I told you so," since you've already alluded to them that their choice and subsequent adverse result was entirely their doing.

Finally, you don't always have to dole out consequences immediately. If they are being defiant, you can state "I'm sorry you feel that way. That gives me a lot to think about. I'm going to have to get back to you about what I think needs to happen next." When they then ask for some act of service, or for you to take them somewhere, or for some privilege, you can coolly bring up their actions from previously and state that you won't give them what they want since their behavior was inappropriate before. Sure they'll whine, beg and plead, but stick to your guns. It will hurt you inside you too that they can't go to their friend Billy's birthday party, but these are very valuable lessons. Plus Billy already has too many toys, won't miss your child's presence and kids' birthday parties suck anyway (for adults at least).

This is the parenting approach I recommend; expand their decision making menu as they get older. This includes expanding their money making decisions as well. I'm not a fan of the concept of an allowance, but instead incorporate a commission for services performed. Now these services aren't hard, but are things like: clean room on Sunday, put away your laundry, empty your room's and bathroom's trash cans, and organize the shoe rack on a weekly basis. If they do those things, they get a commission, if not then no money. It's ultimately their choice. Additionally, the chore list changes as they get older. The older child is now responsible for doing her own laundry as part of her list. It is really not that hard to take the laundry from your room, load the washer, throw in a wash tab, hit start, and then transfer the wet clothes and turn on the dryer.

Hard work is one of the foundations of successful life, and if you don't promote the drudgery of chores, even minor ones, early on, you are doing your child a disservice later in life. How many of us knew college friends who didn't have any clue on how to do laundry? How many had grown-up friends who had no concept of work and was enabled throughout their life by their parents, only to have the harsh realization upon that first real job? How many pigsties have you been in as a young adult (or maybe even older adult) with people who were used to mom or dad picking up after them?

We love our kids, we want them to succeed, but to do so they must think things through themselves and learn by making their own mistakes. They must be given the tools to succeed by encouraging them to think critically and take personal responsibility. Providing parental structure, discipline and life learning opportunities all contribute to the type of child and adult we'd like to raise and will help as they transition from child to teen to adult.

CHAPTER 10

Fathering at Different Ages

Ⓗ ow we behave as fathers need to change as our kids grow older. You don't discipline a 5 year old the same way as a 15 year old. However, involvement as a father is important from birth to adulthood. From J.S. Wallerstein and S. Blakeslee's *The Good Marriage: How and Why Love Lasts*:

> "Children with sensitive, involved fathers surge ahead in their cognitive and social development as they explore their environment and play with other children."

Contrast that with children from absent fathers that have five times the average suicide rate, increased depression, increased incarceration and school dropout rates, lower average income, increased substance abuse and increased divorced rates. Fathers provide the masculine definition for their sons and daughters. If not present, children must overcome this huge gap and may spend a lifetime compensating for their absence. The old stripper adage of "daddy issues" isn't far from the mark. Without an involved and present father, daughters are much more likely to try and get this masculine attention as older teens or young adults through sexual behavior if they don't have other alternatives. I'd say fathering is pretty important to your kids' lives, and the needs change over the years. What doesn't changes are the key values that we provide: presence, involvement, love, discipline, authority, structure.

230 • PART 4: PARENTING

Age 0-2: Infants/toddlers

While often the least enjoyable phase for many fathers, it is an important one. It is critical for a number of reasons, not the first of which is that raising a baby is really hard and you need to support your wife in this endeavor or she will resent your lack of involvement. A Northwestern University study has shown that testosterone drops significantly in men following the birth of a child, and hypothesizes this is the impact of raised bonding hormones such as Oxytocin, which the mother also experiences. During this time, do not let your wife dictate your involvement (or lack thereof) with your child and make sure you have one-on-one time with your child for both your sakes. Skin-to-skin contact, feedings, bathing, even diaper changes are all things you should help with and take over from your wife at least some of the time for the purpose of bonding between you and your new child. Not to mention it can provide a level of relief to your wife. Insist on doing this even if she's apprehensive. She's likely exhausted and could use a break.

It is easy to begin the downward slide of letting your wife slowly start to take charge of the baby, and placing you in a supplementary position. Be cognizant that this is happening and don't let it get too far. Recognize that your testosterone may have dropped and do something about that as well. Be supportive, but still a leader with your wife, while at the same time recognizing her attention will be more focused on the baby (rightfully so) and not your relationship.

Newborn and early toddler years are some of the most trying in a marital relationship as you figure out your newly defined roles. The goal is to simply get through this time with your child in a healthy manner with successful stimulation, love and affection while at the same time maintaining a healthy spousal relationship. Most kids will be more mom-centric, so you must fight for dad-time and learn your own way of feeding them, clothing them, bathing them, diapering them, and playing with them. Your wife will likely challenge how you do things, insisting you do things her way, but you need to stand tall sometimes and tell her that just because your way is different it doesn't make it incorrect. Again these are minor tests on your fitness as a father and provider. Choose your battles judicially, but don't indiscriminately defer to her on all things child rearing. You may not have the natural instincts to parent well, and may often allow her to make many of the child decisions, but at least have an opinion more than "I don't care" when it comes to your child.

Take care of bottle feeding the baby and be an active participant in child rearing. It takes the baby about three months to attach to an adult caregiver. That is, whoever plays a large role in crying feeding and general caretaking. Attachment behaviors include handholding, skin-on-skin contact, eye contact, and being held, which all engage biological attachment mechanisms and reinforce the bond. According to the Jeffrey Rosenberg 2006 article *The importance of fathers in healthy development of children*: "A number of studies suggest that fathers who are involved, nurturing and playful with their infants have children with higher IQs, as well as better linguistic and cognitive capacities." Involved fathers of six-month to two year olds also result in higher scores of motor development.

Just because babies, even your own, make you uncomfortable doesn't mean you should check out and defer this area to your wife. Going down that road is a slippery slope that makes recovering from time consuming and difficult. Despite your lack of confidence in diapering or comforting, it behooves men to continue to make efforts and find a way that works for them. These are the first steps in building that bond, and one that, unfortunately, many men don't even realize.

Ages 3-5: Preschool Years

This is the years where thing start to get a little less difficult on the dependency side, but are more difficult in that the child is now gaining independency as they explore and get into trouble. I always thought the so-called Terrible Twos weren't that bad, but once they got moving and talking for real, look out! Instead of crying, it's crying *and* whining. They learn to talk, talk back, and argue. It's a never ending debate with them to go to the bathroom in the toilet, to put the food in their mouth, to stop eating that, to stop putting that *thing* in that *place* (fork/electrical socket, finger/dog's butt, crayon/nose, I'm sure you have some good ones too). You replace total exhaustion from infant/toddler years with mere tiredness, but mix in the need for tremendous patience, resolve and willpower to make it through this time in a positive mindset toward your child and your spouse. These past few sentences don't do justice this time in a parents' lives, but at least gives basic credit to the difficult though rewarding time we go through. Pure and intense joy as they discover things that you and I take for granted, coupled with the low-lows of a complete meltdown at a store in front of what seems like a million judging eyes. Chasing after toddlers and preschoolers does keep us younger in seeing things in a new way, though also ages us faster than expected at the same time. You likely go from young parent to grizzled veteran in short order. Your growth as a person is accelerated, and even if immature when having the baby, you quickly grow up.

These years are still pretty expensive if you choose outside childcare. The good news is that once potty trained most places reduce your costs and may give you some breathing room on the financial side. The Preschool years are also way more fun as a father compared to the earlier infant/toddler years. Kids are exploring their world and aren't so mom-centric, willing to interact and have dad be much more part of their daily routine. They begin to realize mom and dad play differently, with fathers willing to give them more freedom to explore, and allow them the opportunity to try more things. I let my kids have a pretty long leash on the playground, help them go higher, or faster, or play in ways that begin to show them the extents of the world. I've let them have much more freedom with the poker stick near the campfire (still supervised), let them get skinned knees on big wheels, and in general encourage them to try new things. Sure, like their mom, I've told them to stop climbing or grabbed them if I felt there was danger, but I'm also very encouraging in the development of gross motor skills, showing the boy how to hold his penis when he pees, how dad likes to roughhouse as a form of love, and in general, embracing more physical play is a big part of these years.

Additionally, these are the years where discipline and letting them make decisions start to happen and they go hand in hand. Timeouts in the naughty spot (one minute per year), establishing routines for bedtime, learning to brush their teeth and wipe their butt are all things that need to be drilled in at this age. When, what I call, the Wonder Years (5-11) begin, a lot of the structural patterns are already in place and you've already been playing the dad role and establishing your own relationship with them.

Ages 5-11: The Wonder Years

These are the Wonder Years (no, not the television show with Fred Savage), a term which I first heard from fathering author Armin Brott, and I (personally) have also used the term Golden Years of child rearing. Both seem to describe this wonderful window of time when the kids are finally fairly self-sufficient, going to school, very malleable to parental suggestion and influence, while at the same time establishing their own identity, and still open to snuggling with Mom or Dad. They are curious, loud, often boisterous with energy, and really open to most things. Learning new things in school then carries over to home, and they start to develop passions, interests and goals. Their built-in personality, which maybe you started to notice at the preschool age, really starts to blossom. You'll start to notice introversion, extroversion, thinking methods (more artistic or more logical), and whether they are more of a regimented rule follower or more of a free-spirit. We're in this phase right now and it really is a glorious time. Gone are diapers, total necessity on mom and dad for entertainment, but willingness and desire to be part of Mom and Dad's world.

So what does a father need to do in this great window? In general, give the kids a rock to depend on and introduce them to as many things as possible. Then just stay out of their way. If you don't fuck up too bad, the kids will most likely turn out good. Be consistent with lessons, discipline and structure. Let their waves of emotions wash over you, and give them an even longer leash to make choices and mistakes. Make sure you are spending time with them nearly every day if you can. Teach them to throw a ball, shoot a jump shot, give them tips on ice skating, take them sledding (northern climates), introduce skee ball. The world is a really great place with many fun and exciting and cool things to see that they never have before. Take them to the local fair to ride the rides and see some demolition derby action. Local museums have a lot of cool things, and many even have free admissions sometime. Essentially, be active and present in your kids' lives.

This age they still try to emulate you and model their behavior after yours. If your idea of a good time on a Sunday is kicking back with a six pack and watching a double-header of NFL, then that's something they'll equate with Sunday afternoons in the fall. While every day and every weekend doesn't have to be a lesson, or an introduction to something new, at least continue to listen and draw out their stories about their day. Basically be a steady influence as a parent in their life. These regular, everyday moments sometimes turn into amazing teaching opportunities. Random questions on life, on who we are as people, on what life is like, divorce, death, and babies. They talk to their friends a lot about what happens in their individual lives, so their world view and input into their brains is more expansive than what we may believe.

These are the years to assist them in building general life skills as well. Besides supporting their efforts in school on reading, writing, and math, introduce them further into music if you get the opportunity, or into computers. Our daughter has started to expand from what music her friends listen to (like One Direction) into other musical genres. We find her listening to The Beatles, or other music CDs that we have in our collection, while at the same time she is learning music from piano lessons. She is also been doing some graphic projects on Microsoft Word and it probably won't be long until she's doing Photoshop as well. I was doing basic computer programming in fourth grade and think these extra-curricular activities introduced by Mom and Dad, or supported by Mom and Dad through after-school or summer-school programs, are important for building skills that support further interests and education later in life.

Sports are important as well, and most parents use this age as an introduction. Swimming is both a life skill and a sport, and is one I recommend if it works for your location and budget. Other ball sports help to facilitate gross motor skills, and with the importance of sports as part of adolescence, it is important to at least introduce your children to throwing a ball or dribbling, lest they be the outcast on the playground or in gym class. Organized sports instill great life lessons: following rules, gaining self-confidence with abilities, sportsmanship, perseverance and working as part of a team are foundational. At the end of the day, sports are supposed to be fun.

A word of caution though: many parents take sports way too far and push their kids to excel in just one area way too young. As a result they often push the fun out of the sport. They often live vicariously through their children's exploits and coaches, even at these young ages, worry way too much about winning or being on early traveling teams. Alternatively, taking out scoring from games, and the "everyone is a winner" mentality takes it too far in the other direction. Kids need to learn how to deal with, and process, their emotions when things don't go their way, despite their best efforts. What they don't need is mom or dad harping on them or asking them excessive questions about the sporting event or practice making sure they are "ok," or giving them lectures on what to do better. One study I read stated the number one reason kids quit sports is because they didn't like the car ride home after practice, the game, or competition. More than that, many said they *hated* the car ride home. Sports psychologists say that it is often better to say nothing after a sporting event or practice, and let them bring up the topic. If you must critique, use the sandwich approach – start with a complement or positive affirmation, sandwich in the critique or what they did wrong or could improve on, and finish with another positive affirmation. Instead of critiquing or replaying sport events, the better approach would be to simply say "I LOVE watching you play/practice!" Praise their hard work and not the result; this goes to schoolwork as well.

If you are like us, you may have a child who is more into passive activities at home such as Legos, video games, or reading. Given his own choice, our son wouldn't do any organized activities and instead would spend his time playing with his friends or doing videogames. That's not acceptable either, and even casual sports activities are encouraged, like baseball or soccer pickup games with the neighbors. A Canadian study showed that 81% of kids aged 6-9 were involved in organized extracurricular activities, with a vast majority involved in sports. Those numbers went up as the kids got older too. While we don't really care what our son or daughter wants to do, we feel he should be doing *something*, and if he doesn't choose, then we will. Playing videogames as a standalone activity is fine, but if that is your only activity or hobby, we have a problem. We've suggested to our son options like Cub Scouts, soccer, music lessons, football, wrestling, and other clubs or community groups. Thus far, he's been involved on swim team and in piano lessons, but still hasn't found what he's passionate about so he'll keep trying new things academic, community, and athletic until he finds what fits.

While my wife and I both believe in expanding horizons through organized activities, excessive scheduling is something to really avoid as well. It can be hard running multiple kids around to various activities each evening and on the weekends, so compounding that with multiple activities for each kid is something I just can't support. We believe in a well-rounded and happy life experience, and excessive scheduling is stressful on both kids and parents. Child Psychiatrist Alvin Rosenfeld M.D., author of *The Over-Scheduled Child: Avoiding the Hyper-Parenting Trap*, believes this widespread phenomenon places way too much pressure on kids to achieve to the detriment of childhood "fun." So instead of being allowed to be creative in their down time, and explore their world in their own way, many parents' good intentions stretch the kids thin and place them in a state of constant exhaustion and stress. I remember only being involved in a

236 • PART 4: PARENTING

few organized activities as a child, and my brothers and I explored our rural environment and made up our own games and excitement. Our family ate dinner together every night, and often explored local nature areas, learned to play sports, or did other family friendly activities on the weekends. This unstructured routine introduced us to a lot of new ideas and experiences. As a result, my childhood never felt like "work" that so many kids today must feel.

Being actively involved in our kids' daily life is really important, but we must also take the time to create memories that are outside the normal day-to-day existence. Obviously vacations are one of those opportunities, but think outside the box here. If you typically spend most of your family time as an entire family unit, you should consider breaking off with an individual child for a day or weekend. Having one-on-one dad attention is pretty rare for children from two-parent families, and maybe even more so if you have a multiple kids or are divorced. Taking one child away and do something fun with them, and them alone, leaves a lasting impression with children. It doesn't even have to be anything super extravagant. Watching a minor league baseball game, or going to the zoo and getting ice cream after, or taking them hiking on a local trail (with ice cream after), all gives you the chance to establish that lifelong relationship with your son and daughter. The younger they are when you start these activities the deeper the relationship can be. It's much harder, though certainly not impossible, to establish these relationships with teens after years of neglecting this type of thing, so start this year on these things.

I'd really also encourage those with sons to establish a "guys' weekend" with your son, and maybe your other friends and their sons. We started this when my son was about five years old, and got away from the moms and sisters for a couple of nights. While we usually camp out somewhere, we don't always do that and have gone to amusement parks or done other activities. These are male bonding moments that we can start to counteract the woman culture they are indoctrinated in. As we get older and my son matures, I will be keeping this tradition alive and allowing him to help plan these activities. The goal is to have a strong, loving, and trusting bond with my son and to be able to build a masculine relationship where we can share life lessons with each other for the rest of our lives.

Establishing relationships with our daughters at a young age is also important. As a father, you are the role model for how she'll view and interact with men in her later teen, and then, adult years. Behaving morally, being strong in the face of small or large crisis, working hard, being present, and giving positive feedback are all things that will help to shape how she views the opposite sex. The benchmark for future boyfriends, or a husband, will be as high or as low as you make it. If you are slothenly, fat, and boring with no friends or hobbies, and allow your wife to boss you around, that bar is pretty low. If you aren't around much, or don't have a great relationship with her, she won't even have a male compass to compare to when she begins dating. You may not think these things matter when she's 9 or 10, but most of our ills and disorders do come back to deep rooted issues from when we are kids. Therefore, it's important to take your daughter on father-daughter trips as well, showing her how men act without having to compromise for the wife or rest of the family unit.

Take out disorder, disharmony and dysfunction within your home and family unit. In doing so you're more likely to have sons and daughters that grow up to be morally sound and mentally strong individuals with fewer emotional and personal issues.

Pre-Teens and Teens

I haven't raised a preteen or teen at this stage of my life, and but have some ideas on what that is going to be like. The hormones, the confrontation, the growth as a person. Essentially, at this stage you need to start instilling life's realities into their thoughts. How you do that is up to you. Another thing you need to be aware of is the impact of pornography on young people, especially boys.

Pornography and the Teen Brain

I discussed briefly the impact of porn on marriage, but for boys whose brains are still developing, porn is more powerful by orders of magnitude. Ted Talks stated that boys as young as 10 years old (one in three have seen porn by this age) have started to watch porn. This means by age 11 at the latest you need to start keeping a close eye and monitoring the computer and tablets to minimize the chance of this happening in your house. Four in five 14 to 15 year olds admit to regularly accessing explicit images online. Seeing sex at that age is novel and exciting and will usually lead to more watching due to simple curiosity. With the proliferation of laptops, tablets and smart phones, boys (really anyone) have instantaneous free access to high-speed porn at any time they want. What happens with forming brains is they get rewired through a vicious feedback loop with masturbation playing a key role as well. They watch porn, they orgasm and get a big hit of dopamine, so they think about and watch porn more. The dopamine response dulls with constant use, like with other drugs. The ability of regular porn to excite them and elicit the same dopamine response is lowered. They need more excitement to trigger the response, hence you see then search out more alternative and novel types of sex scenes. Inevitably, reality seems boring by comparison and real-life sex with real-life people can be problematic for the teenager who's a serial porn watcher. Sexual issues like premature ejaculation, or even more common, sexual dysfunction where they can't get or maintain an erection for a real person, is being seen extensively in young men today.

Their brain wires up 11 or 12 billion new neural connections related to sexual association, and after continued watching, this serial porn watching brain prunes neural circuitry to leave him a manageable assortment of choices. So essentially your son trains his brain to get excited at porn, and real life can't compare. The website www.yourbrainonporn.com has a lot of resources to educate you or give you resources to talk to your teen. Don't be in the dark on these issues facing young men today, and get out in front of this topic with them.

Building Life Skills

Besides continuing to provide structure, love and discipline to your pre-teen and teen, you also need to encourage them to continue to learn and develop skills. I highly recommend having them be in an extracurricular activity most of the year. While sports are good, it doesn't have to be sports and kids this age have a lot more options. Music, boy scouts, chess club, debate team, whatever. As long as this activity requires regular meetings/practices, and the need to work hard at accomplishing whatever the goals are for the activity are emphasized, I don't think you can go wrong. Allowing your teen or pre-teen to not do anything but play video games or watching television is a recipe for a lazy grownup, even if they do well at school.

Spend Time

Continue those traditions you've established in the Wonder Years to spend one-on-one time with each child. Maybe you can't find time to spend entire weekend with them anymore, but continuing to make each child feel special and to devote the time and effort to getting to know them better will yield some long-term memories in life. For young women, modeling how a man should be will forever be the example that she holds to when comparing potential suitors.

Rites of Passage

If you have sons, I also strongly encourage you to perform some sort of rite of passage into manhood as he gets in his late teens. While these are nearly extinct in today's modern world, other cultures and societies still utilize this initiation of boyhood to manhood. A rite of passage has three main phases according to sociologists: separation, transition and re-incorporation. The first phase is intended to separate him in some way from his current/former life. During the transition phase, he is taught the knowledge he will need to become a full-fledged adult member of society. Often, this second phase has some sort of ceremony or trial associated with it. Re-incorporation then re-introduces the new adult member back into his community, often with some sort of celebration.

When, and how formal or informal you want to make this rite of passage, is entirely up to you. I believe a good time would be following his graduation from high school or near age 18 when they are legally an adult. Some that I've heard about from peers and mentors have included father-son backpacking or canoe trips, or introduction into the man's hunting camp as a full-fledged member of the group. If other men are involved in the experience, I encourage you to invite them to spend some individual time with your son as well, providing him with advice on what it takes to be a man. One rite of passage I've read about that I may replicate, is a walk through the woods. If my father and father-in-law are still around, I plan to take my son on a short hike through my father-in-law's wooded property. At certain points on the walk, uncles and grandfathers would be waiting to meet up and offer guidance and advice, culminating with everyone meeting back up, grilling and sharing in a bonding environment with the men of our family. How you do this is up to you, but again, set yourself apart from the average dad and average man, and provide a powerful life experience to your soon-to-be man.

Dads and Daughters

For dads, understanding daughters will be a much harder time. We haven't been through the experience, but we can still provide guidance. First, understand that seeing a daughter, your baby, grow up into a woman is incredibly difficult. I expect to feel jealousy and confusion as she starts to break free of the childhood ways and embrace teenage years. Being consistently in their lives and providing an example of moral fortitude, leadership and unraveling how boys their age are thinking or acting are probably the most important roles we'll play as fathers during these years. As they are growing into women, they are taking in societal examples and family examples of how women and men are to behave toward one another and are figuring out their own hormones and sexuality. For a father, it must feel very foreign on how to act.

Fathers sometimes pull back from their daughters as their bodies begin developing. This can be confusing to them, especially if you used to be a hands-on, loving dad who rough housed and are now meek and hands-off. They may read too much into this and equate your lack of touch and affection with lack of love. Transitioning from girl to woman is confusing enough, so don't make it any more confusing by changing your behavior extensively. Be sure to talk about these topics with your daughter, no matter how uncomfortable with them you are.

Something else that most men don't really consider is the pressure girls feel in trying to fit in. Eating disorders are very common in teen girls as many struggle to fit in to society's vision of what is beautiful. Being aware of this fact can help identify red flags before they become serious. It begins with poor body image and insecurity. This can then manifest itself into excessive exercise, self-conscious eating patterns (rarely eating in front of others, or eating small amounts), malnutrition (fuzz or hair growth, lowered body fat, dry or blotchy skin) and weird eating rituals with such as always going to the bathroom right after eating (the purge cycle). Daughters who suffer from these afflictions need to get professional help, as they are classified as a mental or psychological disorder.

While I have a daughter of my own, I feel extremely unqualified to write much more on this subject. I envision my own daughter, a few years from now, spreading her wings and growing up in society today and it scares me. My father-in-law was literally one of those fathers cleaning his guns on the kitchen tables when boyfriends came over. We need to protect our little girls from themselves and from some poor decisions, but they need to learn about life in their own way. That's a tough balancing act to know when to actively throw your weight in as a father versus being an outside observer and letting her learn the hard lessons on her own. Like when you know she's seeing a shithead before she does. All you can do is try to keep her aware of what boys are like at that age, what the ramifications are of poor decisions, and hope they listen enough so they aren't the next episode of "Teen Mom" or "Teen Intervention." An involved leader of a father makes the likelihood of these adverse conclusions much less. Sure, I expect she'll frustrate you and you'd wish she'd move out at times, but be the rock for which she comes back to after all the mistakes she'll made. That's all we can do as fathers of daughters.

Love and Logic with Teens

If you've taken the time to raise your kids in Love and Logic style while the kids were younger, and they've grown up with good structure and life ideals, you'll have a hard time messing up your teens as they transition to adults. Sure, you'll have conflict and they may get into trouble, but avoid bailing them out and let them live with their consequences. The teen version of *Love and Logic* book has a number of real face-palm examples, but is still full of great situations they discuss that will at least get you thinking about how you'll deal with things like drugs, sex, driving, poor work ethic or grades and bad friends that are likely to happen in your life.

Real (Red Pill) World Wisdom

With those base building blocks as a backdrop, the only other thoughts I have on raising a preteen to teenage children is to begin to impart in him or her real-world wisdom that you yourself may still be wrapping your head around. Like some parts of this book, some of these teachings go against the feminist thoughts and typical nice- or sensitive-guy teachings that are so prevalent in our society today. Now, being able to speak frankly with your kids on these subjects will likely be difficult, so taking a softer or less direct route to these lessons may be a better idea. I think these teachings must be passed on to our youth to continue to work towards changing the culture that many find themselves in as adults. Simply put, many on the doorstep of adulthood don't have the ability or tenacity to deal with failure or disappointment or are missing basic life skills or understanding to really succeed once they are out of the nest.

Without further ado, here are some of the lessons I plan to impart on my kids when they get older. In your own way, I feel it would be a good idea to impart or apply these concepts to teaching your teen or young adult, depending on your situation as well. Keep in mind, these are mature topics and how you or I pass these messages on may not be as strong or as straightforward as I note below, but the message themselves are valuable. If you understand and believe these concepts yourselves, passing them on to your kids will come naturally. These are not easy conversations to have, but valuable ones:

1. You will fail. How you bounce back will define you as a person. Are you a fighter, or are you quitter? If you are a fighter, and work hard after failure, you will have success in life.

2. In life, success is determined more by hard work than anything else. It's called grit, look it up. A work ethic and drive to succeed will overcome lack of ability in many cases. It may mean you're working and going to school at the same time, or working a couple of jobs to set the table for your life. This hard work and taking the time to do your best at every task, work or leisure activity, is one of the cornerstones of a successful approach to life.

3. Eating well and exercising growing up will carry over to adulthood. Don't underestimate the importance of looking good. You'll have more self-confidence, be healthier, sleep better, be able to enjoy more recreational activities, and be able to attract a better looking partner. The so-called "sacrifice" necessary to eat well and exercise yield tangible benefits that cannot be underestimated. In college, don't fall into the trap of the "Freshman 15 (pounds)," and continue to carry these good habits into young adulthood. Curb the alcoholic beverage drinking to limit the empty calories and prevent getting fat, a trap that so many college-aged kids and young adults fall into.

4. Gender teachings – *for my son*: don't believe the "nice guy" myth, that people will like you simply because you are nice. This is a covert contract (you do something and you think people should behave a certain way just because of your actions, without discussion of what the cause-effect is). Example: you help a girl with her homework, expecting her to be attracted to you because of your contribution. Usually, you get put in the Friendzone with these types of actions. You are better off treating girls like your sister, teasing them and being funny around them. Every dude is going to be placing attention on the girl of your affection, raising up her self-esteem, but only if you tease her mind, make her laugh, and set yourself from the pack will she even notice you. It's extremely intimidating and scary to put yourself out there, but unless you do, you'll never get anywhere with girls or women. Take the bull by the horns and ask her out. Ask her to do something just you and her. Being overt about your expectations to both girls and guys sets you apart from the rest of the pack and commands respect. If you get shot down, it may hurt, but don't keep wasting time on that girl. Learn from the experience and move on to the next girl. There are many, many fish in the sea, and if one that says "no" the first time, she likely won't say "yes" after that, so stop pining over lost causes.

    For my daughter: being pretty and nice, but respecting yourself and having values that hold in the face of social and sexual pressure, will help you best in the future. You are an attractive girl and will be a beautiful woman with lots of options. Don't make the mistake of chasing after the loser or "player" because they are funny or hot. Choose quality traits, and don't discount the strong silent type or other nice boys/men. As you get older, realize that having long hair and dressing in a feminine way is much more attractive to boys/men than short hair and being comfortably sloppy, despite what your girlfriends say or what the trend is. Instead of the typical self-centered woman of today, be nurturing, supportive, responsible, respectful, and honest in what you want and who you're with. Beware of societal pressures that encourage women to be sluts and put off marriage until later.

You are a super intelligent person, so don't let gender limitations railroad you into gender-defined jobs unless that is your passion. Choose to challenge yourself and don't be afraid to be the smart or brainy girl. Chances are, if you get a smart-person's job, you'll be hanging out with smart and capable potential partners. Don't become married to your job at the expense of a potential family. Family and kids of your own, along with a spouse who you love (and who leads), is the core of what life enjoyment is about, not your job. It's a tough balancing act in today's world for women, but if I had any advice for your adult self, it is to prioritize your family and your future husband at the expense of any job you may have.

5. Social media can be a powerful tool when used properly, but can really adversely impact your life forever if used incorrectly. Digital copies of anything you put on there for public consumption can be there forever. So can things sent privately to individuals. Just because you trust your boyfriend or girlfriend now to keep private things private, all it takes is one thing to piss them off and the whole world can see it. That includes drinking, drugs, and sexual images. Ask yourself "would I be OK with a teacher, parent, or future employer seeing this image?" And keep in mind, if you aren't yet 18, sending, receiving or keeping naked pictures of you, your boyfriend or girlfriend, or any other image of people you may or may not know, could be considered distribution of child pornography. Don't make a dumb decision as a teenager due to peer pressure ("everyone else is doing it") or pressure from your young relationship ("she asked me to send her a naked shot") that can result in you being listed on a sexual offender registry. EVERYTHING ON SOCIAL MEDIA CAN BE PUBLIC FOREVER, MAKE SMART DECISIONS.

6. Financial responsibility, financial planning – you need to know how to balance a checkbook, how to budget, how to save, how to be frugal and say no, and eventually, how to invest in your company's 401(k) or other retirement plan available to you if you have one.

   Being poor starting out is acceptable. Your mom and I have worked a lifetime to accumulate our status and house and furnishings, which we've shared with you for the last 18 years. You need to set their sights lower when starting out, just like we did at your age. For example: when your mom and I moved out to our first jobs after college, we found free curb couches, had a 13" television, slept on an air mattress, furniture consisted of camp chairs, and I drove a $2,000 10 year old car for my first vehicle. When you're starting out you can't try to capture what you had while living at our house. Having a nice television, appliances, furniture or cars is not realistic and you need to understand that lesson early and DO NOT go into debt to acquire these types of things.

7. We will help with college costs to the degree we can, provided you work hard toward a degree with a high potential for gainful employment. The college experience can be personally and educationally fulfilling, but you aren't going to school and going into debt to party and be a Women's Studies or Philosophy Major. You're likelihood of trying to move back in with your mom and I increases with bad university Major choices. See below. If you have a passion or a dream, and you have shown aptitude, passion and the work ethic to pursue that dream at any expense, you'll succeed regardless of your major, or even your education. However, if you don't have this passion, it is better off not going to school at all (not going into debt), or going to school in a STEM field while you work toward something that will pay the bills. Don't be afraid to take an alternative route as well. A skilled trade or technical school training to be a high-elevation utility worker, diesel mechanic or other skilled and limited vocation may end up being a better

long-term job than the traditional white collar gigs the guidance counselor sells you.

8. We will not support you as an adult. You will be expected to educate yourself in a vocation, and upon beginning that vocation, fund any and all living expenses. We recognize that the job market isn't always perfect for graduates, but you will have a job until you find a career. While we may allow you to live with us at home in certain special circumstance while starting out, you will not be freeloading off of us. Room and board will be paid to us, and as one of our roommates/boarders, you will be expected to contribute to housework or your lease may be terminated. Coddling is something I've never been very good at.

9. Birth control – use it. For my daughter, be aware that while hormonal birth control can be a blessing, it may very well upset your hormones and have adverse side effects. However, it is much better than coming home with an unexpected child. For both my son and daughter: while abstaining from sex is an option, at a minimum, use a condom. If you don't have one, don't have sex. Having a kid can be a wonderful blessing if you are ready for one, but at the wrong time, it can have a huge impact on your life and may delay or greatly impact reaching your life goals. Speaking of which...

10. Sex – casual sex has adverse effects for your long-term potential as a husband or wife. You understand now a little about hypergamy, and what being an Alpha male is, and why women like Alpha males, but keep it in your pants. Women may very well be able to attract a more Alpha male for a short term sex-fling, but keeping this type of a man for a long-term relationship is more difficult. The Alpha sex-fling, can be detrimental for your long-term ability to be happy with a husband since he may not quite measure up to Mr. Alpha. And the more short term flings a woman has, the more likely that she will have a hard time bonding mentally (and possibly physically) with a partner that she finally decides to settle down

with. While this may happen to men too, this is usually less of an issue. In general, sex in a long-term relationship with potential for marriage is the preferred choice, or even waiting until marriage, to give you the best chance for long-term success and bonding. This flies in the face of the drunken, slut-filled, hookup, you-go-girl, you-only-live-once culture of today. Don't be afraid to be contrarian. For my son, choose a long-term partner who isn't damaged goods and that hasn't slept with (m)any other men.

11. Settling down – you are very young, I'm sure you aren't looking to settle down right away, but it is also something you shouldn't necessarily discount either. You are as attractive as you will ever be while you are young. If you wait too long, then you waste this youthful vigor, and your hot self, with people who later will only be memories. This is an insult to your future spouse who will feel slighted. Even if they don't know your exact number of partners, they'll know that he or she missed out on something valuable. Hurt feelings are common when thinking about the exes and people who used to sleep with your significant other. The earlier you settle down, with the right partner, the better chance you have of reducing these risks and making a lasting marriage just a little bit easier. Any advantage in this area is a blessing.

12. Marriage – Your mom and I have a very solid marriage, but it took a change in thinking from that shown on television and romantic comedies as well as a lot of effort to get here. Son: If you go into marriage knowing what a quality Alpha males possess, and at least how to play the part and not fall in the traps that are out there, you'll have a good shot of making a marriage work provided you chose your partner wisely. However, most of us don't start out like this and hence, marriage is, at best, a crap shoot; and at worst a life destroying event. Son and daughter: if you get married, realize more "traditional" gender roles as the Alpha man leading is in our lizard brain. Knowing these key thoughts outlined in the marriage section will lay the

foundation for a marriage that has a higher likelihood of success. Don't be afraid of traditional gender roles in marriage, or what your friends will say about it. This structure is more natural for both men (at least those who embrace the leadership – which can be problematic with today's men) and women, versus the current equal power relationship, which often slowly turns into the woman having more power.

13. Partner selection – Choose someone with a low sex partner count. Avoid entitled people, and instead find hard workers. Find someone who places a high emphasis on being healthy, and who treats all people with respect from the CEO to the janitor. For my son, avoid the hard-core, ball busting feminist and instead find someone who will go along with your leadership provided you show you deserve to lead (and you will learn to lead with honesty, quality decision making and strength). For my daughter, avoid "the player" and "the loser" who is tough but without a viable job or values, and instead look beyond the surface and find someone of value that likes you for you and still has a little bit of excitement to them

14. Marriage and Sex - Sex with a long-term partner will likely fade somewhat, but if you are getting warning signs early that you have different priorities about sex, you either need to find out what is killing her or his attraction to you, or get out. So many marriages end up being very difficult due to differing expectations on sex that were known early on, but tried to get over that because they "were in love." Not making changes early about this subject will lead to either a marriage where resentment between partners is very common or to a divorce. Sometimes people who look great on paper are not sexually compatible. That's ok, but when you find that out, don't marry them. It may be hard to walk away when so much else is good, but it is much easier to do that now than to suffer in silence or get divorced over the issue.

15. Be on the lookout for signs of batshit crazy – drugs for psychotic illnesses like bipolar or schizophrenia, manic or

depression episodes, that type of thing. It doesn't matter how hot the sex is if she or he is a ticking time-bomb. And fuck your life if you have a kid with someone like that, so never trust someone like this. No. Not even if she says she is on birth control, or that they can't use a condom because they're allergic but they'll pull out, or if they (boyfriend or girlfriend) ever physically harm you or scream at you. Those are some signs of batshit crazy and not someone who you want to be with in any manner.

The bottom line is that you can feed your kids Red Pill thinking that goes against the grain of common cultural and social teachings in small nuggets as they get older. In many ways, these things will go directly against the feminist agenda most teachers, parents, friends, and society is instilling in their behavior. They will say things to your kids such as:

- "go after your dreams" (in regards to a major that won't yield a job), and
- "you only live once" (to justify drinking, partying and sleeping with many partners), and
- "short hair is so cute" (to get your daughter to look less attractive to men, just like her friends), and
- "a woman needs a man like a fish needs a bicycle" (or similar such feminist statements, to justify all sorts of things to girls, but mostly to bump against male power [even boyfriend or spouse], and promote career over family), and
- "just be nice, be yourself and women will like you" (to keep boys putting women on a pedestal and giving beta comfort instead of promoting being awesome, being a leader, looking good, and amassing Alpha quality mindset and skills), and the corollary
- "women don't like jerks" (to keep boys being nice and supplicating as above, when in reality, women like the bad boy despite what they say)

Contrarian thinking and teachings are needed to give both sons and daughters a better chance at being a success as an adult, having successful long-term relationships with quality mates, having the necessary outlook on life, and avoiding the pitfalls many fall into. I don't expect them to necessarily believe some of these things at first, but by planting these seeds in their brain, and letting them see for themselves, they will likely have a head start coming to the conclusions I, and many others have, reached. Really the best teacher of these life lessons is you and how your kids observe you and your wife interact with each other and live your life. So incorporate Red Pill lessons first into your own life before trying to sculpt a young mind

Part 5: Putting It All Together

CHAPTER 11

The Takeaway

The information in this book contains the tools you need to succeed and improve in how you live your life, but it's up to you to implement them. It will do no good if you read this, put it on your shelf or hide it in your Kindle. It is very scary to see the consequences of not implementing these key principles and what effect they can have on marriage, on life happiness, on finances, health, and children. While this blueprint for your life is fairly straightforward, actual follow-through on implementing all the aspects will take a long time, likely years. You need to prioritize the areas of your life that are the weakest, while at the same time not neglecting the areas you are strong in. Focusing on things that you can control is the key. Realize that you aren't losing weight and getting strong to have more sex with your wife, you are doing it so you are a better version of yourself. The side effect may be that your wife will find you more attractive and have more sex with you, but putting that as your goal will set you up for failure since you can't control her actions.

Like the frog in the pot of water that slowly starts to boil, we don't even realize our slow slide into marital roommates, growth of a spare tire or extra chin, lackadaisical parenting, and financial irresponsibility. We use defense mechanisms to rationalize our behavior, instead of looking at ourselves in the mirror and accepting that we have flaws. Nor do we really believe that we have the ability to correct these flaws. I've provided a solid roadmap to addressing those flaws. And while some of the truths presented here may be difficult to swallow, they are true.

By cutting out wheat and flour, eliminating processed foods, and beginning to eat in a sustainable way with nutrient dense whole foods, you can easily start to shed fat and feel better. It's not easy to go through the transition and to fight the urges of the sandwich tray from a vendor at work. It's not easy to make home-cooked nutritious meals instead of picking up that pizza or take out on the way home from work. It's not easy to cut back on happy hour with your work mates or to pack you and your kids' lunches. Easy is what got you and your family where they are now. The easiest way to begin to feel better and to get to a healthy weight, and potentially greatly reduce your risk of Western diseases, is to modify your diet. Try it strictly for at least 30 to 60 days and see if you don't feel better.

Along with eating better, start lifting weights if you can. No, you won't get "too big," a common misconception of women mostly, but I've heard guys use this as an excuse why they don't want to lift. Growing new muscles, besides feeling and looking awesome, contribute to testosterone production provided you go heavy and use big, compound movements like squatting and deadlifting. I gained 30 pounds of mostly muscle in a relatively short time, getting unsolicited comments of "you're getting ripped" from neighborhood wives (including mine). The secret is simply setting tangible goals, following a good program, eating well, resting well, and being patient. When you look good, you feel good. And when you feel good, you're more confident and carry yourself differently, projecting an aura of superiority. This attitude manifests more positive reactions and interactions and carries over not only to your marriage, but to your interactions with friends and coworkers.

While improving physically, don't forget the mental health part as well. Mindfulness, being present in life, and enjoying the small things are often much more calming than the dopamine and stress inducing electronic device that disrupts your circadian rhythms. Put the tablet and phone down, and do some yoga instead. Your stress will drop, your cortisol will be reduced, you'll sleep better, and recover better from those workouts. In addition, you are more likely you'll be a calmer and better parent and spouse.

Your wife may love you, and you're probably great around the house, provide for the family and help with the kids. But if you don't have the sex life you want, she likely doesn't find you attractive, or you aren't doing things to attract her. In the absence of changed behavior where you begin being more of a leader within your realm, look and behave strongly, and bring some of the cocky/funny attitude back into your lives, she may be receptive to that tingly dopamine feeling from someone else. Many men are surprised when their loving wives, who they've slipped into a comfort-filled marriage with, drops the "I love you but am not in love with you" bombshell. Don't be one of those men. Instead be one of those men who rediscovers their former athletic body post-40 and who stands out compared to all the other average Beta schlubs that populate the masses.

Addressing financial matters that may have been creeping up for years may be a critical path item, is causing undo mental stress that seeps over to other aspects of your life, and will take some time to undo. We all struggle to balance income and spending. We're trying to juggle so many balls like daily living expenses, saving for college and retirement, and simple things like birthday presents for kids or your friends. In general though, we probably don't say "No!" enough to that toy or gadget, or meal out, or vacation, or new car. Instead we often procure something that will lose value versus gain value. These types of things that are wants, not needs. Changing this mentality is key, as are finding cheap and free alternatives to overcome this consumerism. Cut cable and replacing it with Netflix or Hulu Plus. Purchase an automobile that is 5 years old with many good miles left instead of buying that new car. Use the library for books, movies and videogames. Many options exist, but you have to stop consuming and incurring the mindless expenses that add minimal long-term value.

After you can at least save a little each month, you need to put together an emergency fund to deal with unanticipated events so you don't need to use your credit cards and incur more debt. Hold a garage sale and declutter. Sell clothes on e-bay or craigslist. Sell that collection you've been holding on that is simply taking up space in the basement. Once you have an emergency fund, work to pay off credit cards. If you have access to a company sponsored 401(k) plan or other retirement account, contribute up to the match. If your employer doesn't offer one of these plans, open up a Roth IRA and set up automatic withdrawal so you can have your bank add a little bit each month to get the ball rolling. Savings is a habit that you can't start early enough or save enough. "One day" will come sooner than you think.

Making small changes, and small additions to debt reduction and saving, will eventually be large if you are patient enough. The more you can either increase income or reduce living expenses, the faster you can make this happen. If you make it a game, and are creative with your spouse and kids on being frugal, you can still have a very fulfilling and entertaining life. Having your finances in order, an emergency fund and getting on the track to a proper future feel like an elephant is lifted off your back. Don't underestimate how awesome you'll feel when you reach this goal – we feel way happier working toward a totally debt free life than consumption of things that we recognize provide only short-term transient joy. It may be painful at first due to our indoctrinated mindset, but you'll soon find joy in how much you are saving, and the future it is leading to. Being your own master and not being a slave to Visa, student loans, or the mortgage company is enlightening in its own right.

Finally, as you are building up your marriage, health and financial freedom, don't forget the key building blocks to being a good parent. Providing love, structure, and discipline in appropriate amounts are some of the foundational elements to raising kids who will grow up with the chance to be moral and successful adults. We all want to see our children grow up happy and enlightened, to do so, we need to allow them to make their own choices and fail often. Providing them the opportunity to make many decisions, and then to live with their decisions, instead of stepping in and saving them from the consequences, is something that many parents simply can't do. Empathy at their failures and discussing what happened results in them thinking through the cause-effect relationship of those decisions. These inevitably result in them building experiences to draw upon later to make better decisions and are invaluable tools as they get older. Instead of being one of the many entitled children we see every day, they will become a critical thinking, self-sufficient person that isn't relying on us as parents to save the day.

As parents, our children model their world view and behavior after us. Sure, they will be their own personality and have their own interests, strengths and weaknesses. But their world will be shaped by us. We need to be setting an example of how married parents should behave towards each other (flirty, loving and a united bond), what a healthy diet is, what role exercise should play in life, how to manage money, and what gender and personal behaviors lend themselves to life success. Imparting this wisdom will occur over years and years, and the younger we start to model these behaviors and slip pearls of wisdom onto our kids' radar screens, the more likely they will be allowed to marinate. Perhaps one day they will see for themselves how some of the so-called truths about life and love are incorrect. How being a "nice guy" isn't really that nice and often leads to disappointment. How choosing the wrong major and not treating post-secondary education as a vocation will lead to financial servitude and misery. How sleeping with a multiple partners and delaying marriage, especially as a woman, is detrimental to building a lasting bond with your partner.

Final Keys of Success

- Evaluate if you are behaving like a child or a man
- Take care of emotional hang-ups preventing you from being a strong, confident man
- Kid with your wife like a sister
- Be cocky/funny and enjoy explicit/implicit sexual jokes or innuendos with your wife
- Initiate, initiate, initiate
- Try new things to spice up sex, especially being more dominant
- Eat quality real foods with high nutritional density
- Lift heavy weights, walk, add cardio sessions of high intensity and short bursts
- Live frugally, save, and find enjoyment in people, nature, actively living your life, and not "things"
- You are a Mountain of a Man, will not be swayed by your family's emotional storms
- Lead by example (parenting and marriage)
- Just spend time with your kids and introduce them to cool things
- Provide structure for your kids, and discipline accordingly
- Allow your kids to make choices, and live with the consequences of those choices
- Impart masculine values in boys, feminine values in girls – slowly feed them alternative viewpoints of life and have them evaluate critically gender relations, government, fiscal policy, corporations, media, and not swallow the standard societal lies.
- LOVE! (Life, Yourself, Wife, Kids)

Going from an Average Married Dad to an Awesome Married Dad definitely takes some work, but being patient and establishing new patterns of behavior, you too can have health, wealth and a sexy marriage.

Bibliography

Aiken, Richard. Hunting 1991-2006: a focus on fishing and hunting by species: addendum to the 2006 national survey of fishing, hunting, and wildlife-associated recreation report 2006-8. U.S. Fish and Wildlife Service. 2010.

Amato, Paul, Previti, Denise. "People's Reasons For Divorcing: gender, social class, the life course and adjustment." *Journal of Family Issues*, July 2003.

Amen, Daniel. *Sex on the brain: 12 lessons to enhance your love.* New York: Harmony Books, 2007.

Angell, Marcia. *The Truth about Drug Companies: how they deceive us and what to do about it.* New York: Random House, 2004.

Austin, A., Breslow, J., Hennekens, C., Buring, J., Willett, W., Krauss, R. "Low-Density Lipoprotein Subclass Patterns and Risk of Myocardial Infarction" *Journal of American Medical Association*, Vol. 260, No. 13, October 7, 1988.

Berns, Gregory. *Satisfaction: the science of finding true fulfillment.* New York: H. Holt, 2005.

Bernstein, Neil I. *There when he needs you: how to be an available, involved, and emotionally connected father to your son.* New York: Free Press, 2008.

Bloch, L.F. and Silverman, K.K. *Manopause: your guide to surviving his changing life.* Carlsbad, Calif.: Hay House, 2012.

Bogle, John. *The little book of common sense investing.* Hoboken, N.J.: John Wiley & Sons, 2007.

Brott, Armin A. *Father for life: a journey of joy, challenge, and change.* New York: Abbeville Press, 2003.

Brown, Brene. *The Gifts of Imperfection: let go of who you think you're supposed to be and embrace who you are.* Center City, Minn.: Hazelden, 2010.

Buss, David. *The evolution of desire strategies of human mating.* New York: BasicBooks, 1994.

Campbell, T. Colin. *The China study: the most comprehensive study of nutrition ever conducted and the startling implications for diet, weight loss, and long-term health.* Dallas, TX: BenBella Books, 2004.

Chandra, A., Mosher, W.D., and Copen, C. "Sexual Behavior, Sexual Attraction, and Sexual Identity in the United States: Data From the 2006-2008 National Survey of Family Growth." *National Health Statistics Report. U.S. Department of Health and Human Services. Centers for Disease Control and Prevention.* Number 36, 2011.

Clarey, Aaron. *Worthless: The young person's indispensable guide to choosing the right major.* Paric Publishing. 2011.

Cline, Foster. *Parenting Teens with love and logic: preparing adolescents for responsible adulthood.* Colorado, Springs CO: NavPress, 2006.

Cline, Foster. *Parenting with love and logic: teaching children responsibility.* Colorado, Springs CO: NavPress, 2006.

Cordain, Loren. *The Paleo diet: lose weight and get healthy by eating the foods you were designed to eat*. Hoboken, N.J.: Wiley, 2011.

Consumer Reports. Track your teen drivers. July 2014, p.55.

Coyle, Daniel. *The talent code: greatness isn't born, it's grown, here's how.* New York: Bantam Books, 2009.

Davis, William. *Wheat belly: lose the wheat, lose the weight, and find your path back to health.* Emmaus, Penn.: Rodale, 2011.

De Zengotita, Thomas. *Mediated: how the media shapes your world and the way you live in it.* New York: [S.l.]: Bloomsbury ; Holtzbrinck Publishers, 2005.

Dor, A., Ferguson, C., Langwith, C., and Tan, E. "A heavy burden: the individual costs of being overweight and obese in the United States." *George Washington University School of Public Health and Health Services,* 2010.

Duhigg, Charles. *The power of habit: why we do what we do in life and business.* New York: Random House, 2012

Eisenberg, Lee. *The number: a completely different way to think about the rest of your life.* New York: Free Press, 2006.

Farrell, Chris. *The new frugality: how to consume less, save more, and live better.* New York: Bloomsbury Press, 2010.

Farrell, Warren. *The myth of male power: why men are the disposable sex.* New York: Simon & Schuster, 1993.

Ferriss, Tim. The 4-Hour Workweek: escape 9-5, live anywhere and join the new rich. New York: Crown Publishers, 2009.

Fisher, Helen E. *Why him? Why her? Finding real love by finding your personality type.* New York: Henry Holt & Co., 2010.

Gall, T.S. "Custodial Mothers and Fathers and Their Child Support: 2009." Current Population Reports. U.S. Department of Commerce Economics and Statistics Administration. United States Census Bureau. 2011.

Gedgaudas, Nora T. *Primal body, primal mind: beyond the paleo diet for total health and a longer life.* Rochester, Vt.: Healing Arts Press, 2011.

Gilbert, Elizabeth. *Eat, pray, love: one woman's search for everything across Italy, India and Indonesia.* New York: Viking, 2006.

Glover, Robert. *No More Mr. Nice Guy.* Prince Frederick, Md.: Recorded Books, 2004.

Go A.S., Mozaffarian D., Roger V.L., et al. "Statistical Fact Sheet 2013 Update." *American Heart Association*, 2013.

Gottman, John Mordechai. *The seven principles for making marriage work.* New York: Crown Publishers, 1999.

Goulston, Mark. *The 6 secrets of a lasting relationship: how to fall in love again--and stay there.* New York: Putnam, 2001.

Guevremont A., Findlay L., and Kohen D. "Organized extracurricular activities of Canadian child and youth." *Health Reports*, Vol. 19, No. 3, 2008.

Guttmacher Institute. "Contraceptive Use in the United States: Fact Sheet." 2013.

Haltzman, Scott. *The secrets of happily married men: eight ways to win your wife's heart forever.* San Francisco: Jossey-Bass, 2006.

Hansen, Mark Victor. *The one minute millionaire: the enlightened way to wealth.* New York: Harmony Books, 2002.

Hartley-Brewer, Elizabeth. *Raising confident boys: 100 tips for parents and teachers.* Cambridge, MA: Fisher Books, 2001.

Hernandex, J.D. "American Children: resources from family, government, and the economy." *Russel Sage Foundation,* 1993.

Herper, Matthew. "Is Lipitor the new asprin?" *Forbes Magazine,* June 2004.

Horstman, Judith. *The Scientific American book of love, sex, and the brain: the neuroscience of how, when, why, and who we love.* San Francisco: Jossey-Bass, 2012.

Howard, Clark. *Clark Howard's living large in lean times: 250+ ways to buy smarter, spend smarter, and save money.* New York, NY: Avery, 2011.

Kay, Athol. *Married Man Sex Life Primer 2011.*

Kay, Athol. *The Mindful Attraction Plan: your practical roadmap to creating the life, love and success you want.* 2013.

Kelly, Joe. *Dads and daughters: how to inspire, understand, and support your daughter when she's growing up so fast.* New York: Broadway Books, 2002.

Kresser, Chris. *Your personal paleo code: the 3-step plan to lose weight, reverse disease and stay fit and healthy for life.* New York. Little, Brown and Company. 2013.

Lai, J.C.L., Evans, P., et al. "Optimism, positive affectivity, and salivary cortisol." *British Journal of Health and Psychology.* Volume 10, Issue 4, 2005.

Larimore, T., Lindauer, M. and LeBoeuf, M. *The Bogleheads' guide to investing.* Hoboken, N.J.: Wiley, c2006.

Larimore, Taylor. *The Bogleheads' guide to retirement planning.* Hoboken, N.J.: Wiley, 2009

Lewis, Robert. *Raising a modern-day knight: a father's role in guiding his son to authentic manhood.* Carol Stream, IL.: Tyndale House Publishers, 2007.

McAllister, Peter. *Manthropology: the science of why the modern male is not the man he used to be.* New York: St. Martin's Press, 2010.

Minger, Denise. *Death by Food Pyramid.* Malibu, CA: Primal Blueprint Publishing, 2013.

National Survey of Sexual Health and Behavior (NSSHB). *Findings from the National Survey of Sexual Health and Behavior, Centre for Sexual Health Promotion, Indiana University. Journal of Sexual Medicine,* Vol. 7, Supplement 5. 2010.

O'Connell, Mark. *The good father: on men, masculinity, and life in the family.* New York: Scribner, 2005.

Panzer C., Wise S., Fantini G., Kang D., Munarirz R., Guay A., Goldstein I. "Impact of oral contraceptives on sex hormone-binding globulin and androgen levels: a retrospective study in women with sexual dysfunction." *Journal of Sexual Medicine.* January 2006.

Parker-Pope, Tara. *For better: the science of a good marriage.* New York: Dutton, 2010.

Payleitner, Jay K. *52 things kids need from a dad.* Eugene, Or.: Harvest House Publishers, 2010.

Perel, Esther. *Mating in captivity: unlocking erotic intelligence.* New York: Harper, 2007.

Pew Research Center analysis of Decennial Census (1960-2000) and American Community Survey data (2008, 2010, 2011), IPUMS.

Pollan, Michael. *In defense of food: an eater's manifesto.* New York: Penguin Press, 2008.

Poppick, Susie. "How much should you have in stocks?" *Money Magazine,* January/February 2014.

Ramsey, Dave. *Financial Peace Revisited.* New York: Viking, 2003.

Ramsey, Dave. *The Total Money Makeover: a proven plan for financial fitness.* Nashville, Tennessee: Nelson Books, 2013.

Robbins, Anthony. *Awaken the giant within: how to take immediate control of your mental, emotional, physical & financial destiny.* New York, NY: Simon & Schuster Audio, 1991.

Robin Baker. *Sperm Wars: infidelity, sexual conflict and other bedroom.* New York: Thunder's Mouth Press, 1996.

Rosenberg, J., Wilcox, W.B. "The importance of fathers in the healthy development of children." *U.S. Department of Health and Human Services,* 2006.

Rosefeld, Alvin. *The Overscheduled Child.* New York: St. Martin's Griffin, 2001.

Saint-Paul, Gilles. "Genes, Legitimacy and Hypergamy: Another Look at the Economics of Marriage." *Center for Economic Policy Research,* 2008.

Schnarch, David Morris. *Passionate marriage: love, sex and intimacy in emotionally committed relationships.* New York: W. W. Norton & Co., 2009.

Segerstrom, S.C., & Sephton, S.E. "Optimistic expectancies and cell-mediated immunity: The role of positive affect." *Psychological Science,* 21, 2010.

Seib, Jason. *The Paleo Coach: expert advice for extraordinary health, sustainable fat loss, and an incredible body.* Las Vegas: Victory Belt Publishing, 2013

Smith, S.C., Allen, J., Blair, S. et. Al. "AHA/ACC guidelines for secondary prevention for patients with coronary and other atherosclerotic vascular disease: 2006 update (endorsed by the National Heart, Lung and Blood Institute)." *Journal of American College of Cardiology.* Volume 47, Issue 10, May 2006.

Stanley, Thomas; Danko, William. *The millionaire next door: the surprising secrets of America's wealthy.* Atlanta, Ga.: Longstreet Press, 1996.

Taubes, Gary. *Good calories, bad calories: challenging the conventional wisdom on diet, weight control, and disease.* New York: Alfred A. Knopf, 2007.

Tolle, Eckhart. *A new earth awakening to your life's purpose.* Waterville, Me.: Bath, England: Thorndike Press ; Chivers, 2005.

Tolle, Eckhart.*The power of now a guide to spiritual enlightenment.* Thorndike, ME: G.K. Hall, 2000.

U.S. Bureau of Labor Statistics. National Employment Statistics. 2011.

U.S. Department of Agriculture. "Agriculture Fact Book 2001-2002."Chapter 2, 2003.

U.S. Department of Agriculture. "Dietary Guidelines for Americans 2010."Chapter 3, 2010.

Wallerstein, Judith S.; Blakeslee, Sandra. *The good marriage: how & why love lasts.* New York: Warner Books, 1996.

Wolf, Robb. *The Paleo solution: the original human diet.* Las Vegas: Victory Belt, 2010.

Zibergeld, Bernie. *The new male sexuality.* New York: Bantam Books, 1999.

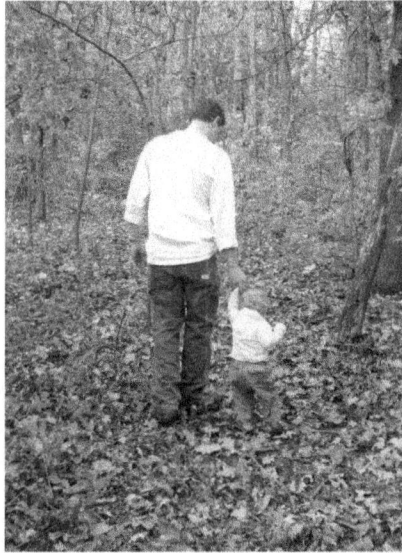

About The Author

Alex Peck is a late-30's father of two and regular blogger on the topics of marriage, sex, family life, personal growth, personal finance, health, and wellness. He's been interviewed for *Men's Fitness* magazine, and invited to appear on podcasts about adult topics for the Huffington Post as well as nationally syndicated radio shows such as Steve Harvey. He's a "Red Pill" subscriber of life – meaning he believes more in the patriarchal structure of marriage and in relationships and thinks feminism, for all its good, is eroding family values and making men into something they weren't ever meant to be: subservient "nice guys" afraid of their own shadows and their wives. Married for nearly 13 years, he's a regular guy trying to balance the rigors of everyday life while still enjoying the fruits of his labor. He lifts heavy things, is kicking ass at life while working on his second book, and encourages other men to stop being average. Check out his on-going blog at www.AverageMarriedDad.com.

www.ingramcontent.com/pod-product-compliance
Lightning Source LLC
LaVergne TN
LVHW011218080426
835509LV00005B/197